V

RUSSIA'S UNDERGROUND PRESS

RUSSIA'S UNDERGROUND PRESS

The Chronicle of Current Events

Хроника Текущих Событий

Mark Hopkins

Foreword by Andrei Sakharov

PRAEGER SPECIAL STUDIES • PRAEGER SCIENTIFIC

Library of Congress Cataloging in Publication Data

Hopkins, Mark.
  Russia's underground press.

  Bibliography: p.
  Includes index.
  1. Khronika tekushchick sobytii. 2. Dissenters—
Soviet Union—Periodicals. 3. Civil rights—Soviet
Union—Periodicals. 4. Soviet Union. Komitet
gozudarstvennoi bezopasnosti. I. Title.
  DK277.A2K4834 1983   947'.005 83-11133
ISBN 0-03-062013-9

OCLC#: 9687200

Published in 1983 by Praeger Publishers
CBS Educational and Professional Publishing
a Division of CBS Inc.
521 Fifth Avenue, New York, NY 10175 USA

56789 052 98765432

Printed in the United States of America
on acid-free paper

Dedicated to

Natalia Gorbanevskaya

and *Chronicle* editors

А. Сахаров

Сахаров Горький Апрель 1983.

Foreword

To tell the story of the *Chronicle of Current Events* and of
the people whose fate has been connected with it is a very
important and difficult task. I have already repeatedly
written—and it is my deep conviction—that the *Chronicle*
during the course of these many years embodies the best in
the human rights movement, its principles and highest
achievements—the defense of human rights using objective
information, and with a principled rejection of violence.
The very fact of the almost uninterrupted publication of the
Chronicle for more than 15 years is a miracle of self-denial,
of wisdom, of courage and intellectual integrity. Undoubt-
edly, people should know the history of the *Chronicle* and
know at what price all this has been achieved. It is that
lucid and bitter knowledge that both elevates people and
makes them more tolerant, and more capable of making the
right decisions in our beautiful and tragic world.

In the circumstances of my isolation in Gorky, I, un-
fortunately, am unable to familiarize myself with the manuscript. But I hope that the author of the book before you
has fulfilled his task, despite all the difficulties connected
with penetrating the world of Soviet reality, which in many
ways is so distant from the western world.

Let this book serve as still another small bridge along
the difficult path of mutual understanding.

A. Sakharov
Gorky
April 1983

[Editor's Note: Andrei Sakharov, the Soviet physicist often
described as the "father" of the Soviet hydrogen bomb, was
awarded the Nobel Peace Prize in 1975 for his dedicated
efforts in behalf of human rights in the Soviet Union.
Soviet authorities subsequently banished him to the city of
Gorky in January 1980, where he has lived with his wife
Yelena Bonner under continuous surveillance of the KGB,
the Soviet secret police. He is denied almost all contact
with the outside world. The original foreword written by

Andrei Sakharov for this book was confiscated by KGB agents in February 1983 when they conducted a personal search of Yelena Bonner aboard a train bound from Gorky to Moscow. Contained herein is a reproduction of that original handwritten foreword which begins just below the solid line. Material above that is Sakharov's acceptance of an award. Writing in Gorky, Sakharov uses ordinary school notebooks for essays, statements and comments sent to the West by private channels. He fills pages to the fullest to reduce the bulk of material brought from the Soviet Union.]

Preface

This book is about a dedicated and remarkable group of
people: the hundreds, probably thousands, of men and
women in the Soviet Union who since 1968 have managed to
report uncensored news of the Soviet Union. The *Khronika
Tekushchikh Sobytü*–the *Chronicle of Current Events*–is
well known to Western correspondents who have worked in
Moscow, to diplomats, and to foreign specialists on Soviet
affairs. The *Chronicle* should be more widely known, for
its founding and continued publication despite concerted
attempts by the KGB (the Soviet security police) to silence
it, have earned it a special place in Soviet political history.

I have used the word "dissidents" throughout this book,
knowing that those to whom it refers reject the word.
They are right to do so. In the United States, "dissidents" has acquired a connotation not all favorable. The
people who put out the *Chronicle*, who wrote for it, who
distributed it, and who read it, and the people who figured
in *Chronicle* news reports–all are "dissidents" in that they
dissent from the practices of an authoritarian regime. Men
and women have been consigned to Soviet labor camps for
no more than that. Many, if not most, Americans would
automatically be "dissidents" in Soviet society. I use the
word because it is a commonly known reference to Soviet
men and women who advocate democratic government.

This book reflects its subject. Much about the *Chronicle*
is still secret. Men and women who have worked with the
Chronicle and who are now living in exile in the United
States, France, or West Germany still will not reveal all
they know about the *Chronicle* for fear that the KGB would
thus be informed. I have withheld some names given to me
for precisely the same reason. Working for the *Chronicle*
has not been, and is not, a dilettante's pastime. As you
read this, there are men and women enduring Siberian labor
camps because they worked for the *Chronicle*.

Like the term "dissidents," I have used the acronym
"KGB" liberally. The KGB is really one arm of the Soviet
ruling structure. Yury Andropov, KGB chief from 1967 to
1982, was a member of the Communist party Politburo for
the last two-thirds of those years, until he succeeded

Leonid Brezhnev as party general secretary. The KGB, in its battle against the *Chronicle*, has carried out Politburo policy. "KGB" is shorthand, then, for the Soviet leadership, as well as for the pervasive Soviet security police apparatus.

As with most books, many people other than the author spent their time in the production of this book. I want to acknowledge especially the following: Professor Robert Sharlet of Union College was the moving force behind this study. He encouraged me to turn an idea into written word. An old friend, Professor Lincoln Furber of American University, painstakingly read the entire manuscript to smooth out awkward writing and thought. It is a richer, more articulate book because of his help. Ludmilla Alexeyeva not only gave her time to recount historical fact, but checked the final work for factual accuracy. Shirley Jones is one of the new breed of "typists." She produced this book on a word processor, making my work easier as she opened up a world of possibilities for rewriting. She has been devoted and uncomplaining.

I interviewed many people for this book. The places and dates are given in the appropriate footnotes and bibliography. The following persons in particular, however, have patiently endured hours of tape-recorded interviews, and without their help and sufferance, the story of the *Chronicle* could not have been told. My appreciation to Ludmilla Alexeyeva, Vladimir Bukovsky, Valery Chalidze, Mario Corti, Galina Gabai, Alexander Ginzburg, Arina Ginzburg, Yury Gastev, Natalia Gorbanevskaya, Tatyana Khodorovich, Victor Krasin, Pavel Litvinov, Kronid Lyubarsky, Peter Reddaway, Galina Salova, Boris Shragin, Vladimir Voinovich, and Yefrem Yankelevich.

Finally, Zora Safir deserves first credit for this history of the *Chronicle*. Her Voice of America news broadcasts and reporting to the Soviet Union in Russian since 1964 have earned her respect among those connected with the *Chronicle*. Her knowledge of the *Chronicle* and its staff, of the events reported in the *Chronicle*, and her entree into "dissident" circles, not to mention her native fluency in Russian and hours of interpreting interviews, are reflected in this book. She also put together the index and indices.

I have studied and written about the Soviet Union for more than 20 years, the last half of them for the Voice of America as one of its foreign correspondents. For the main years covered in this book, I traveled frequently to the Soviet Union on assignments from VOA European bureaus. The experience of those years and the encouragement of my editors at that time, Alan Heil and Bernard Kamenske, in reporting Soviet developments have contributed substantially to this work.

Mark W. Hopkins
Alexandria, Virginia

Acknowledgments

The author is grateful to Amnesty International, London, for permission to quote sections from its copyrighted English translations of *A Chronicle of Current Events* and to Khronika Press, New York, for permission to quote material from issues of the *Chronicle of Human Rights in the USSR*.

Contents

Introduction

Twice in my life I have had the opportunity to read books whose subject was the society to which I belong. The books are *The Russians* by Hedrick Smith, and the book by Mark Hopkins about the *Chronicle of Current Events* and those who established it. I opened both books with exactly the same feeling—well, I felt, it will be interesting to see what the author knows and thinks about us, but, of course, I will read nothing new from him because I know all of this not from the outside, like him, but from within. And both times I have discovered the truth of the saying that "things are seen better from afar."

I remember how I was surprised in just the first pages of *The Russians,* where Smith describes how, soon after he arrived in Moscow, he ended up by chance with a group late at night drinking vodka. Smith described how they were pouring the vodka, in what kind of glasses, what and how they were eating, how men drank and how women drank. Uncounted times, I have seen this ritual and taken part in it. But until I read Smith's description, it never came into my head that this was a ritual, a custom. If I were asked to write about it, I would simply have said, in place of Smith's two page account, "they drank vodka," because I did not know that it could be any other way. Smith was helped in his writing exactly because he had the view of the new person, the outsider. With the same feeling of strange recognition, I read Mark Hopkins' book in which he scrupulously describes how material is collected for the *Chronicle,* how it is typed, how it is read and how it is hidden from authorities. All of this is extremely familiar to me, but with the outsider's view, he has seen much that would not have fixed our attention precisely because it repeated often, it was commonplace.

Mark Hopkins has not only written the history of the emergence and 15 year life of our *Chronicle,* but what strikes me as especially valuable, he has researched all the stages in the production process of a *samizdat* information journal and has shown, in the example of the *Chronicle,* in such detail and so fully, how the *samizdat* mechanism functions. Until now, no one has done this, neither in

English nor Russian literature. The book by Mark Hopkins, despite its readable style, is more precisely not a description, but a study. And it is done so exactingly, that there is no need for me to question the author, or to add any factual additions to the material he has collected. I only want to add to this study, which was conducted as it should have been "from the outside," what the *Chronicle* gave to those of us who participated in it and what it meant for us.

Andrei Sakharov said about the *Chronicle* that it fully reflects the spirit of the human rights movement. The "dissident movement in the Soviet Union" is not only a movement dealing with the rights of man—although they sometimes become one in the same; it is a whole conglomerate of different national and religious movements, as well as a movement for social and economic rights. The merging of these different forces in the Soviet Union began with the *Chronicle*. Until its appearance, the numerous national and religious movements functioned, during the whole of Soviet history, in total isolation from one another.

This can be explained first of all by the lack of information among their participants. In Soviet circumstances, all means of information, from the first children's readers in whatever language to historical and sociological research, not to mention the press and other mass media, are called upon to support the theme of the "unity and monolith" of Soviet society, of "unity around the party and the government." Real problems of real life do not find expression in the press, and therefore they remain concealed not only from those beyond Soviet borders, but they are not seen as well within the country. In such a situation, a Lithuanian, let's say, who knows about the problems of his own nation, of his own church according to his personal experience, still knows nothing about the problems of Ukrainians, or Georgians and so on, even though their problems are very close to his and could become the base for the unity of these national movements.

But lack of information is not the only thing interfering with unity of action in the Soviet Union. National and religious feelings, which cement each movement within itself, do not provide the base for broader unity, but in fact do just the opposite. No one of the Soviet national or religious movements could become the link to all the others. In this, the Soviet Union differs, for example, from Poland. In Polish society, where there is an homogenous nationality and religion, these feelings have united popular protest throughout the country. In the Soviet Union, which is not homogeneous, these feelings lock people within their own national or religious communities, isolating them from others, if not setting them against the others.

In such a society like the Soviet, with many nationalities and religions, only the human rights movement could play a unifying role. It turned out to be the natural point of attraction for all other dissident movements exactly because it applied to all people, and because it was neutral toward national, religious and political movements. The *Chronicle* introduced people to one another who were separated by huge distances, and by different existences and beliefs, who distrusted one another. It became their first common cause and crystalized that which, given time, united them under the common name of the "dissident movement in the Soviet Union." The *Chronicle's* role in forming this unity is an invaluable political achievement. I must acknowledge, that this was not the result of conscious efforts, but was a natural side effect.

All of us in the Soviet Union are pounded in school with the Lenin dictum that a "newspaper is not only a collective agitator, but also a collective organizer." Lenin was attempting to overthrow the existing order, to take power, and he felt that the place to start was with the organization of a newspaper. The members of the Soviet human rights movement do not fight for power, they do not have political goals. The people who created the *Chronicle* neither thought of it as an agitator nor an organizer—but as a source of honest information about the hidden layers of our society. But it turned out that without agitation, and maybe precisely because of it, the *Chronicle* did "agitate" many people toward the human rights position, and they made that their own. Without any particular goal or without organizing anything in particular, the *Chronicle* gathered all other dissidents around the human rights activists, and helped spread the human rights ideas and methods of protest. The first contacts with other movements were served to a significant degree by the willingness of all sides to publish full and detailed information in the *Chronicle* about their movements. Contacts helped them know one another, helped mutual understanding and assistance.

On a personal level, the fate of everyone connected with the *Chronicle* was fixed the moment that the connection was made. For each of us who worked for the *Chronicle*, it meant to pledge oneself to be faithful to the truth, it meant to cleanse oneself of the filth of double-think, which has pervaded every phase of Soviet life. I know of various people who because of different circumstances had to quit working for the *Chronicle*, but I do not know of a single person who, on leaving the *Chronicle*, returned to official activity. The effect of the *Chronicle* is irreversible. Each one of us went through this alone, but each of us knows others who went through this moral rebirth. This creates among people who scarcely know one another, but who were connected with the *Chronicle*, very strong spiritual ties, the kind that probably existed among early Christians, and that in our day exist among those who fight shoulder to shoulder at the wartime front. I don't know which of these analogies is closest to our experience. Even those who have paid with years of imprisonment, consider it a great personal good fortune, I believe, to belong to this brotherhood.

The attempt at this self-liberation by hundreds, let's say even thousands of people who participated in the *Chronicle* probably was not evident in the social atmosphere of a country of 260 million people. The *Chronicle* —using here the words of one of its founders, Anatoly Yakobson— was not a political, but rather a moral struggle. Such phenomenon cannot be put to a political measure in which each action must bring a concrete result or some benefit.

If the day comes when our country will stop repelling others with its insidiousness, and become an honest partner of the democratic West, and the world loses its fear of the "Russians," historians will discover that one of the first bricks in this foundation of a kinder and wiser society was laid by the *Chronicle* staff, who believed that the truth is needed for truth's sake and not for the sake of something else, and that one has to fight evil even when there is no hope of victory.

Ludmilla Alexeyeva
Tarrytown, N.Y.

1
RESISTANCE

Moscow, the end of April 1968. Natalia Gorbanevskaya pushed together a pile of notes lying on the desk alongside her well-used Olympia typewriter. A small, black-haired woman, she always worked intensely, often chain-smoking Russian cigarettes as she penciled poems or typed her manuscripts. Thirty-two years old this spring of 1968, she was also eight months pregnant with a second son.

This day Gorbanevskaya was beginning work on the first issue of a unique publication in the Soviet Union, although it was only one among a number of writing projects she had underway. Pounding the Olympia hard to make the original first pages and six copies with the heavy typing paper and flimsy carbon sheets found in Soviet stores, Gorbanevskaya worked off and on over the next few days. She finally finished the 20-page manuscript the last week of the month. Not wanting to date this first issue May 1—the Communist celebrated labor day—Gorbanevskaya arbitrarily typed 30 April 1968 on the cover page. Along with that, in capital letters reflecting the worn keys of her old machine, she wrote in Russian: HUMAN RIGHTS YEAR IN THE SOVIET UNION, and centered below that in spaced out letters: A C H R O N I C L E   O F   C U R R E N T   E V E N T S. That was followed by the Russian translation of article 19 of the United Nations General Declaration of Human Rights and a brief content list of seven news items. [1]

The underground bulletin—not entirely a newspaper by standard definitions, not wholly a periodical, not quite a

1

journal, but some of all three—was at the time so incidental to events in Moscow let alone the vast Soviet Union that only a handful of Gorbanevskaya's friends and fellow dissidents even knew she was working on the *Chronicle*. The KGB, the Soviet secret police, and the Soviet Communist party apparatus and the Western press corps, the foreign radiobroadcasters—organizations that would later lavish attention on the *Chronicle*—ignored it then and for months afterward, mostly out of ignorance of what it was or that it even existed.

More than a decade later, the *Chronicle* was to gain quiet fame both as a reservoir of factual news untouched by the Soviet censor and as a durable symbol of men and women in the Soviet Union fighting for rule of law. The *Chronicle* became the voice, the press organ, if you will, of the "democratic movement," an ill-defined, but active association of people in the Soviet Union who advocated fundamental human rights—free speech and press, freedom of conscience and belief, freedom of assembly, equality before the law, politically independent courts, honest and fair government—all guaranteed in the Soviet constitution. The movement was to encompass men and women hurled involuntarily into stormy international controversy, caught up in the volatile relations of the Soviet state and the West, particularly the United States. Nobel Peace Prize Laureate Andrei Sakharov was among them, one of the many intellectuals in the Soviet scientific and academic world advocating rule of law. Gorbanevskaya and her friends were among the less established and younger intellectuals who, from another perspective, struggled for the same goal.

The *Chronicle of Current Events* was destined to become the chronicler of this movement, functioning by necessity as an underground press, hunted by the security police, its editors and staff terrorized and punished in erratic application of harsh Soviet state power. The *Chronicle* ultimately became the model of a free press in the Soviet Union, juxtaposed to the huge state media network that served to justify the status quo.

The *Chronicle* was born as Nikita Khrushchev's successor, Leonid Brezhnev, consolidated his power as Soviet Communist party general secretary in the late 1960s and prepared the domestic political ground for diplomatic openings with the West. As part of that political consolidation in the Kremlin, longtime Communist party professional Yury Andropov was given command of the State Committee for Security—the KGB in its Russian acronym.

Andropov, 52 years old when he was named KGB chairman in May 1967, had been Soviet ambassador in

Budapest in 1956 when Soviet tanks put down the Hungarian rebellion. For ten years before 1967, he had headed the party's central committee department for liaison with other Communist countries, and for the last five of those years he had been a member of the select and powerful party secretariat.

Born as World War I broke out, Andropov was said to be the son of a railroad or office worker. Some accounts maintain that his father actually was Vladimir Andropov, an NKVD officer connected with the infamous Smersh, the secret police counterintelligence section. No one really knows. It is known that Yury Andropov came up the hard way. His formal education stopped with studies at a water transport technical school and the "higher party school." He early turned to the party youth organization, the Komsomol, then to the Communist party for a career. He moved steadily upward, and by 1967, Andropov had performed impressively enough at the solid gray stone central committee headquarters in Moscow to be selected KGB chief. By then, Andropov's experience and personal philosophy had made him a staunch traditionalist, if not a conservative.

In 1967, the Soviet leadership observed the fiftieth anniversary of the founding of the *Cheka*–the "Extraordinary Commission"–the original Soviet secret police. The year 1967 was a time when the secret police, whose image had been blackened by Khrushchev's revelations of the Stalinist years, was being rehabilitated. In a speech during official celebrations, Andropov praised the inheritors of the *Cheka* tradition for implacable struggle against state enemies and for stern adherence to duty. He could not say enough to honor the pervasive Soviet security police.

With the "new" KGB under his command, Andropov was responsible for internal security in the Soviet Union, a responsibility covering political protest, *samizdat* literature, worker grievances, religious dissent–virtually any suggestion of opposition to established policy. The *Chronicle* and Gorbanevskaya and her friends were inevitably to fall under Andropov's surveillance. The histories of the *Chronicle* and Andropov's tenure as chairman of the KGB are inseparably entwined.

Natalia Gorbanevskaya was born in 1936, the year that the Spanish civil war erupted, the year that Adolf Hitler ordered German troops into the Rhineland, and the year that Josef Stalin began purge trials that claimed hundreds of thousands of victims. She was a young girl by the time the Great Patriotic War–as World War II is described in

Soviet history—ended, leaving much of her country in ruins and some 20 million people dead. She was 17 years old when Stalin died in 1953. And by the time Khrushchev denounced Stalin, three years later at the famed twentieth Communist party congress, the 20-year-old Gorbanevskaya was turning into a young poet. She had already expressed decidedly troublesome views, at least as the Soviet bureaucracy looked on Soviet youth. Gorbanevskaya wrote *This World*, one of her early poems, in 1956. She talked about "two dimensions" in her world, that for her "three are too few."[2]

Gorbanevskaya was maturing as a writer during tumultuous political years in the Soviet Union. Khrushchev's "secret speech" to the twentieth congress slowly became known throughout the Soviet Union. Party members were told about it in private meetings. The U.S. Central Intelligence Agency obtained a copy from a Polish defector. It was leaked to the *New York Times*, which published the entire text. Western shortwave radio stations broadcast the Russian version back to the Soviet Union, breaking through Soviet jamming signals as best they could and confirming to millions of Soviet citizens what they knew privately about Stalinist terror.

The Khrushchev speech marked the start of reform years in the Soviet Union just as Gorbanevskaya and many of her friends were coming of political age. In 1956, Gorbanevskaya took part in a small protest at Moscow University, where she was a student, against the bloody Soviet suppression of the Hungarian uprising. In 1957, she was taken to Lubyanka prison and questioned by the KGB for the first time. They wanted to know about her friends and her political activities. Gorbanevskaya aroused enough suspicion about her political tendencies that she was expelled from Moscow University, no slight punishment in the Soviet Union of the 1950s when a university degree translated into a life of privilege, benefit, and relative comfort. In 1959, Gorbanevskaya voluntarily submitted to psychiatric examination because of intense fatigue, insomnia, and persistent feelings of irritation. The examination record was to be used against her later when political authorities questioned her mental condition.[3]

By the late 1950s and early 1960s, Gorbanevskaya, along with the rest of her generation, found the Soviet Union changing, but never as quickly as they hoped. Khrushchev toyed with a precedent-making summit with U.S. President Dwight Eisenhower. The historic conflict with China was swirling to the surface. The Berlin and Cuban crises were on the horizon. Inside the Soviet

Union, Khrushchev tried to reorganize the stolid Communist party and government bureaucracies. Liberalization was in the air. Memoirs about Stalin's labor camps were being prepared. Alexander Solzhenitsyn's *One Day in the Life of Ivan Denisovich*, personally read and approved by Khrushchev, was published in the Soviet literary journal *Novy Mir* in 1962. It buoyed the Gorbanevskaya generation but alarmed the older, more traditional generation.[4]

Novels, short stories, poems, political essays, and memoirs that could not get through the Soviet state censorship system began appearing in typewritten manuscripts, spawning a whole Soviet industry known as *samizdat*. The Russian term *samizdat* is a contraction for words meaning "self" and "publishing." Later there would be *radizdat*—material recorded from foreign radiobroadcasts and circulated in typewritten manuscript—*tamizdat*—literature published abroad and smuggled into the Soviet Union—and *magnitizdat*—homemade recordings. The *"izdat"* genre amounted to an underground Soviet world of communications in which ideas and attitudes banned from the official state-censored Soviet mass media found expression.

It was in this world that Gorbanevskaya lived as a student and young "dissident," although the word had not yet come into vogue. These were years in which important friendships were formed among Moscow dissidents. Yury Galanskov, for example, produced a typewritten *samizdat* literary journal. The first of two issues was called *Phoenix-61* and carried some of Gorbanevskaya's poems. By 1961, she had been permitted entry again into Moscow University and was once more expelled. She had in the process met Andrei Sinyavsky, a gentle, quiet-spoken and brilliant lecturer in Russian literature, who also wrote satiric short stories that were published abroad under the pen name Abram Tertz. A friend of Sinyavsky was Yuly Daniel. Daniel's stories, also bitingly critical of Soviet society, appeared abroad under the name Nikolai Arzhak. Another Gorbanevskaya friend was Alexander Ginzburg, a young dissident who by the early 1960s had put out three issues of an underground literary journal called *Syntax*.

Gorbanevskaya and her friends were moving in the direction of democratic reform as the Communist party's reaction to Khrushchev's anti-Stalin campaign set in. Khrushchev's successors overthrew him in a bloodless Kremlin coup in October 1964, and promptly moved to restore more orthodox social order. They arrested Andrei Sinyavsky and Yuly Daniel in 1965 and put them on trial early in 1966. The two were found guilty of "anti-Soviet propaganda and agitation" and were sentenced. Sinyavsky got seven years in the labor camp. Daniel received five.

The Sinyavsky-Daniel trial was a watershed event.[5] It marked the start of the Brezhnev leadership's steady and methodical suppression of internal dissent, even as it grew. Gorbanevskaya and her friends, nurtured with expectations by Khrushchev's anti-Stalin campaign, found themselves caught in the crackdown. In the mid-1960s in Moscow, they formed intimate, small groups based on personal friendships or friendships of families. The Sinyavsky-Daniel trial tended to be the ethical gauge by which these young intellectuals chose one another's association. To denounce the trial privately was to give one an identity badge that like-minded people could recognize. Gorbanevskaya found herself in a circle that included Pavel Litvinov, Larisa Bogoraz, Victor Krasin, Pyotr Yakir, Alexander Ginzburg, Yury Galanskov, and Ilya Gabai. She got to know Andrei Amalrik, Valery Chalidze, and Pyotr Grigorenko, a retired Soviet war hero general, who was generally regarded as the inspiration of the gathering protest movement.

They were all to become famous in the coming years, although in the Moscow of the mid-1960s they were practically unknown. One could not have distinguished any of them from the hundreds of thousands of Muscovites swarming along Gorky Street or other of the capital's main thoroughfares, jamming into wheezing, worn Moscow buses, pushing into food stores along with the sturdy *babushki*—the legions of old grandmothers—to grab whatever supplies of cabbage, sausage, or potatoes were available. Like others in Moscow, they lived in crowded, dim apartment buildings, sharing kitchens and bathrooms. If they occupied newer, Khrushchev-ordered housing developments outside the center, they spent wearisome hours on subways and buses to reach tiny separate flats, already destined to be the future slums because the construction was so shoddy.

Many of their daily hours in Moscow of the mid-1960s were spent simply surviving, merely battling the faceless mob to accomplish each step of the day. The nights, another thing, often were spent in one or another apartment, in very informal settings, with friends coming and going as circumstances dictated. Nights drinking and talking. Nights getting drunk and having affairs. Nights arguing about life, specifically life in Moscow. Nights talking about what to do. It was small-town, very close, gossipy, everyone knowing one another, everyone privy to the others' thoughts. Galanskov and Ginzburg were friends. Litvinov's mother knew Ginzburg's mother. Larisa Bogoraz was married to Yuly Daniel. Gorbanevskaya knew

Galanskov and Sinyavsky.[6] They were a family unto themselves, not without other associations, but they all saw and knew enough of one another that they could tell the strengths and weaknesses of each, and they knew whom to trust. The close-knit relationship was to prove important later, after the *Chronicle* became established and the KGB tried to break the organization.

During 1967, as they all read the Brezhnev leadership's direction and as the *samizdat* piled up along with more and more reports of arrests, and KGB interrogations and trials, the idea of issuing some kind of bulletin to record events and trends took hold. There were some specific events that moved the idea along. Galanskov and Ginzburg had been arrested that January 1967 for producing the *samizdat* journals *Phoenix-61* and *Phoenix-66* and *Syntax*. Also, irritating to authorities, Ginzburg had gotten together a "white book" of documents revealing the Sinyavsky-Daniel trial as a legal sham. Some friends, including Vladimir Bukovsky, a young dissident who had been in trouble with the authorities for years, helped organize a startling public demonstration on January 22 in Moscow's Pushkin Square, not far from the Kremlin. There were fewer than 40 men and women. They carried a few handmade banners that they unfurled to protest the arrest of Galanskov and three others (Ginzburg was to be arrested the next day).[7] KGB agents immediately broke up the unusual demonstration. Arrests began later in the day. Bukovsky was one of those taken, and by September 1967 he had been tried and sentenced to three years in prison. Others already had been sentenced, including Victor Khaustov. By February 1968, Ginzburg, Galanskov, and their friends Alexei Dobrovolsky and Vera Lashkova had also been found guilty of anti-Soviet activities.[8]

The Sinyavsky-Daniel trial thus seemed to have begun an official Kremlin campaign that was reaching into heretofore obscure enclaves to root out persons who were not only discontent with political events in the Soviet Union but were actively writing and demonstrating against them. The group in which Gorbanevskaya had found herself was suddenly being assaulted by the KGB.

Pavel Litvinov, grandson of the Soviet "people's commissar" or minister of foreign affairs from 1930 to 1939, and educated as a physicist and with a mind for scientific precision, had studiously started collecting information about the Pushkin Square demonstration and about the Galanskov-Ginzburg case. There were a number of informal meetings among people like Gorbanevskaya, Litvinov, Yakir, Krasin, Galina Gabai, the wife of Ilya, and others. They felt overwhelmed by the amount of varied information they had assembled or that was circulating about trials, arrests, labor camps, searches, interrogations. It was, Litvinov recalls, as if there were "hundreds of sentences just hanging in the air."[9]

They were all acutely aware that information given to Western correspondents in Moscow about arrests and trials, about ominous reports of hunger strikes in labor camps, and of life there among political prisoners could be transmitted in foreign radiobroadcasts. Sometimes it was just a matter of hours after a document was given to an American news agency in Moscow that a foreign radio report about the event could be heard in shortwave programs in Moscow. The British Broadcasting Corporation, Radio Liberty, Deutsche Welle, and Voice of America Russian-language broadcasts circumvented the Soviet censorship system under Glavlit—the acronym for the government censorship administration for the press, radio, television, literature, and general publishing. These reports in turn attracted new sources of information, nurturing a grapevine of civil rights news. Khrushchev had halted blanket jamming of foreign radiobroadcasts in Russian in 1963, with the exception of the officially despised Radio Liberty, whose special focus on internal Soviet political events made it a category unto itself. People could listen to all the foreign news they wanted in the mid-1960s in the Soviet Union. The tacit alliance of Soviet dissidents and Western correspondents and foreign radio stations was creating a vast information network reporting to the mass Soviet audience independently of the Glavlit organization.

The information network among the dissidents themselves operated on the basis of personal knowledge and trust and sometimes out of sheer chance. It happened like this: Larisa Bogoraz, wife of Yuly Daniel, was on a train traveling to see her imprisoned husband. She met the wife of Valery Ronkin, who also, it turned out, was on a trip to visit her imprisoned husband in the same Siberian labor camp. Ronkin was an unfamiliar name to Moscow dissidents. A Leningrader, Ronkin had been arrested in 1965 for antistate activities after the KGB broke up a clandestine group that he led. It was called the Union of Communards and preached a truly workers' state. In the conspiratorial fashion of earlier illegal Russian Marxist circles, the group met in secret. It published a *samizdat* journal called *The Bell* on a clandestine printing press. In Russian it was *Kolokol*, after the famous journal of the same name produced by Alexander Herzen in the nineteenth century in London and smuggled into Russia. Even after the KGB penetrated the Union of Communards and imprisoned Ronkin, not many in the Soviet Union, let alone the outside world, knew about him or his group, such was the compartmental quality of Soviet life, especially concerning dissident political and police matters. The Moscow dissidents thus learned of the Ronkin case only when two wives met to share common information about their imprisoned husbands.[10]

What was happening, then, as trials picked up in the Soviet Union of the late 1960s and as dissidents met and talked was a growing awareness of a pattern of events. That some of this information was obtained by Western correspondents and that some of it was broadcast back to the Soviet Union in Russian served to document and enlarge the dissidents' picture of their society. For they suffered from a sense of isolation and ignorance of daily events in the Soviet Union, where authorities ensure that the mass media present a narrow and particular portrait of the country. In the late 1960s, Soviet dissidents only gradually assembled facts to convince them that the post-Khrushchev leadership was undertaking a deliberate policy of repression.

Pavel Litvinov was a central figure in these circles, and for his political activities he was later sent into internal exile and then banished from the country in 1972. He made his new home in Tarrytown, N.Y., where he taught at a private boarding school. In an interview, he recollected the Moscow years, the sense of isolation, the paucity of information:

I mention the wife of Ronkin—Nina Ronkin—as an example. The Soviet press did not write about them. There was nothing we could learn about them because only their close friends knew the story, and they were afraid to talk. And suddenly when two wives of two prisoners meet each other on the train, that is a different story. Suddenly we get the information. And suddenly Ronkin and Daniel meet each other and become friends in the labor camp.

So we picked up information about other political trials through these channels, through meetings of relatives of prisoners. And of course at the same time, when I gave to foreign correspondents the record of my questioning by a KGB officer,[11] I signed my own name and put my address on it. And then together with Larisa Bogoraz, I wrote an "Appeal to the World Public Opinion." It was transmitted by the Voice of America. Suddenly people started to come to us, write us letters. I received about 100 letters from Soviet people before my mail was cut off.

We got this information and we couldn't do much with it. Most of the information was not of much interest to the American and Western press, at least in that form. So we started to say that we have to publish some sort of bulletin. We called it a "bulletin" in the beginning. The word "chronicle" appeared later.[12]

There were a series of get-togethers among the increasingly active dissidents in the late winter and early spring of 1968. There was no organization, no specific leaders, no agendas, no records—none of the paraphernalia that goes with planned, orderly action. Natalia Gorbanevskaya remembers talking with Ilya Gabai, among others, before the first issue of the *Chronicle* appeared and deciding that a bulletin of some kind must be issued to publicize the mounting information they had on hand. She reminisced about the origin of the *Chronicle* while sitting in her Paris apartment amidst stacks of books and papers:

[A friend] was saying that it is necessary to organize regular information, but she was too busy. She was in charge of contacts with the labor camps, and sending packages to the prisoners. She really didn't have the time. The reason I could do it was because I was pregnant and I had pregnancy leave from work. Because of that I had more time. There were a number of people, it is true, who had been fired from their jobs. But these were high-level intellectuals who could not do "blue collar."

There was a meeting with Ilya Gabai at the end of March, maybe the beginning of April, I don't remember. But I want to say there was no specific meeting where we decided to issue the *Chronicle*. There were regular, just normal meetings where we discussed whatever was interesting at the time. They were friendly chats about a lot of subjects. I remember they said, "Well, you start it and we'll help you." It wasn't formal, it was just in the conversation.[13]

Gorbanevskaya does not recall that it was even particularly important when by consensus she agreed to take on the job of issuing the *Chronicle*. It was just another thing to do in the day's activities. A name had not even been chosen for what was referred simply as a "bulletin." The group had no particular form in mind, let alone an agreed-upon purpose except to publicize the increasing frequency of secret police actions against friends or acquaintances who were speaking out on human rights.

Recollections focus on a particular meeting in late February or early March 1968, in Dolgoprudny, an area of enormous apartment house complexes ringing the older, central Moscow. The apartment in which the dissidents met belonged to a friend of Major General Pyotr Grigorenko, a lavishly decorated World War II hero who as early as 1961 had openly criticized the Khrushchev leadership. By 1968, Grigorenko had been demoted, confined for 15 months in a Leningrad prison psychiatric hospital, and expelled from the Communist party. At the age of 61, he was old enough to be the father of most of the *Chronicle* group, but he was extraordinarily fearless and active, and besides protesting against the trials of Ginzburg and Galanskov and Khaustov and Bukovsky, he had taken a special interest in the Stalin-era expulsion of the Crimean Tatars from their homeland.[14] Grigorenko's friend was not himself involved in the human rights cause, but allowed his apartment to be used for meetings.

In the early evening, when it was already getting dark, seven people arrived at the apartment in Dolgoprudny for at least the last, if not the decisive, meeting before Gorbanevskaya put out the *Chronicle*, issue no. 1. Besides Gorbanevskaya and Grigorenko, the others were Litvinov, Krasin, Yakir, and Gabai. The seventh person cannot be identified for the person's own protection.[15] The setting was some 15 miles from the center of Moscow. Snow covered the ground still, reminding them of long Moscow winters. Litvinov recalls the scene:

> It was an apartment building, six stories, maybe four. It was a brick building, a typical Moscow apartment. They are all alike, but it had reasonably good Finnish furniture. The reason we met there was that we were pretty sure that our apartments were all very well bugged. We didn't want our activities interrupted in advance, although all of our activities were open. That's why we took that minimum of precaution, to go to an apartment where there was reasonable expectation that there were no bugs. They [the KGB] probably could have listened to us if they had been there. . . . What I want to stress was that it was not a decisive meeting. It was not like a politburo meeting. Natasha [Gorbanevskaya] said she would do it. She was very well organized. She was

efficient. She had literary experience. And she started to do it. [16]

The Dolgoprudny meeting ended with an understanding that Natalia Gorbanevskaya would produce some sort of "bulletin" reporting information from friends of the group and anyone else about the persecutions underway. It still had no name. It would be typed because that was how virtually all *samizdat* was produced in the Soviet Union. The general Soviet public, then or now, did not nor does not have access to printing presses or even mimeograph machines, let alone electronic copiers. Anything produced on Soviet state presses, in any case, is censored by Glavlit. This is to say that the talk in 1968 of putting out a private, unofficial "bulletin" readily translated in the minds of those involved into a few typed carbon copies of *samizdat* that would be circulated among friends, one of the copies being reserved for a contact in the Western press corps in Moscow.

As Gorbanevskaya began collecting material for the first issue of the new bulletin, the founding group was already caught up in a paradox. Its main intent was to publicize violations of human rights in the Soviet Union, especially the lesser known incidents, and thereby draw what dissidents thought would be curative world public opinion to the Soviet malady. The group set out to be neither clandestine nor deliberately secretive. The dissidents put a premium on public activities and confined itself scrupulously within the limits of written Soviet law. [17]

They all well knew from experience that the KGB watched them. They all assumed that their telephone conversations were monitored, that their private correspondence was probably read, and that their daily movements around or outside of Moscow were reported. Litvinov had been questioned by the KGB as recently as the previous September, in 1967, about notes he was assembling on the Pushkin Square demonstration and on the Galanskov-Ginzburg case. Most of the others had also had encounters with the KGB or its predecessors. Both Yakir and Krasin had already served sentences in labor camps, and Grigorenko had been subjected to drug treatments in a Leningrad psychiatric hospital.

These particular individuals thus had no illusions about the chances of succeeding in the Soviet Union with a conspiratorial or revolutionary movement, even if they chose that path. Actually, as the Soviet human rights "movement" was then forming, the *Chronicle* group shunned conscious, planned secrecy. They regarded that tactic as too similar to the Bolsheviks, to the Leninist concept of a political movement. They later would reject the suggestion that the *Chronicle* was at all analogous to *Iskra*, the underground paper that Lenin edited outside of Russia during czarist years before the 1917 Bolshevik revolution and smuggled into the country. The *Chronicle* group believed more in public action, in holding a mirror to the Soviet social system built by Stalin. They wanted little more than the civil liberties ensured in the 1936 "Stalin constitution" and repeated in the 1977 "Brezhnev constitution."

Yet, as Gorbanevskaya began preparing the first issue of the *Chronicle*, the work was per force and by habit and practice more of a clandestine operation than a public petition. It was the opposite of how the dissidents, in their more idealistic moments, hoped to function.

In Moscow in those years, living arrangements were necessarily flexible. Housing was in short supply, although Khrushchev had approved a rapid building program that saw mass-produced brick or prefabricated concrete apartment complexes mushrooming in and around the city. While Muscovites were abandoning the worst of old housing in the late 1960s, they often enough crowded together in apartments that had been sliced into spaces for several couples or families who shared the original kitchen, toilet, and bath. The closeness and lack of privacy, the continuous arguments about using kitchens, about storing foods, about irritating noises and habits of neighbors almost living on top of one another contributed to a deep, continuous fatigue. Gorbanevskaya, for example, was living in one room of a communal apartment with her young first son and her mother at Novopeshaniya 13/3. Life was a struggle already as she undertook editorship of the *Chronicle*.

Gorbanevskaya earlier had assembled some information for the bulletin she had now promised to compile, and she began collecting more. The focus was almost inevitably on the Galanskov-Ginzburg trial. Litvinov had put together precise notes of those proceedings.[18] The trial was special for invoking not only article 70 of the Russian republic's criminal code but two newly and secretly adopted laws directed against free expression and assembly. Articles 190-1 and 190-3 of the Russian republic's code came into force in September 1966.

The one concerning assembly, 190-3, made it a crime to organize or actively participate in "group activities involving a grave breach of public order, or clear disobedience to the legitimate demands of representatives of authority. . . ."[19] The maximum penalty was three years' imprisonment.

This new law on assembly seemed clearly designed to be used against unsanctioned public gatherings that worried Soviet authorities. In the early and mid-1960s, a number of young intellectuals, including Bukovsky, Vladimir Osipov, and Edward Kuznetsov, had organized and taken part in poetry and literature readings in Moscow's Mayakovsky Square. The latter two had been convicted under article 70 on antistate propaganda and agitation. The new law 190-3 dealing with public gatherings carried less severe penalties and was more narrowly construed so that police could break up Mayakovsky Square assemblies or any others and have a written law clearly on their side.

Articles 70 and the newer 190-1 dealing with press and speech were immediately important to the *Chronicle* group. They became a legal sparring point between dissidents and the KGB as the *Chronicle* developed.

Article 70 describes as a crime: "Agitation or propaganda conducted for the purpose of weakening or subverting Soviet power for the purpose of committing particularly dangerous state crimes; dissemination for the same purpose, of slanderous fabrications that discredit the Soviet state and social system; as well as dissemination or preparation or possession for the same purposes of literature with a like content."[20] Article 70 had been used to imprison Sinyavsky and Daniel. But Soviet authorities, ever concerned about maintaining a facade of legality in political cases, were working with a law designed for far more serious activities in the official view than publishing a few short stories or *samizdat* leaflets. Could these really be said to fall under article 70; did they convincingly weaken or subvert the huge, powerful Soviet state?

Article 190-1 was drafted in less global terms and therefore seemed designed to deal with lesser forms of political protest. It outlaws "The systematic dissemination by word of mouth of deliberately false statements derogatory to the Soviet state and social system, and also the preparation of dissemination of such statements in written, printed or any other form. . . ." Whereas the penalty for violation of article 70 is a maximum of seven years in prison and/or two to five years in internal exile, the lesser sentences in article 190-1 are three years in prison, one year of corrective labor, or a fine of up to 100 rubles.[21]

Two specific phrases proved important to the *Chronicle*—in article 70, the words "slanderous fabrications that discredit," and in article 190-1, "deliberately false statements derogatory" to the Soviet state. The KGB and Soviet courts were to use these time and again to argue that the *Chronicle* was an illegal publication.

There was more than enough information on hand for the first issue of the *Chronicle*. The problem was more selection than quantity. Litvinov had his detailed report of the Galanskov-Ginzburg trial, or the "Trial of Four." Reaction to the trial within the Soviet Union, Gorbanevskaya recalls, produced a "torrent of the most varied kinds of letters from both individuals and groups, and of protests against the handling of the trial, against the verdict and the sentence, and against mendacious articles in the newspapers."

Besides putting together the Galanskov-Ginzburg trial information, Litvinov traveled to Leningrad in the weeks before the *Chronicle*. Leningrad authorities were cracking down on dissidents there, and Litvinov picked up what information there was of arrests and trials to pass on to Gorbanevskaya. Bits and scraps came from Yakir and Krasin. But Gorbanevskaya was the workhorse. She collected the longer written scripts, the few lines about an arrest, the protest letter with a dozen or more signatures. She talked with friends and acquaintances, storing information in her memory or jotting down notes.

What may appear to be an undemanding task of putting together a 20-page neighborhood newsletter with items about who is doing what and where was enormously time-consuming, exhausting work in Moscow of the late 1960s. In compiling a bulletin about protests and objections to the Soviet government and about reprisals against individuals who challenged authorities, Gorbanevskaya had to conduct herself carefully. She could not use the telephone to obtain information, for everyone knew that the KGB tapped private telephones. She could not, without some risk, carry notes with information on her person. It was risky for her, and it was risky for those who supplied her. KGB experts could trace people by their handwriting. Traveling around spread-out Moscow in crowded buses or the metro took hours out of a day if one wanted personally to talk with friends. Gorbanevskaya had to keep a file of information in her apartment. The KGB could search apartments whenever they chose. She had no readily available reference books on Soviet law to check criminal proceedings. She had no archive, no file of newspaper or magazine clippings against which to check names, dates, places, and events. It was like putting together a bulletin out of a shoebox, relying on one's own memory or the memory and exactness of others.

Besides the work of getting the *Chronicle* contents together, Gorbanevskaya faced the normal struggle for survival in Moscow. She, her young son, and her mother, living in a cramped room, shared a toilet, bath, and kitchen with neighbors. There was food to buy, clothes to wash, a child to care for. Although Gorbanevskaya's mother, in the tradition of the Russian *babushka*, or grandmother, could do much of this, Gorbanevskaya had to keep her activities from her mother.

In the last days of April, then, she sat down with material in hand, carbon sheets, paper, and the old Olympia typewriter that she had bought in a *kommission*, the Soviet consignment shop network, to produce the first issue of the *Chronicle*. The typewriter had been purchased in 1964 for 45 rubles with what is called "black cash." Soviet wages were so low that it was impossible to save money for a major purpose except by scrimping for months. A Slavic linguist and young writer, Gorbanevskaya, for example, worked in an organization that compiled bibliographies and earned only 83 rubles a month. She and her colleagues would get together on payday and contribute five rubles each to the "black cash" fund. Everyone drew from the fund by turn, the order determined by lottery. One could thus acquire 50 rubles or more quickly. It was like buying something on the installment plan.

The old portable Olympia on which Gorbanevskaya typed poetry already portented a problem as she began the *Chronicle*. The KGB could connect documents and typewriters. Each machine, like fingerprints, has its own typeface characteristics. One had to be careful in writing *samizdat* that it could not be traced through other items typed on the same machine. Later, Gorbanevskaya went to the Soviet underground economy to pay a private craftsman to change the type faces on her Olympia, so that previously typed copies of her poetry could not be matched to copies of the *Chronicle*.[22]

As Gorbanevskaya began work on the first issue of what came to be known as the *Chronicle*, the form, name, or purpose had not been determined. While the word "bulletin" had been used, that still was not a title. It was Krasin who suggested calling the news periodical the *Chronicle*. There reportedly was a foreign radio Russian-language program by the name—*Khronika* in Russian—and the program, in giving factual, varied news items, seemed to describe what they were setting out to do. The program title was expanded into the fuller, more descriptive name *Khronika Tekushchikh Sobytii*, the *Chronicle of Current Events*.

But in the beginning this was almost secondary. The year 1968 had been declared "Human Rights Year" in observance of the twentieth anniversary of the United Nations General Declaration on Human Rights. Gorbanevskaya and her fellow dissidents thought it particularly timely to identify with the year-long observance. Hence, on the top of the title page of the first issue of the *Chronicle*, Gorbanevskaya typed, in Russian, "Human Rights Year in the Soviet Union." It was decided to add, on the same front page, the Russian translation of article 19, of the UN Declaration on Human Rights:

Everyone has the right of freedom of opinion and expression. This right includes freedom to hold opinions without interference and to seek, receive, and impart information and ideas through any media regardless of national frontiers.[23]

Working at odd moments, Gorbanevskaya finished the original and six carbons a few days before the end of April. At times she would check information with friends, always concealing the work from her mother. Completing the 20 pages, she then typed the cover page, dating the first issue April 30, 1968. She and Litvinov handed out six copies to friends. At least one was given to a Western correspondent. All the original notes, Gorbanevskaya's and others', were burned so that handwriting could not be traced by the KGB.

Gorbanevskaya, about two weeks later, began to produce another pressrun of issue no. 1. She was now almost nine months pregnant; the baby could come at any time. Gorbanevskaya transferred her work to Litvinov's apartment, to ensure that her mother did not discover what she was doing. It was May 13, 1968. Alone in the small apartment that afternoon, Gorbanevskaya was working on the *Chronicle* when she felt the first labor pains. She left what she had typed, and a note to Litvinov to finish the work. Still feeling labor pains, Gorbanevskaya went to her apartment and finally to the hospital. She gave birth to her second son, Osik, at 1:30 A.M. on May 14.

Several weeks later—Gorbanevskaya does not recall precisely when—she had returned home with the baby and one day reappeared at the Litvinov apartment to find it crowded with friends. It says something of the times, the people and the inauspicious birth of the *Chronicle*, that Gorbanevskaya found the typewriter where she had left it, a partly finished page of the *Chronicle* still in the machine, and no one particularly concerned about it. None could then envision how seriously Soviet authorities would come to view the *Chronicle*, or how long the *Chronicle* would survive, or that it was that important at all.

The summer of 1968 Gorbanevskaya was 32 years old. A photograph taken about that time shows her with her older son, Yasik, dressed in shapeless cotton pants, high ankle tennis shoes, and a nondescript dark sweater, almost Maoist in simplicity. Diminuitive, short, sandy hair, firm chin. Not much the picture of a revolutionary. Before the summer was out, Soviet troops marched into Czechoslovakia and the future of both the *Chronicle* and Gorbanevskaya was forever changed.

NOTES

1. The author is indebted for much of this information to Natalia Gorbanevskaya in several interviews. The last concerning the circumstances of the first issue of the *Chronicle* was conducted on June 3 and 4, 1982, in Paris. See also Natalia Gorbanevskaya, "The Founding of the Chronicle of Current Events," *Chronicle of Human Rights in the Soviet Union,* no. 29, pp. 52-56 [hereafter *Chronicle/ Rights*].

2. Natalia Gorbanevskaya, *Poberezhye: Stikhi* (Ann Arbor, Mich.: Ardis, 1973).

3. See Sidney Bloch and Peter Reddaway, *Psychiatric Terror: How Soviet Psychiatry Is Used to Suppress Dissent* (New York: Basic Books, 1977).

4. For a description of the Soviet literary scene in the 1960s, see John Dornberg, *The New Tsars: Russia Under Stalin's Heirs* (New York: Doubleday, 1972), pp. 118-51. Dornberg spent two years in Moscow as *Newsweek*'s correspondent before he was expelled.

5. For an analysis of the Sinyavsky-Daniel trial in the context of Soviet politics at the time, see Frederick C. Barghoorn, "The Post-Khrushchev Campaign to Suppress Dissent: Perspectives, Strategies and Techniques of Repression," in *Dissent in the USSR: Politics, Ideology and People,* Rudolph L. Tokes (Baltimore: Johns Hopkins University Press, 1975), pp. 35-95.

6. See Dornberg, *The New Tsars,* pp. 70-71.

7. Pavel Litvinov, *The Demonstration in Pushkin Square: The Trial Records with Commentary and an Open Letter* (Boston: Gambit, 1969), pp. 1-20, contains an instructive essay by Karel van Het Reve and details of the demonstration.

8. For discussion and description of these events, see

Litvinov, *Pushkin Square;* and Peter Reddaway, ed. and trans., *Uncensored Russia: Protest and Dissent in the Soviet Union* (New York: American Heritage Press, 1972), pp. 72-94.

9. Both Pavel Litvinov and Natalia Gorbanevskaya, in interviews with the author, remember being impressed with the flood of information in Moscow at that time.

10. This information comes from Litvinov interview. Some of the information about Ronkin appeared in the first issue of the *Chronicle* after he joined Daniel and other prisoners in a Mordovian labor camp to protest inhumane conditions. See *Khronika Tekushchikh Sobytii: Vypuski 1-15* (Amsterdam: Alexander Herzen Foundation, 1979), p. 16. The volume reprints the first 15 issues in Russian of the *Chronicle*. See also Reddaway, *Uncensored Russia,* pp. 65-67, 203-08, for translations of *Chronicle* reports, in addition to background information.

11. For the Russian and English versions of Litvinov's questioning by the KGB on September 26, 1967, and 63 of the letters he subsequently received, see *Dear Comrade: Pavel Litvinov and the Voices of Soviet Citizens in Dissent,* Karel Van Het Reve, ed. (New York: Pitman, 1969).

12. This section quotes Litvinov interview.

13. Gorbanevskaya interview. Her reference to the "high-level intellectuals" and "blue-collar work" was said cynically. See also Gorbanevskaya, *Chronicle/Rights,* no. 29 (January-March 1978):53-54.

14. See *Chronicle*, no. 8, in *Khronika,* pp. 158-64; and Bloch and Reddaway, *Psychiatric Terror,* pp. 105-27.

15. These names were mentioned in independent interviews by the author with Litvinov, Victor Krasin, and Ludmilla Alexeyeva. Alexeyeva was not present. She says she was given the information during interrogation by the KGB.

16. Litvinov interview. Litvinov says that possibly Yury Gendler, a Leningrad dissident, also was at this meeting. Gendler did have contacts with Litvinov, Krasin, and Grigorenko, and they were used against him when he was tried in Leningrad in December 1968. See Reddaway, *Uncensored Russia,* pp. 380-85.

17. Valery Chalidze argues this point with particular force concerning his own dissident activities. See Valery Chalidze, *To Defend These Rights* (New York: Random House, 1974), pp. 50 ff.

18. See Reddaway, *Uncensored Russia,* pp. 72 ff., for the *Chronicle's* account of the proceedings. See also Litvinov's fuller account, originally 200,000 words, published in condensed form in 1972 after being smuggled out

of the Soviet Union in *The Trial of Four,* ed. Pavel Litvinov and Peter Reddaway, trans. Janis Sapiets et al. (New York: Viking Press, 1972).

19. See Litvinov, *Pushkin Square,* pp. 13-14, for a translation of both 190-1 and 190-3. Although each of the 15 Soviet republics has its own criminal code, the provisions of the Russian republic's are found in those of other republics, usually under different numbers. The Russian republic code normally sets the legal pace.

20. See Mark W. Hopkins, *Mass Media in the Soviet Union* (New York: Pegasus, 1970), pp. 129-30, for a translation of article 70 from the Russian republic criminal code and for a discussion of the law.

21. Litvinov, *Pushkin Square,* p. 13, contains the text. The ruble was worth about $1 at the official rate at the time article 190-1 came into force. An average monthly wage was about 100 rubles in the mid-1960s.

22. This section is drawn mostly from Gorbanevskaya interview.

22. See *Khronika,* the title page of the first issue. Gorbanevskaya says that Krasin suggested the name *Chronicle,* or *Khronika* in Russian, after a BBC program. Russian service staffers do not recall such a title. Litvinov says he proposed adding the Russian version of article 19 of the UN Declaration on Human Rights. Gorbanevskaya says it was her idea.

2
THE SPARK

In the history of the Soviet press, the first issue of the *Chronicle* was a remarkable publication. Although modest in scope and appearance, the *Chronicle* contained real news, uncensored news, gathered by a staff of sorts that had talked with unfettered sources of information and that, in some cases, had directly witnessed events and freely written about them. Here was information that Soviet authorities had chosen either to conceal or to present in a particularly biased way for their own political purposes. What the *Chronicle* reported one would not find in *Pravda*, *Izvestia*, or other of the Soviet Communist party and state-monitored mass media. Issue no. 1 was the birth of an uncensored periodical issued in the Soviet Union by Soviet citizens directly exercising the Soviet constitutional right of free press. There was nothing like it in the Soviet Union of the 1960s, and one would have to search back in Soviet history to the 1920s for its journalistic predecessors.

It was true that Baptist dissidents had been producing a bulletin in the Soviet Union since 1964. The unofficial Council of Churches of Evangelical Christians and Baptists was a breakaway group that refused to accept Soviet government registration of religious groups and restrictions on their practices. After declaring their autonomy in the early 1960s from the officially sanctioned Baptist church, the dissenters quickly became objects of official Soviet harassment. A number of persons was arrested and imprisoned. In 1964, a Council of Prisoners' Relatives associated with the larger council began issuing what was simply titled *Bulletin* to document violations of Baptists' rights and to gain publicity for appeals to Soviet government and international organizations on behalf of imprisoned Baptists.[1] The *Bulletin* appeared regularly, on the average of once every two months from 1964 through 1980. Like other Soviet *samizdat*, the *Bulletin* circulated underground, from hand to hand. Its contents were deliberately focused on Baptist activities. Unlike the *Chronicle*, it purposely did not aim for a larger audience. Indeed, there is no evidence that any of the Moscow group involved in the original *Chronicle* had ever heard of or seen a *samizdat* issue of the Baptist *Bulletin*.

From the start, then, the *Chronicle* was set apart from other and plentiful *samizdat* literature, political tracts, petitions, statements, and reports. It was unique, writes Soviet specialist Michael Meerson-Aksenov, because it was the "first *samizdat* journal which, for the first time in the history of the Soviet regime, began the collection and the publication of significant data relating to violations of personality, illegal incarcerations, imprisonment in psychiatric hospitals, and firing from work for ideological, political and religious reasons."[2] Soviet and foreign journalists could get this type of information in Moscow in the late 1960s only on a sporadic basis and only if they were involved in *samizdat* and dissident circles. Even then, information was unstructured, obtained by chance, and sometimes incomplete. If one were outside established dissident circles, the most one knew about official actions besides rumors was contained in cryptic Soviet press reports. They told one virtually nothing except that something had happened. Or one found out about dissidents in polemical broadsides in state-controlled newspapers that were so deliberately distorted that it was difficult to know precisely what was involved.

The *Chronicle* was from the beginning an alternative to official information. A style was established with the first issue that distinguished the *Chronicle* from the Soviet press certainly and that ultimately survived successive changes of editorial groups to lend the *Chronicle* an air of detached, dispassionate reporting.

For that, the *Chronicle* gained widespread credibility in an area of Soviet information not known for either precision or thoroughness. The style of the *Chronicle* was heavy on facts—names, ages, dates, places, specific events. It was light on both judgments and speculation or opinion. Years later, interviewed in Paris, the exiled Gorbanevskaya reflected:

> To a certain extent the [*Chronicle*] style already had
> been worked out in *samizdat* letters of protests.
> Basically there was an attempt in all the letters to be
> very exact, to lay out the facts, to describe the
> violation of rights, to quote articles of law. Nothing
> was exaggerated. The love for objectivity was in the
> air. Was this un-Russian? I don't think so.
> Herzen's *Kolokol* contained a mass of pure informa-
> tion. Journalism before the [Soviet] revolution was
> varied, and objective information was a considerable
> part. We were educated in communist propaganda—
> exaggeration, lies and the like. And we felt that we
> had no right to either lie or to exaggerate. The
> *Chronicle* put itself outside of any polemics. There
> was the idea that the *Chronicle* was a common voice,
> not the voice of an individual person or a specific
> group. Therefore, the *Chronicle* had to be put
> together so that no personal opinions entered into the
> information. [3]

Most of the people around the *Chronicle* were of like
mind on violations of civil rights. They felt that fully
documented, passionless statements to Soviet authorities,
including specific points of law, ultimately would be more
effective than emotional complaints. Indeed, a whole segment of the emerging Soviet human rights "movement" put
the legal approach before all. The then young, brilliant
Soviet physicist Valery Chalidze, although not directly
connected with the *Chronicle*, particularly argued this
theme. The homemade banners unfurled during the brief
Pushkin Square demonstration on December 5, 1965,
Chalidze contends, were typical of those advocates of human
rights emphasizing Soviet constitutional guarantees. One
banner, Chalidze notes, read "Respect the Constitution, the
Basic Law of the USSR." Another said, "We Demand that
the Sinyavsky-Daniel Trial Be Public."[4] These were ex-
pressions of persons who far from a violent revolution
advocated rule of law.

With this approach to reform of the Soviet system went a
style that reflected both the reaction to typical bombast in
the Soviet media and the intellectual background of many of
those involved with the *Chronicle*. Litvinov, for one, was
a trained physicist. His scientific style was apparent in
the voluminous report on the Galanskov-Ginzburg trial.
Much of what appeared in the first *Chronicle*, including
segments of the trial record, were written by Litvinov.

The report on the trial of Galanskov, Ginzburg, Dobrovolsky, and Lashkova began:

> All four were charged under article 70 of the Russian criminal code, and Galanskov was additionally charged under article 88-1. All four were arrested in January 1967 and had spent nearly a year in Lefortovo prison, in violation of article 97 of the Russian criminal code, according to which the maximum period of pretrial detention may not exceed nine months.[5]

The clinical, aloof writing of the *Chronicle* report contrasted sharply with official Soviet newspaper accounts of the trial under such headlines as "The Lackeys" and "No Indulgence!" These suggest the tone of vitriolic Soviet press commentary designed to discredit ideas or individuals opposed by the Soviet government.

The first issue of the *Chronicle* also established a form for the publication. The issue carried seven items, in this order: "(1) the trial of Galanskov, Ginzburg, Dobrovolsky and Lashkova, (2) protests in connection with the trial, (3) repressions in connection with the protests, (4) statements to the Budapest Conference of Communist and Workers Parties, (5) political prisoners, (6) Leningrad trial, and (7) arrest of Valentin Prussakov."[6] There would be additions to these news categories later, as the *Chronicle*'s information network expanded and its editors changed, but the basic format remained the same. The *Chronicle* would include reports of major trials involving civil rights, statements of grievances, news notes from the labor camps holding political prisoners, and documents bearing on civil rights.

The first issue drew heavily on actions against the *Chronicle* group and its friends and acquaintances. Besides the Galanskov-Ginzburg proceeding with which some of the *Chronicle* people were closely connected, protest statements reproduced in that first issue revealed a pattern of signatures. Many of those who encouraged founding of the *Chronicle* turned up as co-authors of grievances. The statement to the Budapest Conference was signed by, among others, Bogoraz, Litvinov, Ilya Gabai, Grigorenko, Krasin, and Yakir. The section about political prisoners included information about Yuly Daniel and Andrei Sinyavsky, friends of the *Chronicle* dissidents. This is to say that when it came time to put together the *Chronicle*, Gorbanevskaya used what was available, and most of that information came from or was collected by one relatively small Moscow group.

Contents of this first *Chronicle* suggest more. The isolation in which most of the dissidents found themselves showed in their rather narrow knowledge. They were cut off from larger areas of Soviet events, unaware of sympathizers in other Soviet cities, or only dimly informed of official persecution of these people. Thus, the first *Chronicle* tended to be a record of some specific events over roughly the previous six months. It would be many more issues before the *Chronicle*'s information network expanded.

The months between April 1968 and December 1969 are largely the Gorbanevskaya era of the *Chronicle*. She edited or substantially compiled the 11 issues put out in that time, although others helped with the final stages of nos. 3, 10, and 11. Once begun, the *Chronicle* appeared every two months, carrying the last date of the month. Issues fluctuated in size, but the trend was to fuller, longer, and more varied contents. Number 3, only nine pages long, was the exception. It reflected a disruption when Gorbanevskaya was preparing for a demonstration in Red Square against the Soviet-led invasion of Czechoslovakia. Except for this, the first 11 issues of the *Chronicle* averaged 34 double-spaced typewritten pages, the smallest being 20 and the largest 60.[7] It is a little deceptive to measure the *Chronicle* this way because copies were typed by different hands. Depending on the typewriter and on whether the typist used single or double spaces and narrow or wide margins, successive copies of the *Chronicle* varied in length. Thus, a tabulation of page numbers drawn from existing reproductions of the *Chronicle* is only approximate. Nonetheless, it is clear that the *Chronicle* was growing in volume as Gorbanevskaya and fellow dissidents developed an information network.

Ludmilla Alexeyeva, who was involved with the *Chronicle* from the start and then with the unofficial Moscow Helsinki-monitoring group, concludes in a statistical and content analysis of the *Chronicle* that from the first few issues it is apparent that the editors had limited information to the mainstream Moscow dissidents. Five of the seven sections of the first issue dealt with events in Moscow and two with events in Leningrad. The pattern of information in subsequent issues showed a noticeable expansion in the range of reporting. In 1969, Alexeyeva notes, there were *Chronicle* items about political trials not only in Moscow and Leningrad but also in Simferopol, Kiev, Riga, Perm, and Kharkov—cities scattered over the Soviet Union west of the Ural Mountains.[8]

Although it is clear from these facts that the *Chronicle* in 1968-69 was reaching an increasingly larger audience and extending its network of information sources, *Chronicle* workers in Moscow could not themselves trace the *Chronicle* distribution routes. Production of the *Chronicle* from the very first was along the lines of a "chain letter." Gorbanevskaya typed the first seven copies. One went to a Western correspondent, another was saved in order to produce more copies, and the remaining five copies were given out. In the already established form for distributing *samizdat*, recipients were expected to reproduce further copies. Commonly these were typed, but homemade photocopying of *samizdat* was increasingly popular. How many copies of a particular *samizdat* item were made could not be said, the work being done privately and separately. The same held true as the *Chronicle* came on the scene. Ultimately there might have been several hundred copies of a single issue of the *Chronicle* produced, and they could have made their way to dozens of Soviet cities across thousands of miles. Rough estimates of the *Chronicle*'s circulation could be made from news items reaching Moscow from readers, but there are no precise statistics.

After the first few issues, as it became apparent that the *Chronicle* would survive, a method evolved for transmitting information. And this in turn touched on the very nature of the *Chronicle*.

From the beginning, dissidents expected the *Chronicle* to have a relatively short life. Born of immediate concern with a rising frequency of arrests and prosecution of dissidents, it was nurtured by the fact that 1968 was the UN "Year of Human rights." As the first *Chronicle* was being readied, no one thought much beyond 1968. Gorbanevskaya, for one, never supposed that the *Chronicle* would survive as long as it did.[9] When the first issue of 1969 was prepared, no. 6, the UN "Year of Human Rights" had ended. Gorbanevskaya revised the *Chronicle* slogan to say, "Human Rights Year in the Soviet Union Continues."[10] With the first issue of 1970, after Gorbanevskaya had been arrested and new editors had taken over the *Chronicle*, the connection with the human rights year was abandoned entirely. The new slogan read: "The Movement in Defense of Human Rights in the Soviet Union Continues"[11]—thus reflecting a permanency that the *Chronicle* scarcely enjoyed in the first months, when Gorbanevskaya was tenuously putting form to an idea.

An important problem at the outset was the *Chronicle*'s legal and political status in the Soviet state. None of the people involved inclined to conspiratorial practices, not like the Ronkin anti-Marxist group in Leningrad. Yet normal fears made them cautious in the world of *samizdat*. Even with the first issue, there was apprehension about operating publicly: "We would appreciate it if, in using the materials in this issue," it was written on the front sheet of issue no.1, "you do not refer to this journal, and do not mention its existence pending the appearance of the next issue."[12] Ludmilla Alexeyeva traces these words to surviving Russian underground tradition and its romantic appeal among dissidents in Moscow. That the dissidents often felt it wiser to adopt standard underground practices is unmistakable. The people working on the *Chronicle* had deliberately chosen anonymity, rather than risk KGB investigation and prosecution. By the end of 1968, with issue no. 5, this question had been discussed, and the *Chronicle* informed its readers about both its editorial objectives and its system for assembling information. Gorbanevskaya wrote anonymously in a final editorial note at the end of the issue:

> December 10 was observed as human rights day all over the world. Human rights year, declared by the United Nations, has now come to an end. From the five issues of the *Chronicle* to date, one may form at least a partial impression of how the suppression of human rights and the movement for them has been taking place in the Soviet Union. Not one participant in this movement can feel his task is ended with the end of human rights year. The general aim of democratization, and the more particular aim pursued by the *Chronicle*, are still to be achieved. The *Chronicle* will continue to come out in 1969.[13]

Although the content of the *Chronicle* revealed its intent, this was the first time that Gorbanevskaya as editor had told readers specifically of the *Chronicle*'s purpose. As well, she and her fellow writers were prepared to commit themselves publicly to continued publication. If it was not clear to the KGB and Soviet political authorities earlier, it was spelled out for them in issue no. 5 that the *Chronicle* was an established organization.

Gorbanevskaya, now looking ahead and influenced by continuing controversy among dissidents over legal and illegal methods of advancing human rights, felt compelled to emphasize that the *Chronicle* operated within Soviet law. That was the dissidents' interpretation. In any case, Gorbanevskaya stressed that the *Chronicle*'s mode of operation was forced upon the editors:

The *Chronicle* is in no sense an illegal publication, and the difficult conditions in which it is produced are created by the peculiar notions about law and freedom of information which, in the course of long years, have become established in certain Soviet organizations. For this reason, the *Chronicle* cannot, like any other journal, give its postal address on the last page.[14]

Not until then, at the end of 1968, did the *Chronicle* assert its legality. There were particular circumstances operating at the time, as we will see, that influenced Gorbanevskaya's choice of words. They were the opening gambit in a battle with Soviet authorities over the status of the *Chronicle* and other *samizdat* material, a battle that persists today. The legality issue and the question of the underground character of the *Chronicle* were inevitably entwined with its system of collecting information. Gorbanevskaya said in the closing of her editorial note in issue no. 5:

Anybody who is interested in seeing that the Soviet public is informed about what goes on in the country may easily pass on information to the editors of the *Chronicle*. Simply tell it to the person from whom you received the *Chronicle,* and he will tell the person from whom *he* received the *Chronicle,* and so on. But do not try to trace back the whole chain of communication yourself, or else you will be taken for a police informer.[15]

As much as the *Chronicle*'s editors hoped to shun underground practices, there was a conspiratorial tone in these instructions. Certainly to the KGB the system that the *Chronicle* had devised was not only shrewd but smacked of a secret organization. The system was so simple it was brilliant. By creating a chain of information among persons who knew one another personally, it was virtually impossible for the KGB to infiltrate the *Chronicle*'s reporting network. In the Soviet Union of the late 1960s, one did not generally share confidential information or private political opinions with anyone except trusted friends. What one really believed and what one read in *samizdat* were not discussed openly. Under these conditions, one received a copy of the *Chronicle* only from a close friend and passed it on only to a close friend. The system slowed circulation of information, but it was a reliable channel of facts and opinions not otherwise available in the Soviet Union. The system struck the *Chronicle*'s compilers, as they gained experience in putting together five issues, as a practical way of collecting information, proven in practice and reliable enough to recommend to readers who had no direct connection with *Chronicle* people in Moscow. Gorbanevskaya's counsel to readers proved an important development in the history of the *Chronicle*. The people of the *Chronicle* had hit on a way to enlarge news coverage without making themselves or reporters vulnerable to Soviet secret police discovery.

The price for that system, however, was a secrecy and confidentiality that amounted to an underground publication. The *Chronicle* group disliked that. It too much recalled the communists—Lenin's Bolsheviks and their clandestine newspaper *Iskra*, for example—for whom they had no admiration. And the secrecy engaged in by the *Chronicle* seemed to deny the claim to legality. If the *Chronicle* was legal, why be secret? If the *Chronicle* was secret, could it be legal? The quandary continued to plague its editors and writers.

By issue no. 11, dated December 31, 1969, the *Chronicle* had developed into a readable, structured news source. It appeared regularly, in increasing numbers of copies, as professional and amateur typists were hired to reproduce the *Chronicle*. Editors were persistently concerned about accuracy, and in another editorial note to readers, this one at the end of issue no. 7, Gorbanevskaya reminded readers that the reproduction system begged errors, as typist after typist copied issues of the *Chronicle* independently of the *Chronicle* staff. There was simply no system devised for authorized versions of the *samizdat*. "A number of inaccuracies occur during the process of duplicating copies of the *Chronicle*," Gorbanevskaya cautioned readers. "There are mistakes in names and surnames, in dates and numbers. The quantity of them grows as the *Chronicle* is retyped again and again, and they cannot be corrected according to the context, as can other misprints."[16]

Although Gorbanevskaya was not conscious of the future significance of that explanation at the time, the defense of inaccuracies on the grounds of unintentional human error was to be important in the dispute over the *Chronicle*'s legality and its alleged violation of Soviet law. For Soviet law banned "intentional" untruths. Gorbanevskaya urged news sources to be precise in their reports and committed the *Chronicle* to a code of accuracy. In the editorial note in no. 7, dated April 30, 1969, a year after the first issue, she wrote:

The *Chronicle* aims at the utmost reliability in the information it publishes. In those instances when it is not absolutely certain that some event has taken place, the *Chronicle* indicates that the piece of information is based on rumor. But at the same time, the *Chronicle* requests its readers to be careful and accurate in the information they provide for publication.[17]

As early as issue no. 2, in June 1968, Gorbanevskaya had taken to correcting information of previous issues or adding to an earlier news item as the item yielded additional information. In no. 2, several references to the Galanskov-Ginzburg case, to Sinyavsky, and to Bukovsky, for example, were corrected or expanded upon. A section dealing with additions and corrections appeared in nos. 5, 6, 10, and 11 as Gorbanevskaya worked to build a record of accuracy and honesty with a mostly faceless, unknown readership.[18]

What was even more noticeable to the Soviet reader of the *Chronicle* during the Gorbanevskaya editorship was the impressive coverage of politically sensitive events, compared with the normal fare in the Soviet press. Not only the now standard arrests and interrogations were reported; political documents and statements, internal disputes involving Soviet policy, and protests and grievances from among an increasingly broad spectrum of the Soviet population were reported as well. The information, moreover, was assembled in one readable source, in direct and unambiguous Russian. There was no need to read between the lines as Soviets routinely did when the official Soviet press reported some specially sensitive issue.

A survey of the *Chronicle* from the spring of 1968 until the winter of 1969, when Gorbanevskaya was arrested, reveals several important innovations. Beginning with issue no. 2, Gorbanevskaya included a section titled "News in Brief." This became a regular source of items about continuing human rights cases, censorship, KGB activities, searches, arrests, questionings, and demonstrations—short reports that gave readers both specific information and a cumulative picture of official actions against citizens that generally were never revealed in the state-controlled media. Some representative examples, from issue no. 7, follow:

The supreme court of the RSFSR heard an appeal April 15, 1959, in the case of Irina Belogorodskaya. The previous sentence remains in force.

The Prosveshchenie publishers have fired the deputy editor for literature for including poems of Nikolai Gumilev and Osip Mandelshtam in the book *Three Centuries of Russian Poetry*.

According to rumors, three students of the MGU [Moscow University] economics department have been arrested, all of them children of high level officials. One of them is the son of the editor of *Ekonomicheskaya Gazeta*, Rumyantsev. According to the same, unconfirmed rumors, they organized a pro-Chinese group.

In Kharkov, authorities continue to call persons for questioning as witnesses without citing the case, but only article 187-1 of the criminal code of the UkSSR, analogous to article 190-1 of the criminal code of the RSFSR. The questioning deals with *samizdat*.[19]

The "News in Brief" section eventually became a channel for a wide range of facts from throughout the Soviet Union. Complementing that section, another titled "News of *Samizdat*" offered a sampling of major *samizdat* documents and writings inaccessible to most Soviet readers. Making its debut in issue no. 4, "News of *Samizdat* extended *Chronicle* coverage of Soviet events and amplified dissident activities and ideas that otherwise might have been confined to small circles. Gorbanevskaya and her colleagues, being in Moscow, were at the best single point for sampling *samizdat* as it passed from hand to hand or was brought by dissidents from other Soviet cities.

There were further changes or additions in these early months of the *Chronicle* that reflected an experimental and maturing process. Issue no. 5 had carried for the first time a section titled "Extrajudicial Political Repressions 1968." The section continued into the following year, the year "1969" being added. In issue no. 8, however, the section was retitled, with the word "persecutions" being substituted for "repressions." By this, the *Chronicle* took note of the fact that there were other ways of intimidating Soviet citizens than by censuring them, or removing them from their jobs, or expelling them from the party, institutes, and universities. The technique of public criticism of a person at factory or office meetings, for example, was also just as effective. The *Chronicle* decided therefore to expand this area of reports to include the less direct forms of political repression. It thus reported in no. 8 that one Leonid Petrovsky, an historian at the Lenin Museum in

Moscow, had been expelled form the Communist party for signing a protest, and that a certain Maria Petrenko, a geologist at a Moscow institute, had been summoned by authorities for a "talk" about signing a petition.[20]

There were exchanges with unidentified readers in these early issues that clarified the *Chronicle*'s objectives and provided some evidence that an interested audience was responding to the still little known publication. There was reaction, for example, to a *Chronicle* editorial comment on a letter attributed to Lenin that ordered harsh measures against the Russian Orthodox church. The purported letter had appeared recently in *samizdat*. Gorbanevskaya added an unsigned editorial note in issue no. 10:

> Readers were critical of the fact that the commentary to this document abounded in value judgments. The *Chronicle* agrees with these comments by readers, thanks them for their criticisms, and will try in the future to keep to fact and avoid judgments. Some readers have also expressed the opinion that the *Chronicle* carries on religious propaganda in its pages. The *Chronicle* does not agree with this, and considers it necessary to clarify that matter thus: It is not the aim of the *Chronicle* to carry on either religious or antireligious propaganda since it considers that the question of religious belief is a matter for the conscience of the individual. However, insofar as there are in the Soviet Union various forms of persecution of believers, and restrictions on freedom of conscience, which are violations of the General Declaration of Human Rights, the *Chronicle* considers it necessary to publish these facts.[21]

A few months before, in the early summer of 1969, the *Chronicle* responded to a Leningrad reader who had analyzed the first issues. They carried too many value judgments, the reader said, and his friends detected an "hysterical tone" in the publication. To this, Gorbanevskaya answered, again in an unsigned note:

> The *Chronicle* makes every effort to achieve a calm, restrained tone. Unfortunately, the materials with which the *Chronicle* is dealing evoke emotional reactions, and these automatically affect the tone of the text. The *Chronicle* does, and will do, its utmost to ensure that its strictly factual style is maintained to the greatest degree possible, but it cannot guarantee complete success. The *Chronicle* tries to refrain

from making value judgments—either by not making them at all, or by referring to judgments made in *samizdat* documents. In certain cases, one is obliged to give an appraisal of the facts, otherwise, their true significance might escape the unsophisticated reader.[22]

In the same editorial note, Gorbanevskaya defended the *Chronicle* against the criticism that its content had moved beyond the realm of the human rights movement by, for example, including the "News of *Samizdat*" section. *Samizdat* has a twofold right to figure in the *Chronicle*, she noted:

First, insofar as a part of it is expressly devoted to the question of human rights; secondly, the whole of *samizdat* is an example of freedom of speech and the press, of creative freedom and freedom of conscience, put into practice. The *Chronicle* has to admit that Soviet legal practice, for example, is given very narrow coverage in its pages—only those arrests, searches and legal proceedings which clearly represent acts of political repression. . . .[23]

In exploring the relation of the idea of the rule of law to human rights, the *Chronicle* found itself defending the obvious perhaps—that all information is connected. It was to prove out, as the *Chronicle* matured, that one could not, for example, deal with even a small officially sanctioned Soviet violation of political rights without dealing with the whole of Soviet society.

The information flow to and from the *Chronicle* developed in important ways under Gorbanevskaya. First, the volume of facts increased as friends and readers caught on to what the *Chronicle* wanted and was willing to publish. Also, a sort of "beat" system of reporting emerged. It was not planned, but developed simply because of personal interests and contacts. Thus, the Crimean Tatars' claim to their homeland was covered by the *Chronicle*, especially because General Pyotr Grigorenko and to some extent Ilya Gabai had made that their cause. Pyotr Yakir had contacts among Jewish dissidents and he became the channel for information about Soviet Jews' demands for emigration and constitutional rights. Ludmilla Alexeyeva had friends among Ukrainians and she supplied news about dissident activities in Kiev. Others had contacts with Armenians or political prisoners.[24]

Another valuable connection developed, this one between *Chronicle* people and Western correspondents in Moscow.

Andrei Amalrik was probably best known among Western journalists in early years, when the word "dissident" had yet to be coined. Amalrik was never directly connected with the *Chronicle*, but he was friends with a number who were, including Pyotr Yakir. Yakir in turn developed his own contacts among correspondents, as eventually did many of the dissidents. Litvinov, for example, was known among American and other Western journalists. Hedrick Smith, the *New York Times* bureau chief in Moscow during the *Chronicle*'s early years, remembers Yakir as "an important channel of information and for obtaining the bimonthly *Chronicle of Current Events*."[25] Through this connection, the contents of the *Chronicle* moved through an already established information network of Moscow correspondents, Western news agencies and newspaper, radio, and television reports to editorial offices and media abroad. Abroad, foreign shortwave broadcasters picked up *Chronicle* information, and individual news reports based on *Chronicle* items or contents of whole issues found their way back to the Soviet Union in Russian-language broadcasts of the BBC, Deutsche Welle, and Voice of America. Radio Liberty broadcast readings of entire issues of the *Chronicle*. Although foreign radio signals were heavily jammed from the summer of 1968 to the fall of 1973, broadcasts could still be heard throughout the Soviet Union. These broadcasts generally served the *Chronicle* well, as audiences numbering in the tens of millions in the Soviet Union heard the news from the *Chronicle*.

Another reproduction of the *Chronicle*'s contents was not so helpful. A Russian-language publication titled *Posev*, issued in West Germany, reprinted each issue of the *Chronicle* from the start. Copies were not only available then in the west but were smuggled into the Soviet Union. *Posev* was (and is) connected with the NTS—the Russian-language acronym for People's Labor Union, a conservative Russian emigre organization dating to 1930. Soviet authorities regularly accused the NTS of being a front for the U.S. Central Intelligence Agency. *Posev* reprints of the *Chronicle* were to haunt the *Chronicle*'s editors in years to come. In later trials, the KGB seized on the *Posev* reprints as evidence of the *Chronicle*'s ties with foreign intelligence services.

By the end of 1969, when Natalia Gorbanevskaya was arrested, the *Chronicle* was an established publication, well known in small but influential Soviet and foreign circles in Moscow and elsewhere. Its editorial objectives and operations had been tested and were being refined. The *Chronicle* was appearing regularly, chiefly because of the persistence and hard work of Gorbanevskaya. Its scope of information was expanding, as it gained readers and supporters. The *Chronicle*—rough-hewn, typed news sheet that it was, an amateurish job compared to the giants of journalism—nonetheless had come of age. And precisely because of that it drew the KGB's attention.

From the start, of course, the *Chronicle*'s editors and writers were also human rights activists. That duality was to persist as editors changed and as unofficial civil rights organizations emerged. Gorbanevskaya had been editor of the *Chronicle* for a little more than four months when Soviet troops invaded Czechoslovakia, and she joined a small but historic demonstration in Red Square against that invasion. On August 25, 1968, four days after the invasion, Gorbanevskaya and seven other men and women quietly assembled in Red Square near the famous St. Basil's Cathedral and unrolled several banners denouncing the Soviet military action. One, for example, said: "Down with the Occupiers;" another: "Hands Off Czechoslovakia, For Your Freedom and Ours." Gorbanevskaya had arrived in Red Square pushing a baby carriage holding her three-month-old son. Besides Gorbanevskaya, the demonstrators, as identified later in the *Chronicle,* were Konstantin Babitsky, a linguist; Larisa Bogoraz, a philologist; Vladimir Dremlyuga, a factory worker; Vadim Delone, a poet; Pavel Litvinov, a physicist; Victor Fainberg, a fine arts specialist; and Tatyana Bayeva. The demonstration was quickly broken up by policy and plainclothes KGB agents. Six of the eight were brought to trial in Moscow from October 9 to 11 and sentenced either to prison or internal exile. Neither Bayeva nor Gorbanevskaya were arrested—Bayeva because police did not think she had participated in the Red Square demonstration, and Gorbanevskaya because she had two small children.[26]
The Red Square demonstration is well known in Soviet dissident history. It has been described fully and there is no need to go into it here, except to note two results. First, both Bogoraz and Litvinov were exiled from Moscow to Siberia where they were assigned to common manual labor. That put them out of touch with the *Chronicle* and deprived the publication of two valuable channels of information. Second, the Red Square demonstration drew the KGB's attention anew to Gorbanevskaya, although it is not known whether at that time the KGB linked her with the *Chronicle*. Some of those involved with the *Chronicle,* like Pavel Litvinov and Ludmilla Alexeyeva, believe that the

Chronicle had not yet, in the summer of 1968, generated KGB interest.[27]

Issue no. 3, dated August 30, 1968, was a mere nine pages. Gorbanevskaya had left material for the issue with a friend for final typing and assembly. Preparing for the Red Square demonstration, she feared that she would be arrested and that someone else per force would carry on the *Chronicle*.[28] Gorbanevskaya resumed her *Chronicle* work, however, putting together increasingly larger issues.

Moreover, there were other events that combined to make the dissidents apprehensive. We can see the pattern now, with the perspective of history. In late 1968 and into 1969, it was as if there was a change of mood in high Soviet political circles. The Red Square demonstration was, from the Kremlin's perspective, part of a greater problem. It can be readily supposed now that Kremlin debate leading up to the Soviet invasion of Czechoslovakia in the summer of 1968 pitted different factions against one another. Much has been written about this, and it may never be known precisely who argued for suppression of the Dubček "Prague Spring," or why, or when. The important consequence for Soviet dissidents, nonetheless, was that the hard line won out. With that came a campaign inside the Soviet Union denouncing imperialism, the CIA, counterrevolutionaries—the full panoply of the orthodox, Stalinist view of the outside world. Moreover, there was still lingering debate about Stalin himself, an issue that had come up at the twenty-third Communist party congress in 1966—that the traditionalists among party, government, and KGB bureaucrats intended to rehabilitate Stalin and impose tighter internal security. The invasion of Czechoslovakia seemed one eruption of the power of this element in the Soviet leadership.

In the aftermath of the invasion, in the three years leading up to the twenty-fourth Communist party congress in 1971, at which General Secretary Leonid Brezhnev renewed a policy of coexistence and cooperation with the West, important debates were held over the implications of this policy. On the one side, the benefits of détente in terms of Western trade and financial assistance for the lagging Soviet economy were attractive to a number of groups in the Soviet Union. But there also was the argument, frequently made in the Soviet press, that in times of closer relations with the West, greater vigilance was required within the country. This was an old problem for Soviet leaders—how to adapt useful ideas selectively from technologically advanced but ideologically hostile societies. They attempted to solve it in the late 1960s and into the

1970s with a two-track policy: Détente would guide foreign policy toward the West, and ideological conformity would direct domestic political affairs.

The continuing objections by Soviet citizens to the invasion of Czechoslovakia could only concern the party leadership. In December 1968, a letter protesting the sentences given to Red Square demonstrators was signed by 95 Soviet intellectuals and sent to the Soviet parliament, the Supreme Soviet. Signatories included the writer Victor Nekrasov and the mathematician Alexander Yesenin-Volpin. General Pyotr Grigorenko had openly approved of the attempted democratic reforms in Czechoslovakia. Several dozen persons had been arrested or questioned earlier in 1968 in Leningrad for passing out leaflets decrying Soviet policy toward the Dubček leadership. In the vast Soviet Union with a population of about 230 million, these protests were comparatively minor. But they were picked up by the Western press and broadcast by foreign radio stations and thus magnified.

Other events were also disturbing to an already nervous Soviet leadership. In January 1969, a Soviet soldier shot at a line of limousines carrying Brezhnev and Soviet cosmonauts into the Kremlin. The incident was quickly hushed up. It was said the soldier was mentally unbalanced. The shooting, whether or not it was an attempted assassination of Brezhnev, had nothing directly to do with Soviet dissidents. But it could only alarm a political leadership and a KGB already concerned about domestic disorder.

By this time, Yury Andropov had been made a candidate member of the ruling Communist party Politburo and had directed the KGB for nearly two years. As a candidate or nonvoting member of the select Politburo, Andropov did not participate in final policy decisions, but his agency was responsible for advising the Politburo of internal security matters. Once policy decisions were made in the concerning domestic political security, Andropov's KGB was, of course, responsible for carrying out those decisions. This is to say, that a wave of repression that was about to engulf Soviet dissidents originated certainly at top levels of the Soviet leadership and would be overseen by Andropov. The campaign against internal dissent was to be one of Andropov's tests of his management of the huge KGB apparatus. He managed it well, it will be seen, for within a few years, as the campaign reached a peak, he was promoted to full status, to voting member of the party Politburo.

On May 7, 1969, a series of searches was carried out in Moscow apartments, and Grigorenko was arrested in Tashkent, in Soviet central Asia, where he had flown to witness a trial of another dissident. In connection with the arrest, authorities went through the apartments of Gabai, Krasin, Alexeyeva, Amalrik, Nadezhda Emelkina, and Zampira Asanova. The latter was a doctor from Uzbekistan involved in the Crimean Tatar rights campaign. Nadezhda Emelkina was active in *samizdat* circles and was among the typists who helped Gorbanevskaya produce the *Chronicle*. The other four were also connected with the *Chronicle* in the emerging human rights movement. The searches did not focus on the *Chronicle*, but, as was to happen often later, on people who were at once connected with it and other civil rights organizations or activities.

On May 19, just a few days later, Ilya Gabai was arrested. The next day, a group of Moscow dissidents announced the formation of the Initiative Group for the Defense of Human Rights. In a statement to the UN commission on human rights, the group appealed for an inquiry into rights violations in the Soviet Union. Among the 15 founders of the Initiative Group, at least seven were or soon would be editing or writing for the *Chronicle*. Besides Gorbanevskaya, Krasin, and Yakir, there were Tatyana Velikanova, a mathematician, and Sergei Kovalev, a biologist, both of whom later were to associate themselves openly with the *Chronicle*. There were also Anatoly Yakobson, a translator, and Leonid Plyushch, a mathematician in Kiev.[29] The Initiative Group rapidly took up the role of unofficial public spokesman for Soviet human rights. By January 1970, it had sent five appeals to the United Nations and gained the support of foreign organizations. The *Chronicle* published summaries and news items about the Initiative Group. A clear connection existed. There was a publicly functioning, unofficial human rights organization with its own press in the Soviet Union. Modest as their combined activities were, measured against Soviet state agencies and mass media, the two operated beyond official control.

To the KGB and Soviet political authorities, all these facts could not be but unsettling as they weighed the opportunities of détente with the West against probable growing penetration into Soviet society of foreign ideology. As if to confirm such apprehension, one of the most widely known Soviet writers, Anatoly Kuznetsov, asked for political asylum in London while on a trip in the summer of 1969. In a statement published in a British newspaper, he denounced censorship in the Soviet Union and brutish restrictions on free thought.[30] About the same time, a campaign begun in March 1969 by *Pravda*, the Communist party's main newspaper, against the liberal literary journal

Novy Mir was stepped up. Under Alexander Tvardovsky, the monthly journal had published not only Solzhenitsyn's *One Day in the Life of Ivan Denisovich* but the works of Andrei Voznesensky, Yevgeny Yevtushenko, and Victor Nekrasov, among others. The more orthodox Soviet newspapers attacked *Novy Mir* for giving aid to the "anti-Soviet camp" and mocking Soviet ideals. In November, a branch of the official Writers' Union expelled Solzhenitsyn, as the campaign against the liberals intensified.

All of this had been duly recorded in the *Chronicle*. By the spring of 1969, Gorbanevskaya was producing issues of 30 pages. As the year progressed, and as KGB interrogations and arrests of dissidents persisted, she concluded that she was likely to be formally charged. She decided to transfer responsibility for the *Chronicle* to someone else. She chose Galina Gabai, the wife of Ilya Gabai, who then was in prison under investigation for anti-Soviet activities. Galina Gabai, a special teacher for handicapped children, had been involved with the *Chronicle* almost from the start. She knew Gorbanevskaya, Litvinov, and Yakir through her husband and had supplied items for the *Chronicle* and reproduced issues as she received copies. Before Ilya Gabai had been arrested, Gorbanevskaya had talked with him about editing the *Chronicle*. After her husband was jailed, Galina continued her association with the *Chronicle* and had supplied information especially for issues nos. 8 and 9. Gorbanevskaya, fearful of imminent arrest, asked her to complete issue no. 10 and possibly take over the editorship of the publication.[31] In the then established procedure, Gabai collected the individual items for the issue. Some were typed, some were handwritten on scraps of paper, and and some of the information came by word of mouth. In the latter days of October, she recopied the contents by hand for no. 10. Then she burned, bit by bit, in a kitchen stove the original handwritten and typed news items. Handwriting and typefaces could be traced by the KGB, and it was important to destroy anything that could lead police to the *Chronicle*'s contributors. Then Gabai typed the final master copies of issue no. 10. Some copies she gave to Yakir, the only other person besides Gorbanevskaya who knew that Gabai edited the issue. Gorbanevskaya had told her to save one copy for Andrei Amalrik, to pass to Western correspondents.

By this time, unknown to the *Chronicle* group, the KGB had begun probing. Sometime after October 31, 1969, when issue no. 10 was out, the KGB searched Gabai's apartment. She was living with her mother in a small flat of two rooms and a kitchen near Moscow's Byelorussia rail station. The doorbell rang early, shortly after 7 A.M. Gabai already had some information collected for the *Chronicle*, no. 11, a handful of papers with some news jotted down or typed on them. She grabbed the papers and put them inside her bulky bathrobe. There were perhaps ten KGB agents at the door when Gabai opened it. Some were dressed in sweat suits, apparently members of a surveillance team, and some were in suits and ties. They moved into the small apartment for the standard, thorough KGB search. Gabai's mother had started a large pot of borscht that morning. It was simmering on the stove. Frightened and anxious lest she be found with material linking her to the *Chronicle*, Gabai edged into the kitchen. When she was certain none of the KGB agents was watching, she quickly pulled the packet of papers from her bathrobe and stuffed them into the hot, dark red soup cooking on the stove.

Gabai had gone through several searches and this last was too much for her. She readily admitted to Gorbanevskaya that she was afraid she was targeted for arrest. Should that happen, there would be no one to maintain the essential link between her imprisoned husband and the outside world. Moreover, she feared she would be the KGB conduit to the *Chronicle*. Gabai continued to supply information for the *Chronicle*, but she no longer had a direct editorial role.

The KGB was interested by now in the *Chronicle* generally and Gorbanevskaya in particular. In the early months of the *Chronicle*, Gorbanevskaya and her friends were relatively open about the publication. "Everyone in Moscow knew I edited the *Chronicle*," Gorbanevskaya recalls, meaning everyone involved in the human rights cause. The KGB as well suspected that Gorbanevskaya at least helped compile the *Chronicle*. The KGB's information had come from a certain Vilko Forsel. He had been released from the KGB's Vladimir prison in June 1969, after serving a ten-year sentence for, according to the *Chronicle*, refusing to cooperate with the KGB.[32] Gorbanevskaya had traveled to the Soviet republic of Estonia in the late summer of 1969 to gather information. Forsel met her there through a mutual friend and, he later testified in a Moscow court, Gorbanevskaya had shown him several copies of the *Chronicle*. He shortly thereafter reported the encounter to the KGB.[33]

On October 21, 1969, Moscow authorities searched the apartments of Gorbanevskaya, Tatyana Khodorovich, and Anatoly Yakobson. The three were publicly associated with the Initiative Group for the Defense of Human Rights and they were privately working with the *Chronicle*. In

Gorbanevskaya's flat, officials confiscated issues of the *Chronicle*, plus personal correspondence and some of her poems. The pattern of other arrests and searches suggested that the KGB was more concerned about the Initiative Group than the *Chronicle*. A month earlier, in September, the KGB had summoned Initiative Group members Velikanova, Alexander Lavut, Maltsev and Khodorovich, among others, for questioning. And on December 20, 1969, KGB agents arrested Victor Krasin; three days later he was sentenced to five years in exile for "leading an anti-social, parasitic way of life."[34]

Thus, when the KGB arrested Gorbanevskaya on December 24, 1969, after another thorough search of her apartment, it appeared that the KGB was continuing a case against the Initiative Group, striking at the *Chronicle* editorial group only by coincidence. Nonetheless, the *Chronicle* figured prominently in Gorbanevskaya's trial six months later, on July 7, 1970, in Moscow, where she was accused of antistate activities, but more ominously was alleged to be suffering from schizophrenia. The eight-hour-long trial included prosecution evidence that Gorbanevskaya had been closely involved in producing the *Chronicle*, as this segment on her trial in issue no. 11 explains:

> The procurator further pointed out that it had been established by the documents in the case that Gorbanevskaya had been one of the compilers of the collections of a *Chronicle of Current Events*, which appeared in *samizdat*. These collections dealt tendentiously with events in the Soviet Union and accumulated information about arrests for antisocial activities, representing these arrests, moreover, as unlawful. Gorbanevskaya had procured information for these collections and even traveled to other cities and republics of the [Soviet] Union for this purpose. Thus [Yury] Gendler had testified that the information which he had personally given to Gorbanevskaya was later included in the first issue of the *Chronicle*. The witness, Forsel, had testified that Gorbanevskaya traveled to Estonia especially to gather information and that she also circulated these documents. Gorbanevskaya had duplicated and circulated these collections. A search of her flat on December 24, 1969, revealed copies of these collections typed on a typewriter belonging to her, a fact confirmed by the findings of a forensic science examination. In October 1969, Gorbanevskaya traveled to the places of

exile of Bogoraz and Litvinov, and in January 1970 issues of the *Chronicle* typed on a typewriter belonging to Gorbanevskaya were confiscated from them.[35]

Gorbanevskaya was found guilty of antistate activities under article 190-1 while being of "unsound mind." Gorbanevskaya, Grigorenko, and at least five other dissidents, who were tried and sentenced in 1970, formed a group that authorities decided was mentally incompetent. Officials had decided to use psychiatric clinics as prisons for some human rights activists.[36] For most of the two years and two months after her arrest, Gorbanevskaya was confined to the Serbsky psychiatric institute in Moscow and the mental hospital in Kazan, east of Moscow, where she was treated with drugs. On the basis of a pretrial examination, Serbsky psychiatrists had concluded, and testified in court, that Gorbanevskaya was suffering from a "form of schizophrenia." The Gorbanevskaya case was among early trials that stirred revelations among both Soviet and foreign psychiatrists and lay people of KGB attempts to stamp an insanity label on the dissident movement.

Gorbanevskaya had left the *Chronicle* abruptly. To go back in time, to December 24, 1969, the day she was arrested, she had gathered most of the material for issue no. 11. Her apprehension of imminent arrest had intensified. She had asked Vladimir Telnikov to her apartment at Novopeshaniye 13/3 that night. They had agreed that she would go over the material for no. 11 and she would show him how to produce the *Chronicle*. Telnikov was among the many Moscow civil rights figures, and Gorbanevskaya believed he could take over the *Chronicle*.

It was 11 A.M. when KGB agents knocked on the door and, using official police rather than KGB identification, Gorbanevskaya recalls, announced that they would conduct a search of her apartment. Agents probed for documents, personal papers, address books, letters—anything that would reveal to the KGB a person's associations and activities. Agents rapped on walls and floors, looking for hollow places where documents might be hidden. They searched bookcases and a work desk in the room Gorbanevskaya used for her study.

She had assembled some raw information and drafted a table of contents for no. 11 and had put them into a 6 × 9 inch envelope. She had placed it in the center drawer of her work desk under some other papers to show later to Telnikov. Other *Chronicle* information newly collected she had left in the jacket of a coat hanging on a hook at the apartment entrance. Gorbanevskaya was swept with foreboding as she watched the head of the KGB search team go through her desk. The agents put together a bundle of her documents a foot thick. In the meantime, three friends had arrived by chance, breaking into the unexpected search. It was only as the KGB finished that Gorbanevskaya was told she was under arrest. The agents had wrapped the file of her personal documents, and Gorbanevskaya looked at it anxiously.

Now living in Paris in a tiny walk-up flat, an exile from her native country, Gorbanevskaya recalled vividly the scene as KGB agents prepared to take her and the seized documents:

> They closed the file and sealed it. I didn't know if the *Chronicle* envelope was there or not. But I couldn't believe that they had missed it. But when I was saying good-by to my friends, I whispered to one of them, "Go through the desk." I had no hope, honestly speaking, that they had not taken the envelope with the *Chronicle* notes.[37]

What particularly worried Gorbanevskaya was the fact that the envelope not only contained a content list for no. 11 but also slips and scraps of paper with information in the handwriting of persons who had given her the news items. She knew the KGB would attempt to identify the informants from the script if they found the envelope. There was other equally sensitive information in her coat.

> The day before, I had been with a family of a political prisoner with whom the family had met at a labor camp. I had a good deal of information from them on the latest situation of political prisoners in different labor camps, but in particular about a hunger strike in one of the Mordovian camps. I had left this in one pocket of my winter coat. For some reason, they [the KGB] did not check the coat, although it was hanging at the door. As I left then I put on another, a light jacket, even though it was Christmas Eve and you know it's very cold. I couldn't whisper anything then to my friends. But while I was putting on my jacket, I caught the eye of one and pointed with my own eyes toward the coat.[38]

Gorbanevskaya learned only when she returned to Moscow from the mental hospitals in February 1972 that the KGB had inexplicably overlooked the envelope of *Chronicle* materials in her desk. Her friends had later found it and the papers in her coat. The *Chronicle*, no. 11, came out shortly afterward, dated December 31, 1969. The ninth item in the table of contents on the cover page read simply: "The Arrest of Natalia Gorbanevskaya." The news item of about 20 lines briefly reviewed the facts of her human rights activities, details of the search, her arrest, and the criminal code article under which she was charged. It went on to say that after the Red Square demonstration of August 1968, Gorbanevskaya had been declared mentally unstable and that she was now threatened with confinement in a prison hospital.[39] There was no hint of Gorbanevskaya's connection with the *Chronicle*. Nor would any of the *Chronicle*'s editors and writers ever be identified as such by the *Chronicle*, unless the KGB directly accused them, although in the coming years many of their names were to appear in *Chronicle* reports.

Later, after she returned to Moscow, Gorbanevskaya quietly contributed information to the *Chronicle* until she immigrated to Paris in December 1975. But her editorship ended on December 24, 1969. New editors followed, and within months it was clear that the KGB not only had opened a special case file on the *Chronicle* but intended to silence it.

NOTES

1. See Amnesty International report dated May 1982, "Imprisoned Leaders of the Unregistered Baptist Church in the USSR."
2. Michael Meerson-Aksenov, ed., "The Debate Over the Democratic Movement: Introduction," in *The Political, Social and Religious Thought of Russian "Samizdat"—An Anthology* (Belmont, Mass.: Nordland, 1977), p. 228.
3. Gorbanevskaya interview.
4. Valery Chadlize, *To Defend These Rights* (New York: Random House, 1974), p. 53.
5. Peter Reddaway, ed. and trans., *Uncensored Russia: Protest and Dissent in the Soviet Union* (New York: American Heritage Press, 1972), p. 73.
6. *Khronika Tekushchikh Sobytii: Vypuski 1-15* (Amsterdam: Alexander Herzen Foundation, 1979), cover page of no. 1.
7. These figures are derived from issues in *Khronika*.
8. Ludmilla Alexeyeva, "Chronicle," *Chronicle of Human Rights in the Soviet Union* [*Chronicle/Rights*], no. 29, pp. 58-60, 1978.
9. Gorbanevskaya interview.

10. *Khronika, Chronicle,* no. 6, following p. 276.

11. See *Khronika, Chronicle,* no. 12, following p. 336.

12. Ludmilla Alexeyeva, "The Evolution of the Dissident Movement," *Chronicle/Human Rights,* no. 31, p. 43, 1978. Alexeyeva quotes these words from a *Chronicle* available to her. They do not appear on the retyped copy of issue no. 1 reproduced in *Khronika.*

13. Translated in Reddaway, *Uncensored Russia,* pp. 53-54. The original in Russian is in *Khronika,* p. 102.

14. Ibid.

15. Ibid.

16. Reddaway, *Uncensored Russia,* p. 59; and *Khronika,* p. 153.

17. Ibid., p. 58.

18. *Khronika,* pp. 48-49, contains the corrections published in issue no. 2. See p. 102 for no. 5; p. 121 for no. 6; pp. 275-76 for no. 10; p. 333 for no. 11.

19. *Khronika,* pp. 148-50.

20. *Khronika,* pp. 179-80.

21. Reddaway, *Uncensored Russia,* p. 57.

22. Ibid., pp. 54-55.

23. Ibid.

24. Grigorenko's interest in the Crimean Tatars is a public fact; as for Gabai, when the KGB carried out a search of his apartment on May 7, 1969, agents seized a "file of Crimean-Tatar documents." See *Khronika,* p. 164. For Yakir's contacts with Jews, see Joshua Rubenstein, *Soviet Dissidents: Their Struggle for Human Rights* (Boston: Beacon Press, 1980), p. 159. Ludmilla Alexeyeva noted in an interview with the author, July 25, 1981, in Tarrytown, N.Y., that she reported Ukrainian dissident activities.

25. Hedrick Smith, *The Russians* (New York: Quadrangle, 1976), p. 461.

26. For the fullest account of this incident see Natalia Gorbanevskaya, *Red Square at Noon,* trans. Alexander Lieven (London: Andre Deutsch, 1972). The events were also covered in the *Chronicle,* nos. 4 and 5. See *Khronika,* pp. 59-66, 80.

27. Litvinov interview; Alexeyeva interview, July 25, 1981.

28. Gorbanevskaya interview. Gorbanevskaya will not identify the final editor of issue no. 3 because the person is still in the Soviet Union.

29. Reddaway, *Uncensored Russia,* pp. 150-52.

30. *Sunday Telegraph,* London, August 3, 1969.

31. This section is drawn from Gabai interview.

32. *Khronika,* p. 333.

33. *Khronika,* p. 466.

34. See Reddaway, *Uncensored Russia,* pp. 150 ff., for actions against the Initiative Group.

35. *Khronika,* pp. 459-60.

36. See Ludmilla Alexeyeva, *The Tenth Anniversary,* p. 58. Sidney Bloch and Peter Reddaway, *Psychiatric Terror: How Soviet Psychiatry Is Used to Suppress Dissent* (New York: Basic Books, 1977), pp. 127-45, contains a detailed analysis of the Gorbanevskaya case from the perspectives of a psychiatrist and a political scientist.

37. Gorbanevskaya interview.

38. Ibid.

39. *Khronika,* pp. 307-8.

3
CASE 24

Late in 1969, the Kremlin leadership secretly ordered KGB chairman Yury Andropov to crush the burgeoning dissent inside the Soviet Union. Thereby was created the KGB's Fifth Chief Directorate. And thereby was born Case 24, specifically directed against the *Chronicle*.

The years 1970, 1971, and 1972, as the KGB undertook its new assignment, were thus critical for Soviet dissidents. By the summer of 1973, following the infamous public trial and confessions of Pyotr Yakir and Victor Krasin, the dissident movement, what there was of it, was shattered, dispirited, and leaderless. Andropov, meanwhile, was elevated to full membership in the select ruling Communist party Politburo.

These were, nonetheless, the same years that witnessed dramatic Kremlin foreign diplomacy playing out the dual policy of détente abroad and more rigid political controls at home. When Richard Nixon arrived in Moscow in May 1972, the first visit of an American president to the Soviet Union, the KGB had completed interrogations, trials, or convictions of literally hundreds of men and women connected with *samizdat* literature, the *Chronicle*, grievance petitions, political documents, and religious or ethnic protests. Hundreds of men and women had been sent to labor camps. The KGB's Fifth Chief Directorate fully meant to destroy the dissident movement. It was the price very likely demanded by orthodox, conservative members of the Politburo for a compromising relationship with the West,

47

first and foremost with the United States.

Gorbanevskaya's arrest and conviction, along with those of other dissidents, heralded many more KGB actions. The *Chronicle*, passed to new editorial compilers, faithfully documented the mounting KGB campaign until 1972, when the *Chronicle*, too, was forced into silence in what many then believed was its demise.

The KGB Fifth Chief Directorate was formed early in 1970 by decree of the Politburo. One of several main KGB elements, the new directorate assumed operational divisions and files previously responsible for students, the intelligentsia, and Jews. The new directorate also inherited KGB political security service offices dealing with religious organizations, the Soviet Union's numerous nationalities, citizens with relatives abroad, Russian emigre groups, and unauthorized literature and publishing.[1]

The directorate thus concentrated in one KGB element investigators and dossiers concerned with many of the same matters that occupied the *Chronicle*. The very harassment and persecution of Soviet political reformists, of religious dissenters, and of outspoken nationalists by the KGB were the *Chronicle*'s editorial fare. The KGB could not delve into internal dissent without coming into contact with the *Chronicle*. It was thus inevitable that one target of the directorate was the *Chronicle* itself. Tracking the *Chronicle* became all the more essential to the KGB as agents collected evidence linking the *Chronicle*'s editors and informants to the entire underground network of dissent rapidly spreading throughout the Soviet Union.

After Gorbanevskaya's arrest in December 1969, the increasingly hazardous job of producing the *Chronicle* was taken over by Anatoly Yakobson, a poet, translator, and teacher of Russian language and literature. Then 34 years old, Yakobson had risked his career by objecting publicly to the Sinyavsky-Daniel trial in 1966. He was a founding member of the Initiative Group for the Defense of Human Rights. By the winter of 1969, then, he was well known to the KGB. Although, as always, many others helped during the final stages of preparing any given issue of the *Chronicle*, it was Yakobson who was responsible for collecting and producing the first typewritten copies.[2]

Among those closely involved with Yakobson was Irina Yakir. A onetime student at Moscow's Institute of Historical Archives, she was the daughter of Pyotr Yakir and granddaughter of the late Soviet general Iona Yakir. Irina became involved with the *Chronicle* and dissident activities through her father. She herself had been expelled from the Komsomol, the Soviet Communist youth organization, after she boldly went to the Moscow courtroom where the Red Square demonstrators were being tried in October 1968, to express her support for them. Her husband, Yuly Kim, a Russian-language and -literature teacher in Moscow and a well-known singer, was also enmeshed in the human rights cause.

Irina Yakir figures into the *Chronicle* story in the early 1970s. According to *her* testimony to the KGB, she edited 16 issues of the *Chronicle*, from February 1970 to October 1972. In fact, she did not. Furthermore, the KGB ultimately discovered that although Irina Yakir was intimately associated with the *Chronicle*, it was Yakobson who was really putting out the publication in those months.[3] Irina Yakir, by taking responsibility for early issues of the *Chronicle*, attempted to divert the KGB's attention from her father. For at this time, all the dissidents were denying connections to the *Chronicle*. Pyotr Yakir, then imprisoned and under investigation, felt he would have to take full blame for the publication. In one of the moments of family tragedy that often befell dissidents, Irina sought to help her father by claiming editorship of the *Chronicle*. She told Yakobson that it was better that she do so, for if the worst came and she were sentenced to prison, it would be easier for her to endure the punishment for through her father's past she was familiar with the labor camp system.

These were dramatic, often tragic months for the men and women who had taken the step of publicly protesting the Communist party's authoritarian rule. The *Chronicle* documented some of the most notable human rights episodes in the Soviet Union. These were months, from 1970 through 1972, during which Andrei Amalrik, author of *Will the Soviet Union Survive Until 1984?*, was seized and sent to a labor camp. Vladimir Bukovsky was imprisoned. Pyotr Yakir and Victor Krasin were arrested. The famed Soviet physicist (and future Nobel Peace Laureate) Andrei Sakharov joined with fellow scientists Valery Chalidze and Andrei Tverdokhlebov to form the Committee on Human Rights. The KGB, meanwhile, pursued members of the newly established Initiative Group.

Among other events in the years 1970-73, the twenty-fourth congress of the Communist party was held in March 1971. It was newsworthy for acclaiming Leonid Brezhnev's "Western" policy, while proclaiming as well generally orthodox domestic goals, among which were tighter restrictions on dissent that went beyond vaguely defined official limits. The party's most authoritative voice, *Pravda*, already had directly denounced novelist Alexander Solzhenitsyn because of his Nobel Prize for literature. In now all too familiar official rhetoric against the dissidents, the party daily called Solzhenitsyn a "spiritual emigre, alien and hostile to the entire life of the Soviet people."[4] A party central committee resolution argued that, given Soviet foreign policy objectives, the ideological struggle was all the more important. The juxtaposition of détente with the West and harsher control of internal dissent was by then commonplace.

The pattern of arrests and imprisonment suggested KGB concentration on those publicized dissidents who associated with Western correspondents—hence, the Amalrik trial and conviction in November 1970, in remote Sverdlovsk after publication in the West of his book.[5] Amalrik was perhaps the best known dissident among Western journalists in Moscow in the late 1960s, when the word "dissident" still was unfamiliar and when any Soviet citizen who routinely saw foreigners was regarded suspiciously by the KGB. To the KGB, Amalrik had become a regular and plentiful source of "anti-Soviet" information for the Western press. Vladimir Bukovsky, who twice had been confined to psychiatric hospitals and once to a labor camp for protesting violations of civil rights, was arrested again in March 1971. After another incarceration in a psychiatric clinic, he was convicted of antistate activities and sent to a labor camp in January 1972.[6] Bukovsky, like Amalrik, had developed contacts with Western correspondents. With Amalrik and Yakir, he had participated in a secretly filmed interview in early 1970 with CBS's Moscow correspondent William Cole. As with much of the dissident material, the interview was politically amplified after the film was smuggled out of the Soviet Union and broadcast in the United States. Soviet state prosecutors used the interview against Bukovsky in his trial to prove that he "libeled" the Soviet Union.

By the end of 1971, then, the Soviet leadership's assessment of internal dissent had taken on new gravity. Even to foreign observers, it was apparent that dissidents were bolder in their public activities. A few distinguished Soviet citizens, symbolized by Sakharov, still were committing themselves to the human rights movement, despite government persecution. Their statements, seemingly more aggressive and damning by the month, were drawing international attention and support. Dissidents, moreover, were organizing associations independent of Soviet authority, outside of state control.

It was also clear to foreign observers, not to mention the better informed Soviet leadership, that the *Chronicle of Current Events* had become the most consistent, reliable, and renowned source of what the Kremlin regarded as hostile and politically dangerous information. The final issues of the *Chronicle* edited by Gorbanevskaya in late 1969 had included summaries of a *samizdat* publication called *Crime and Punishment* that intended to expose former NKVD secret police officials who had terrorized and tortured during Stalin's dictatorship.[7] Under Anatoly Yakobson, the *Chronicle* hewed to the established consciously detached style, persisting in detailed reports of trials and labor camp conditions and enriching its reportage with new insights into Soviet political life. Issue no. 17, dated December 1970, carried a report of KGB suppression of a previously unpublicized Ukrainian nationalist group that had put out 15 issues of its own underground journal between 1964 and 1966 promoting Ukrainian independence.[8] Issue no. 19, in April 1971, listed 16 films produced in the Soviet Union that either had been censored before showing or whose distribution had been restricted.[9] Issue no. 21, dated September 1971, reported contents of a *Political Diary*, a typewritten underground journal that contained authoritative private political information, including a transcript of the closed Communist party meeting that ousted Nikita Khrushchev in October 1964.[10] The *Chronicle*, numbering on the average about 40 typewritten pages, was by now something more than a recitation of trials of a small Moscow group. Appearing regularly every two months, it had developed a solid network of informants that now routinely funneled more and more news through *Chronicle* channels to the final editor.

The *Chronicle* record was available, then, to the Communist party's central committee when it reportedly secretly approved a plan during a December 30, 1971, meeting to suppress the *Chronicle*. There has never been official confirmation of the central committee's decision. Assessing a flurry of KGB actions, dissidents told correspondents in Moscow that the Soviet leadership had directed the KGB to once and for all silence the *Chronicle* and a number of other *samizdat* periodicals that had come on the scene. The *New York Times* and the *Times* of London so reported the dissident judgment on February 4, 1972.

By then the KGB had mounted a full-scale investigation, Case 24, into the *Chronicle*. Between January 11 and 15, 1972, KGB agents made coordinated searches of the homes of at least 30 men and women in at least eight Soviet cities, including Moscow, Leningrad, and Kiev. More than 100 persons were interrogated. Some were arrested. One was Kronid Lyubarsky, an established Soviet astronomer who had quietly been reproducing and circulating issues of the *Chronicle*. The home of Pyotr Yakir was searched. So was that of Yury Shikhanovich, a Moscow University lecturer in mathematics, who was to have a long association with the *Chronicle*. Recounting details of this wave of KGB actions, the *Chronicle* reported:

> The order for searches in connection with case No. 24 stated that proceedings had been instituted in relation to a crime covered by article 70, para 1, of the Russian criminal code. *Samizdat* literature, typewriters, rolls of film and personal correspondence were confiscated during the searches. . . . During the following one-and-one-half months all of those whose homes had been searched (except Yakir) were summoned by the KGB for questioning, as were their relatives and friends. It has become clear from the interrogations that the matter of principal concern to the investigation is the preparation and circulation of the *Chronicle of Current Events*.[11]

Ultimately dozens of KGB agents pursued Case 24. The *Chronicle* itself, routinely reporting Case 24 as if standing apart and watching the KGB press its investigation to a finale, counted more than 200 persons who had been summoned for interrogations. The *Chronicle* listed the names of more than 100. They included many of the now familiar Soviet dissidents who have been publicized in Western media.

The *Chronicle*'s tabulation confirmed the geographic range of Case 24. Interrogations were carried out from Leningrad, in the north, to Odessa, in the south, to Vilnius, in the west, and to Khabarovsk, in the east.[12] In other words, the KGB's investigation encompassed the entire Soviet Union. KGB agents diligently assembled transcripts of interrogations for nearly two years before the Kremlin arranged the show trial of Pyotr Yakir and Victor Krasin, which the KGB, and indeed many foreigners, believed finally smashed the *Chronicle*.

Case 24 turned out to be more a battle of wits and intelligence than a fight with KGB thugs. Many persons later suffered terribly in labor camps because they worked for the *Chronicle*. Many who edited and wrote for the *Chronicle*, or who typed and distributed it, lived in stark fear of arrest and imprisonment. One person is known to have been driven to suicide by unrelenting KGB pressure. Husbands and wives, parents and children, whole families were divided. But in putting together Case 24, the KGB rarely resorted to physical punishment—commonplace with Stalin's NKVD. Investigators instead used psychological tactics of persistent questioning, of alternating kindness and hostility, of warnings and threats, of harassment and intimidation, of incessant surveillance and wiretapping. It became apparent that the KGB was building a legal case against the *Chronicle* and its staff, "legal" at least within the bounds of Soviet political trials. The objective was less to fill the labor camps than to stop the *Chronicle*, although the latter did not preclude the former.

Case 24 symbolized a refurbished Soviet secret police whose ranks, in Moscow in any case, contained educated, intelligent, sometimes even cultured investigators and agents. There were still sufficient thugs for clumsy surveillance work, young toughs uniformly outfitted, it seemed, in synthetic fabric raincoats or bulky wool coats and porkpie hats. There were still KGB goons assigned to occasional beatings or threatening encounters along dark streets. But once called for questioning by the KGB at the Lubyanka in Moscow, the Lefortovo prison outside of the capital, or other KGB offices, dissidents were handled with conspicuous propriety. KGB investigators probed for names and places, for confirmation of their own conclusions or speculations about the *Chronicle*. They wanted to know who edited the *Chronicle*, who wrote for it, how it was reproduced and distributed, who received it. Some of the information was already in dossiers: KGB technicians bugged apartments, and they tape-recorded telephone conversations. Agents followed the more publicized, active dissidents. So it was not that senior KGB investigators had nothing in hand. They knew a lot. They seemed, from questions consistently put to people associated with the *Chronicle* (although not always known as such then to the KGB), to be looking for a pattern.

It is easy for an outsider to imagine a smoothly performing Soviet secret police state that, on the model of Arthur Koestler's *Darkness at Noon*, knows the most personal acts and thoughts of each Soviet citizen. Both Soviets and foreigners are, indeed, often stunned by the breadth and depth of information in KGB files, information revealed by the KGB for one or another purpose. Often, too, it is surprising how little the KGB knows, how inept its surveillance, how snarled in bureaucratic infighting it becomes, and how, as a practical matter, Moscow's 6 million residents go about their daily business with the KGB having only the vaguest idea of what they are doing.

There were repeated close calls by dissidents as Case 24 developed, when the KGB by accident or ignorance or both missed opportunities. There was, for example, an incident involving Vladimir Bukovsky, Valery Chalidze, and Ludmilla

Alexeyeva. Alexeyeva's parents both were Communist party members. Raised in Moscow, she studied at Moscow University, and in 1952, she herself joined the Communist party. But growing awareness of what she believed was opportunism and corruption in the party led to a break and Alexeyeva was expelled in 1968. By the spring of 1971, Alexeyeva was routinely involved in retyping, distributing, and editing parts of the *Chronicle*.

Now an exile in the United States, the energetic Alexeyeva lives with her husband north of New York City. She retains sharp memories of events in Moscow:

It was the same day they arrested Bukovsky, March 29, 1971. That day I had gone to see Chalidze. I had with me three copies of issue no. 18. They were typed on thin onionskin paper, but still made a package of over 100 pages. Just as I arrived at Chalidze's, he told me he had just talked to Bukovsky. Bukovsky had telephoned to say, "They've come for me." And we decided to go to Bukovsky's.

I had those three copies of the *Chronicle*. It was better not to leave them at Chalidze's. The KGB might search his apartment. So I rolled them up and stuffed them under and around my bra. The KGB normally won't conduct a body search.

As we got to Bukovsky's street, it was dark and quiet. We were walking along when two men appeared, as if out of the air. They pushed Chalidze into a car. I could do nothing. I couldn't stop, because I had the copies of the *Chronicle*. But I hadn't taken five more steps when they grabbed me and put me in the same car. They took us to the closest police station. We were put in a small room to wait. I was afraid to move because of the rustling noise that the onionskin sheets would make. I asked to go to the bathroom, thinking that once there I could flush the *Chronicle* copies down the toilet. But a policewoman went with me and made me keep the bathroom door open. When I came back to the room, they took Chalidze away to search his apartment. Then a man asked for my documents. Well, they let me go with no more questions.

I told this story several times over the next months. A year passes. I'm called in for questioning by the KGB. My interrogator, Alexander Mikhailovich, says, "Don't you know the KGB treats you very well?"

I answered, "I haven't noticed that."

And he says, "Don't you remember the day of Bukovsky's arrest and you had copies of the *Chronicle*, excuse me, in your bra. They were making noise. But we let you go."

Well, I don't think they really did know I had those copies. But the KGB was probably eavesdropping and later heard me tell the story.[13]

With persistence and an unlimited budget, the KGB built its *Chronicle* file. With Case 24 officially sanctioned by senior party ranks, the KGB began new arrests and trials almost immediately. The *Chronicle* was not the only target in the intensified campaign against internal dissent. However, by 1972, the KGB acknowledged, and dissidents well knew, that the *Chronicle* was politically dangerous.

Kronid Lyubarsky was arrested on January 14, 1972, held in a KGB prison for more than nine months, put on trial October 26-30, found guilty of anti-Soviet activities under article 70 of the Russian republic's criminal code, and sentenced to five years in a strict regime labor camp.[14]

Lyubarsky was a representative *Chronicle* case. An accomplished astronomer, he not only had numerous scholarly articles to his credit but was working in the Soviet program of interplanetary exploration of Mars. Like many Soviet intellectuals, he also was read widely in *samizdat* literature—books, articles, miscellaneous essays. He also personally arranged a network of typists and photographers to reproduce the *Chronicle*. Beginning with no. 3, in 1968, and ending with no. 22, in 1971, Lyubarsky managed to produce about 50 copies of each of 19 issues. This was a private enterprise. Although Lyubarsky knew some of the *Chronicle* circle, he neither contributed to nor wrote for the *Chronicle* until after his release from prison.[15]

The indictment against Lyubarsky in his five-day trial in October 1972 contained 54 items. They all dealt with possession, reproduction, or dissemination of *samizdat* materials, including the *Chronicle*, as well as copies of Chalidze's *samizdat* periodical *Social Problems* and Andrei Sakharov's essay *Thoughts on Progress*. The state prosecutor's arguments and witnesses' testimony in what amounted to a closed trial had two objectives: (1) to create trapping of a legal procedure, complete with dates, places, names of persons, and evidence of illegal actions; and (2) to demonstrate that *samizdat* materials were, in fact, anti-Soviet and therefore banned under article 70. Typical of Soviet political trials of dissidents, Lyubarsky's conviction was a foregone conclusion. Although he argued that neither *samizdat* publications nor his own actions were anti-Soviet, the trial basically came down to his assertions against the state's.

Lyubarsky's trial also revealed, typically, how intertwined the *Chronicle* had become with the diverse Soviet world of *samizdat* and dissident activities. Seldom in these years or later did the KGB accuse a given person of solely working for the *Chronicle*. Virtually everyone who wrote for, edited, or circulated the *Chronicle* also was engaged in other *samizdat* authorship or distribution. So when indictments were read in courts, association with the *Chronicle* usually was listed amidst a litany of allegedly criminal political acts against the Soviet society.

The Lyubarsky trial led off Case 24 court proceedings. Many more trials followed. Number 24 was the trunk of an investigation tree that developed branches, each with a different KGB case number. Thus, other underground periodicals that originally were part of Case 24 grew into separate investigations, as did the most celebrated of the *Chronicle* cases, that of Yakir and Krasin. At the same time, the KGB persisted in amassing courtroom evidence against a number of men who eventually were tried under the Case 24 rubric. It took the KGB and the Soviet state prosecutor's apparatus almost two years—from January 1972, until November 1973—to complete the investigations and trials directly linked with the *Chronicle*. In the process, the KGB so terrorized, intimidated, and demoralized the *Chronicle* group that, by late fall of 1972, the *Chronicle* was halted. Leading up to that decision on the *Chronicle* and continuing beyond were these trials that served to intimidate countless other dissidents or those even considering protests:

• *Victor Khaustov*. Arrested January 17, 1972. Tried in the city of Orel, March 4–6, 1974. Charged with transmitting information about an underground group in Orel to the *Chronicle* and possessing or transmitting other *samizdat* literature. Khaustov had already served three years in a labor camp for participating in the 1967 Pushkin Square demonstration in Moscow. In Orel, the KGB believed he was associated with a small group intending to publish an underground periodical called *The Russian Patriotic Front*.[16] Khaustov was convicted of anti-Soviet activities, apparently under article 70, and sentenced to four years in labor camps and two years of internal exile. Internal exile normally meant assignment to a remote village in Siberia.[17]

• *Alexander Bolonkin* and *Valery Balakirev*. Bolonkin was

arrested on September 21, 1972; Balakirev, the following day, in Moscow. They were tried together November 19-23, 1973, in Moscow, under article 70. They were charged with preparing and circulating various anti-Soviet literature, including the *Chronicle*, Robert Conquest's book *The Great Terror*, leaflets, and other *samizdat* documents. They were said to have used several means of production, including a homemade rotary press. About 20 witnesses were called. Bolonkin, an established scholar at the Moscow Institute of Aeronautical Engineering, pleaded not guilty. Balakirev, a lecturer at the Moscow College of Metallurgical Technology, recanted. He thus received a suspended sentence of five years' imprisonment. Bolonkin was given four years in labor camps and two years internal exile.[18]

• *Georgy Davydov.* Davydov was arrested on September 22, 1972, at a Moscow airport en route to Leningrad. According to the KGB, he had picked up several parcels of *samizdat* literature in Moscow from Alexander Bolonkin. Davydov was tried in Leningrad, July 10-16, 1973, with a friend, Vyacheslav Petrov. A geological engineer, Davydov was charged with entering into a criminal conspiracy with Bolonkin and Balakirev, as well as Petrov, to prepare, distribute, and possess *samizdat* literature. Among the items were the *Chronicle* and several underground social journals, including 20 copies of *Free Thought*, said to have been printed on a clandestine flatbed press. He also was charged with possession of photographic reproductions of the *Chronicle*, no. 25, and the NTS journal *Posev*. Balakirev was brought from prison to testify that, in Petrov's presence, he had taught Davydov how to use a mimeograph and had received two documents from Davydov—"Program of the Estonian National Front" and "Russian Colonialism in Estonia"—to summarize for the *Chronicle* in Moscow. Davydov was sentenced to five years in a strict regime corrective labor camp and two years in exile.[19]

• *Yury Shikhanovich.* Arrested on September 28, 1972, he was tried in Moscow on November 26, 1973, under article 70. Originally investigated under the broad tent of Case 24, Shikhanovich had become separate Case 380 by the time of his trial. Shikhanovich, a longtime friend of such noted human rights activists as Sakharov, had been under investigation for almost two years by the time of his trial. He had been examined at Moscow's notorious Serbsky Institute and diagnosed as tending toward mental illness. Among the specific charges against him were reproduction and circulation of the *Chronicle*, distribution of no. 18, and delivery of a *Posev* reprint of a *Chronicle* issue to another person. He also was charged with disseminating other *samizdat* works. The court ordered Shikhanovich to a hospital for compulsory psychiatric treatment.[20]

• *Gabriel Superfin*. A young and privileged writer, Superfin had edited memoirs of former leader Anastasis Mikoyan and had done research for Alexander Solzhenitsyn. He was arrested in Moscow on July 3, 1973, and brought to trial May 12-14, in Orel, under article 70. Superfin was accused of editing and writing for the *Chronicle*. Irina Belogorodskaya, a well-know figure in the *Chronicle* group and under arrest at the time, so testified. Superfin did not deny the charge, although it was not made clear what was meant by editing. Superfin himself had revealed during eight months of interrogations names of persons involved in the *Chronicle*. He later withdrew his statements, in November 1973, saying they were extracted under duress. But some of his earlier remarks to investigators about the "anti-Soviet" character of the *Chronicle* and other *samizdat* were used against him. Superfin also was charged with making editorial comments on galley proofs of Peter Reddaway's book *Uncensored Russia*, an analysis and annotated English translation of the first 11 issues of the *Chronicle*. Given Superfin's associations, there were international appeals to Soviet leaders to spare him. Nonetheless, he was sentenced to five years in labor camps and two in internal exile.[21]

• *Sergei Pirogov*. Arrested on July 11, 1973, he was tried May 15-22, 1974, in the northern city of Arkhangelsk. Pirogov was charged under the relatively new article 190-1 of the Russian republic's criminal code with circulating the *Chronicle* and other *samizdat*. The indictment called attention to a Moscow city court ruling of September 1, 1973—the Krasin-Yakir verdict—that held the *Chronicle* to contain, per se, deliberately false information defaming the Soviet system. It was an important ruling, clearing the way for Soviet courts in these political trials to assign guilt after 1973 for the mere possession of the *Chronicle*. It no longer was necessary to go through the charade of "proving" the *Chronicle* anti-Soviet. The Pirogov case took months to put together. KGB agents questioned more than 120 people in Moscow, Leningrad, Kiev, Novosibirsk, Ahkhabad, Omsk, and Vilnius, among other cities. Pirogov pleaded not guilty. State witnesses called to testify that they had received the *Chronicle* from Pirogov reportedly failed to support the state's case. Nonetheless, Pirogov was convicted and he was sentenced to two years in a labor camp.[22]

• *Lev Ladyzhensky* and *Fyodor Korovin*. A doctor of physics and mathematics, Ladyzhensky was arrested in the Latvian capital of Riga on December 7, 1973. He was brought to trial there September 25-October 10, 1974, along with a Russian engineer, Fyodor Korovin, on charges of engaging in anti-Soviet agitation and propaganda. An all-night search of Ladyzhensky's home when he was arrested turned up some 50 *samizdat* titles, including the *Chronicle*. Korovin was arrested a few days later, and both were charged with possession of and retyping and distributing books, essays, documents, and underground periodicals like the *Chronicle* between 1966 and 1973. Both men pleaded guilty. Ladyzhensky said he had been influenced by anti-Soviet foreign radiobroadcasts, and Korovin said he had been influenced by Ladyzhensky. Despite their cooperation with investigators, Ladyzhensky was given three years in the camps and three years exile; Korovin got two years' imprisonment and two in exile.[23]

These cases suggest the breadth of the KGB investigation into the *Chronicle*. And they underscore that, by 1972, the *Chronicle* reached *samizdat* readers far beyond Moscow. A loosely woven network had been created to pass information between the *Chronicle* group in Moscow and supporters in most parts of the country. The last issue of the *Chronicle* before it was forced into silence, no. 27, carried news reports from 35 locations in the Soviet Union.[24] KGB investigations and trials also documented that the *Chronicle* was also being reproduced in widely separated regions of the country.

Case 24 had far more ramifications than one would imagine from a summary of persons ultimately brought into court and sent to labor camps. Literally hundreds of people were being questioned. KGB teams searched scores of apartments for *samizdat* material. Thousands of documents were carried off to KGB offices to be meticulously recorded, examined, and filed for use as evidence. One issue of the *Chronicle* recorded KGB activities in just the first six months of 1973 dealing with Case 24. A sampler of *Chronicle* items about the case follows:

Victor Krasin's wife Nadezhda Emelkina, who was exiled to eastern Siberia, was brought to Moscow early in January to be interrogated about Case No. 24.

In February, the following were also interrogated in connection with Case No. 24: L. Alexeyeva, T. Velikanova, L. Ziman, I. Kaplun, L. Kardasevich, S. Kovalyov, L. Kusheva, P. Litvinov, G. Podyapolsky, G. Superfin, T. Khodorovich, I. Yakir, and A. Yakobson. Some of them were presented with an order "on the taking of specimens of handwriting for graphological analysis," because of the great amount of "handwritten materials figuring in the case."

On March 30, Alexander Lavut was questioned by investigator Rastorguyev, who described Case No. 24 as a case involving the preparation, possession and distribution of the *Chronicle*. Lavut refused to testify. His grounds: investigations of this sort obstruct the free dissemination of information.

Valentina Savenkova was interrogated, on the basis of testimony from Yakir, Krasin and Emelkina, about 4,000 rubles which were transmitted from abroad.

The interrogation of Irina Yakir was completed. Frequent interrogations were conducted over a period of two and one half months, sometimes every day.

In [KGB arranged] confrontations with I. Belogorodskaya, L. Alexeyeva and N. Kravchenko denied Belogorodskaya's testimony about their part in the preparation of the *Chronicle*.[25]

Although these particular events occurred early in 1973, as the KGB prepared the Yakir-Krasin trial, they describe an atmosphere nurtured with Case 24.

The *Chronicle*'s compilers watched as one by one friends, informants, and their own number were called to Lubyanka for questioning or seized and imprisoned to await months in uncertain solitary confinement for show trials that routinely resulted in years at hard labor in remote, harsh camps. Foreboding, fear, anger, and helplessness spread as KGB pressures increased.

The unexpected death of Yury Galanskov in the late fall of 1972 added to deep anxieties. It shocked and saddened Moscow dissidents. Moreover, it reminded, if a reminder was at all necessary, that the human rights campaign in the Soviet Union ultimately dealt in life and death. Galanskov died in a Mordovian labor camp on November 20. Friends believed that camp authorities refused proper medical care for a series of illnesses, and that his death during an operation, possibly for perforated ulcers, was a result of poor treatment. The *Chronicle* published an obituary written by his fellow political prisoners who charged that Galanskov "was killed by constant persecutions, by an unjust verdict, by the slander of provocations, by the harshness of the camp regime. And then he died on the operating table under the indifferent knife of a surgeon from the Mordovian camp hospital.[26]

By the fall of 1972, the *Chronicle* was in a tenuous position. To edit, write for, or even be associated with the *Chronicle* put one's life in jeopardy. Yet the *Chronicle* group had frustrated all KGB efforts to silence the publication. No matter threatening trials and nerve-wracking interrogations, the *Chronicle* continued to appear approximately every two months after Gorbanevskay's arrest in December 1969.

Evidence suggests that in the fall of 1972, the KGB decided to tighten the screws. Issue no. 26 was dated July 5, 1972. It began to appear in Moscow later in the month, as copies were reproduced and circulated. Yakir was already in the Lefortovo prison in Moscow undergoing continuous questioning, and Krasin soon would be. Both would eventually break from the particular strains of prison isolation and interrogation.

In November 1972, Irina Yakir was allowed to visit her father at Lefortovo, the KGB facility where those charged and under investigation are held for pretrial interrogation. With two KGB investigators present, Pyotr Yakir told his daughter that he was convinced that the *Chronicle* published factually inaccurate and distorted information. It was a serious and significant accusation, for article 70 of the Russian republic criminal code outlawed, among other things, "slanderous fabrications" intended to weaken the Soviet state. Yakir, then, was providing the KGB corroborating testimony about the *Chronicle*'s criminal content. Just as important, Yakir warned his daughter during this purposeful meeting that "each future issue" of the *Chronicle* would make his and Krasin's eventual prison terms longer, and that as each *Chronicle* appeared, new arrests would result. The investigators confirmed the latter statement, according to a later *Chronicle* report, "pointing out that those arrested would not necessarily be those directly participating in the publication of the new issue."[27]

News of the KGB's "hostage" policy, as Moscow dissidents called it, rapidly spread. That was the intent, of course, of Yakir's meeting with his daughter. The KGB assuredly hoped to raise sufficient apprehension in the *Chronicle* group to halt its publication. Some dissidents believed that the hostage policy reflected the KGB's own inability to narrow its investigation of the *Chronicle* to the actual editor or editors. Others believed that KGB investigators acted on the basis of outdated information about the

Chronicle staff and thus resorted to a blanket threat. There is no way to say for certain.

Chronicle issue no. 27 was already late as word came of the KGB's hostage policy. To maintain the bimonthly publication schedule, an issue should have been dated about September 5, 1972. Number 27 was finally dated October 15, a month late. It began to appear in Moscow over the next few weeks. Given the tedious retyping necessary to produce the *Chronicle,* the date of an issue was only a rough indication of when it might be in the hands of readers. Any given issue was actually seen weeks, even months, after master copies were typed.

Precisely who produced issue no. 27 remains a secret. Anatoly Yakobson, having edited the *Chronicle* until then, finally succumbed to KGB-instilled fear and after putting together issue no. 26 in the summer of 1972, decided against the risk of editing the *Chronicle.* Others of new *Chronicle* compilers who had taken up the work after Gorbanevskaya's arrest assumed responsibility for issue no. 27. Even now, according to some of those involved, they cannot be identified. *Chronicle* work, then, was extraordinarily secretive, for everyone felt the KGB pressure. During the final step, when material was assembled to type the first and master carbon copies, the *Chronicle* editors were especially vulnerable. In a surprise search, KGB agents could seize not only the editor but documents, manuscripts, often the raw handwritten material, from which the *Chronicle* drew.

At this tense moment, the anonymous editor of issue no. 27 retreated to the apartment of a friend, Boris Shragin, on Vernadskogo Prospect in southwest Moscow, to produce issue no. 27. Shragin was a onetime Communist party philosopher who eventually was allowed to immigrate to the United States. Interviewed there, he recalled the clandestine preparation of no. 27:

It was a time of troubles for the *Chronicle.* There had been a delay in publication even before no. 27. It was not easy to find an apartment that the KGB did not know. My apartment was not one of them, but there was no choice. I helped him, with the editing work, putting it together, making corrections. It was a one bedroom apartment. He worked in the separate room. People visited, but they didn't know he was there. My wife secretly gave him food.

There had to be complete secrecy because it was very dangerous at this time. The KGB did not know who personally was editing the *Chronicle* at this time. Maybe they don't know even now about this issue.[28]

Number 27 began showing up in Moscow in late October and early November. On November 13, just nine days after Irina Yakir had met with her father in Lefortovo prison and had been warned about the *Chronicle*, KGB agents searched Pyotr Yakir's apartment and found a copy of no. 27. In swift order, the KGB arrested Irina Belogorodskaya in an act of retaliation. And Yakobson was warned that if issue no. 28 appeared, he too would be arrested.

A known dissident, Belogorodskaya had already served a year in a labor camp for circulating materials in defense of Anatoly Marchenko, the Russian worker whose book *My Testimony* graphically describes Soviet labor camp life. But she had had nothing to do with producing no. 27. Taken to Lefortovo prison, Belogorodskaya was told bluntly that she had been arrested in reaction to issue no. 27, although investigators knew that she had no part in its production.[29] The KGB thus made good on its earlier threat, driving home to those working with the *Chronicle* that the policy of taking hostages was no bluff.

Yakobson's position became precarious. He was summoned by the KGB for questioning. His Moscow apartment was searched, and materials intended for the *Chronicle* confiscated. Not only was he vulnerable because of a *Chronicle* connection, but also because he was a founding member of the Initiative Group, whose activities authorities regarded as anti-Soviet. KGB investigators, questioning Yakobson a few weeks after Belogorodskaya was arrested, took samples of his handwriting for analysis—a sure sign that they were prepared to build a case against him.[30] The KGB increased the pressure on Yakobson in other ways, according to Tatyana Khodorovich, who later became publicly associated with the *Chronicle*. A cosmopolitan, self-assured woman, Khodorovich reminisced in precise Russian as she sat in her Paris apartment:

He was told straight out—either the *Chronicle* does not come out, or you'll be arrested. He was very honest and he was outraged. He told them blackmail wouldn't work on him. But the KGB had no limits. They began calling his friends and telling them the same thing. Moreover, Yakobson's favorite son was very ill; one kidney did not function. Yakobson feared the second would fail. Soviet doctors said they could not treat the boy, and Yakobson's friends told him to take his son abroad. He loved Russia and he refused.

Well, the KGB knew all of this. And when they summoned Yakobson's friends, they were told to make him leave because of his son's illness. The KGB said that despite the illness, they would arrest Yakobson and put him in the labor camp, because they were sure he was putting out the *Chronicle* and they could not allow the *Chronicle* to continue. All of us were shocked. We loved Yakobson. We started telling him he should leave the country.

As it turned out we were "blackmailing" him, too, because we said if he refused to leave we'll halt the *Chronicle*. If he refused, we said, we'll announce that the *Chronicle* will stop. And while he was deciding what to do, the *Chronicle* did not appear.[31]

A consensus emerged among the *Chronicle* intimates in early 1973. Faced with the moral dilemma of persisting with publication at the cost of more arrests, and—given the Galanskov tragedy—even deaths of innocent people, they decided to cease publication of the *Chronicle*. Dissidents told foreign correspondents in Moscow on February 28, 1973, that issue no. 28 would not appear for fear of KGB reprisals.

It was a wrenching moment. By this time, the *Chronicle* had become a symbol of resistance to Soviet official persecution. So long as the *Chronicle* appeared, many Soviet human rights activists believed, there was still hope. Its editors and writers were as aware of its symbolic significance as anyone. Yet there was Belogorodskaya already in Lefortovo, and Yakobson was certain to be arrested if no. 28 should appear. The *Chronicle* thus fell silent for 18 months. Still darker days awaited Soviet dissidents before the *Chronicle* reappeared.

NOTES

1. See John Barron, *KGB: The Secret Work of Soviet Secret Agents* (New York: Readers Digest Press, 1974), pp. 16, 84-85; and Harry Rositzke, *The KGB: The Eyes of Russia* (Garden City, N.Y.: Doubleday, 1981), pp. 253-55.

2. Alexeyeva interview, October 18, 1982.

3. *Chronicle of Human Rights in the Soviet Union* [*Chronicle/Rights*], no. 2, p. 10; no. 9, p. 5. Also Alexeyeva interview, October 18, 1982.

4. *Pravda,* December 17, 1970.

5. For his own account of these events written shortly before his death, see Andrei Amalrik, *Notes of a Revolutionary* (New York: Knopf, 1982), chap. 7-13.

6. For his recollections of this time, see Vladimir Bukovsky, *To Build a Castle—My life as a Dissenter* (New York: Viking Press, 1979), pp. 377-401.

7. Peter Reddaway, ed. and trans., *Uncensored Russia: Protest and Dissent in the Soviet Union* (New York: American Heritage Press, 1972), pp. 427-31.

8. [*Chronicle/Amnesty*], *A Chronicle of Current Events*, no. 17, pp. 64-65.

9. Ibid., no. 19, pp. 196-97.

10. Ibid., no. 21, p. 294.

11. *Chronicle/Amnesty*, no. 24, p. 120. For information on the KGB searches, see ibid., pp. 119-26.

12. *Chronicle/Amnesty*, no. 30, p. 85.

13. Alexeyeva interview, July 25, 1981.

14. For details of the Lyubarsky case, see *Chronicle/Amnesty*, no. 28, pp. 16-22. This section also draws from the author's interview with Lyubarsky.

15. Lyubarsky worked on the *Chronicle*, nos. 44, 45, and 46, issued in 1977. Lyubarsky interview.

16. *Chronicle/Amnesty*, no. 29, pp. 55-56.

17. *Chronicle/Amnesty*, no. 32, pp. 12-14.

18. *Chronicle/Amnesty*, no. 30, pp. 88-89.

19. *Chronicle/Amnesty*, no. 29, pp. 49-53.

20. *Chronicle/Amnesty*, no. 30, pp. 87-88; and *Chronicle/Rights*, no. 2, p. 10.

21. *Chronicle/Amnesty*, no. 30, pp. 91-93; no. 32, pp. 14-17; and *Chronicle/Rights*, no. 3, pp. 12; no. 7, pp. 9-14.

22. *Chronicle/Amnesty*, no. 32, pp. 21-26.

23. *Chronicle/Amnesty*, no. 32, pp. 85-86; no. 34, pp. 8-10.

24. *Chronicle/Rights*, no. 29, p. 60.

25. *Chronicle/Amnesty*, no. 29, pp. 62-29.

26. *Chronicle/Amnesty*, no. 28, pp. 11-12.

27. *Chronicle/Amnesty*, no. 28, p. 14.

28. Shragin interview.

29. *Chronicle/Amnesty*, no. 28, p. 61.

30. *Chronicle/Amnesty*, no. 28, p. 63; and *Chronicle/Rights*, no. 1, p. 13.

31. Khodorovich interview.

4
BETRAYED

The show trial of Pyotr Yakir and Victor Krasin in a small district court in Moscow lasted five days, from August 27 to September 1, 1973. That they would be convicted under article 70 for antistate agitation and propaganda was assumed. They had admitted guilt during months of questioning. Those confessions and evidence they gave against others involved with the *Chronicle* and human rights cases in the Soviet Union demoralized, shocked, and angered dissidents. The trial amounted to a public demonstration of the KGB's success in suppressing the *Chronicle*. More, it reflected handsomely on KGB chief Yury Andropov's ability to crush internal dissent. Just four months before the Yakir-Krasin trial was staged, Andropov was selected by his political cohorts to become a full member of the ruling party Politburo. His accomplishments as KGB chief transformed him into one of the most powerful men in the Soviet Union and ultimately propelled him to the pinnacle of Kremlin power, the post of party general secretary.

The state-controlled Soviet mass media gave the Yakir-Krasin trial unusual publicity. Newspapers used purposefully written TASS reports that constructed a picture of two renegades selling out their country to foreign organizations. TASS reported:

Conclusive evidence was presented at the first court session showing that Yakir and Krasin were used by the anti-Soviet emigre organization "People's Labor

Union" (NTS) and other subversive centers. . . . At the same time they played the role of informants to certain foreign correspondents in Moscow, regularly providing all sorts of rumors and speculation. . . . In turn, the defendants supplied NTS with libelous materials, many of which appeared in the illegally published *Chronicle of Current Events* and which were systematically reprinted by the anti-Soviet journal *Posev*.[1]

KGB investigators assembled some 150 volumes of evidence for the Yakir-Krasin trial. In just one search of Yakir's apartment, 3,000 items of written or printed material were seized. KGB agents interrogated hundreds of people believed to be associated with Yakir and Krasin and the *Chronicle* group. The investigation stretched nearly two years, the last year of which Yakir and Krasin were imprisoned. Krasin says that he alone was questioned for 1,500 hours, during which he broke and implicated himself and others. Yakir likewise betrayed his friends. The Yakir-Krasin case, so voluminous that it was separated from Case 24 into its own Case 63, was a KGB triumph.[2]

Yakir and Krasin devastated the *Chronicle* group long before the two were brought into a Moscow city courtroom to recite their political crimes in a proceeding reminiscent of the Stalin show trials in the 1930s. Months earlier, they gave KGB investigators information about individual dissidents connected with the *Chronicle*. So, too, to a lesser extent did Irina Belogorodskaya after her arrest in January 1973. In some instances, they were asked to confirm information that the KGB already possessed from surveillance, wiretaps, or searches of dissidents. Other times, they elaborated on their own and others' use of *samizdat*, including the *Chronicle*.

It is difficult to determine precisely the harm that Yakir and Krasin did to the *Chronicle*, for it is impossible to say how effective the KGB would have been in silencing the *Chronicle* without their information.[3] But as it became known in the fall of 1972 among Moscow dissidents that Yakir and Krasin had been broken, a natural and intimidating fear spread. As countless persons were summoned to KGB offices, it was apparent that the secret police were nearing the heart of the *Chronicle*. The KGB threat in early 1973 to arrest Yakobson, whether or not it derived from Yakir's or Krasin's confession, seemed part of an ominous pattern. The *Chronicle* might have survived an isolated Yakir-Krasin case, but it was not isolated. Hedrick Smith, of the *New York Times*, who reported from

Moscow in these months, concluded: "Two many had regarded Yakir as a rock of reliability and were unbearably
disillusioned when he began to talk. . . ."[4]

Pyotr Yakir was a former *zek,* Russian slang for
"prisoner." His father, Iona Yakir, a Red Army general,
had fought with distinction in the Russian civil war. The
father was arrested and shot in 1937, during Stalin's
purges of the Soviet Army Officers Corps. Pyotr was
thrown into a labor camp the next year, guilty by association. He was freed only in 1954, after Stalin died and
Khrushchev ordered the release of thousands of Stalin's
innocent victims. Yakir was then 31. He had already
spent 16 years in the camps. He enjoyed a privileged
position by virtue of his father's record and because
Khrushchev had been his father's friend. But Pyotr Yakir
refused to accept passively the retrenchment of Stalinist
orthodoxy in the late 1960s. After the arrests of
Grigorenko, Bogoraz and Litvinov, Yakir had emerged as a
visible acknowledged leader of the human rights movement.
Thus his arrest on June 21, 1972, shook fellow dissidents.
The *Chronicle* published a letter from a "group of Soviet
citizens," in which they tried to thwart mounting feelings of
despair: "The arrest of Yakir, a man who consciously
placed himself at the spearhead of the struggle, does not
mean that 'all is lost,' that the authorities have achieved a
victory with their policy."[5]

Victor Krasin, too, was a former *zek* and a child of
Stalin's terror. Krasin's father died in a labor camp in the
1930s. Krasin studied in the Moscow University economics
faculty in the late 1940s. He was arrested in 1949 and
spent six years in the camps before he was rehabilitated.
He had been sent into exile in 1969. Krasin, like Yakir,
was almost a generation removed from most other Moscow
dissidents of the 1970s. At the time of his trial, he was
44. Yakir was 50. They both carried psychological scars
from the camps, the "Gulag" labor camp network that
Alexander Solzhenitsyn has recorded.

Their personal histories are important because the KGB
almost certainly regarded Yakir and Krasin as weak links in
the *Chronicle* chain. Yakir was notorious for his drinking
and that presented the KGB with a particular advantage
over him. But, more important, KGB investigators knew,
as Krasin later believed, that years in labor camps had left
them both with special weaknesses. Krasin, now an exile,
living in a crowded apartment complex in New York, was
interviewed about his tragic past. Sipping tea one day, he
recalled in accented English the *Chronicle* years and the
KGB campaign under Andropov against the *Chronicle:*

We tried to participate in a rebellion. But we always had a fear in our bones. And we couldn't overcome this fear. The new generation to which Litvinov and Amalrik and my wife belong doesn't have this fear. Yes, they had a fear when they were followed by the KGB, and knew that the KGB could beat them. Of course, they felt fear. But I call this just a pragmatic fear. But we had some mystical fear. A fear of the KGB as an organization. I think all the people who grew up under Stalin, and especially those people like Pyotr and I who spent a lot of years in concentration camps, and saw how they kill and how they die . . . we have this special feeling, a special feeling that I can describe only as a feeling of slaves.

The KGB understood this clearly. [KGB interrogator] Alexandrovsky once asked me, "Why do you think Yakir behaved this way?"

I said, "Very simple. He is mystically afraid of you, you meaning the KGB as a whole, and you and his own investigator as persons."

He smiled and said, "Yes, you're right."[6]

Andrei Amalrik, for one, agreed with this interpretation. He thought that Yakir's and Krasin's labor camp years sharpened their survival instinct and, at the same time, convinced them that once arrested, the secret police could do what they wished, kill the two of them if that was necessary.[7]

Yakir had already been held incommunicado in the KGB's Lefortovo prison for three months before Krasin was arrested on September 12, 1972. Neither of them was seen outside Lefortovo until the following August, almost a year later. In the intervening months, dozens of "confrontations" were staged as individuals were brought to Lefortovo to face Yakir or Krasin personally and to hear an accusation and then and there deny or confirm the charge. It was a way of extracting information but also of crushing human spirits as friends openly betrayed friends. Men and women who had known and trusted one another for years found themselves forced by KGB threats and fear to inform on each other, knowing that by sparing themselves, they probably doomed their friends.

Most of Yakir's and Krasin's first months in Lefortovo were spent in near isolation. Interrogators slowly instilled sufficient fear, despair, and resignation and thus, they confessed. Yakir had predicted that he might cooperate with the KGB if arrested. He earlier told David Bonovia of the *Times* of London in a tape-recorded interview: "If they beat me, I will say anything. I know this from my former experience in the camps. But you'll know it will not be the real me speaking."[8] In fact, there is no evidence that Yakir was beaten or otherwise subjected to physical punishment to make him confess. Krasin acknowledges that KGB investigators neither used nor even threatened torture. KGB techniques were more subtle. The KGB relied on patient, intense interrogation to reduce a person's will to resist. Krasin has described how he was broken.[9] It appears that Yakir went through approximately the same procedure.

Krasin spent his 11 months in Lefortovo prison in a cell just large enough to hold three cots, a small table, and a bucketlike toilet. During these months, he was isolated from all human contact save for his chief interrogator, KGB Major Pavel Alexandrovsky, two successive cell mates, nameless guards, and those persons later brought to Lefortovo for confrontations. Alexandrovsky was about 40 years old. Ironically, he studied in Moscow University's law faculty the same years Krasin was in the economics faculty. Alexandrovsky's assignment was to take material collected by 25 to 30 KGB agents assigned to the Yakir-Krasin case and gain Krasin's confession, a confession to be repeated in open court.

Questioning began at 10 A.M. and lasted often until 10 P.M., seven days a week with breaks for two meals and a walk. The interrogation room was small and doubled as Alexandrovsky's office. "Even the KGB does not have enough space," Krasin recollected with amusement, alluding to the common Moscow complaint of apartment shortages. The room held two tables, Alexandrovsky's near a window, Krasin's near the door. There was a heavy metal safebox where Alexandrovsky kept documents related to the case.

Krasin, like Yakir, was charged under article 70, which provided for a maximum sentence of seven years in prison and five in exile. But early in his interrogation, Krasin was threatened with article 64—treason. The penalty for treason in the Soviet Union is death. Alexandrovsky pressed Krasin on the seriousness of his situation. Krasin recounts:

His job was to put in my mind that the threat of the death penalty is not a joke, no bluff. At the end of two months, he was concentrating on two points.

The first was that it was not his initiative to threaten me with the death penalty. Our case, he said was being reported to [the then KGB chief Yury] Andropov himself every week. So, I had to realize the situation and those threats are coming from the top. And the other line was that I deserved this, I really deserved this. The connection with NTS with the purpose of overthrowing the Soviet government and so on and so on . . . this is not article 70, this is article 64. And if we charge you with this, don't be surprised, he would say. Well, he was very direct.

He said something like this: "If we shoot you, your dissident movement will stop tomorrow. It will be a very good example for others."

So they consistently put in my mind that I was chosen as an example to stop the others. It was a problem of whether to believe or not to believe. With all my Stalin concentration camp experience I finally believed him—that my price would be the death penalty. So finally, I began to make some concessions. At the time, I thought that I could give them only as much as I wanted, no more. It was maybe the biggest mistake I made, because, you know, there is no limit. As soon as you start, it is difficult to stop.

At the same time, because they have experience and because they knew me very well, he began to establish very friendly relations with me. It included tea, cigarettes, permission to get special food—I had an ulcer. Then they permitted me to get parcels twice a month from my wife, instead of once a month. They permitted me books in my cell.

One of the ideas that he consistently repeated, and which I finally accepted, though it was wrong and false, was that Pyotr and I should tell our friends that we were wrong, that in thinking we were fighting for truth, we actually started an anti-Soviet movement and were fighting against the Soviet government, meaning the Soviet people.

If we recognize this, Alexandrovsky would say, and tell our friends stop—and they would listen, they would stop because they considered us their leaders—you will save their lives. Because if they don't stop you can be sure we will arrest everyone. We have such instructions now, to stop your activities. You know what the KGB is. It is not hard for us to arrest a couple hundred people in one night. You can save their lives. Many of your old friends will say you are a traitor, that you betrayed the ideals and the movement. But you have to accept this, because your satisfaction will be that you saved their lives.

At first I laughed, but then as I began to look for moral approval of my actions, I accepted these ideas. I even wrote a letter to my friends and argued that we are surrounded, so to speak, and it is better to capitulate without losses.[10]

In the beginning, Krasin gave the KGB information only about himself. The KGB had files of names, dates, events. Major Alexandrovsky persuaded Krasin that to confirm what the KGB already knew would do no harm. Krasin further was encouraged by his cell mate, a man convicted of speculating in gold and brought from a labor camp to Lefortovo specifically to help break Krasin, presumably in return for a lighter sentence.

His job was to do what Alexandrovsky did in the interrogations, to tell me in a friendly manner, "Listen, Victor, you are an old prisoner. You understand this is the KGB. They will shoot you without any doubt. And what will happen? Your friends will put your picture on the wall, and that's it. You've had experience. It's no joke. If they tell you they will kill you, they will kill you. You have to make some concessions."

Well, you hear this day after day, every evening, in a friendly manner, like old friends. "You're a *lagernik*, I'm a *lagernik*. It's no joke. It's a serious matter. They'll kill you."[11]

The next step was to press Krasin to implicate others. He had hidden *samizdat* books and about 100 rolls of film negatives of *samizdat* material in apartments of a friend and a brother and in the Siberian village of Eniseisk, where his wife remained in exile. In mid-November, about two months after he had been arrested, Krasin agreed to tell the KGB where the books and film were stashed. That implicated the friend and his brother.

Major Alexandrovsky himself flew to Siberia, where, after Krasin had talked with his wife Nadezhda Emelkina by telephone, he seized Krasin's *samizdat* books. Krasin had buried the books outside Eniseisk when he had lived there with Emelkina. With instructions from Krasin, she led Major Alexandrovsky and several police guards through snow-covered taiga to a spot where they dug up a parcel. Alexandrovsky personally carried them back to Moscow. The books were used as evidence in the Yakir-Krasin trial.

Emelkina had burned incriminating notes of Krasin's before
Alexandrovsky arrived in Siberia.[12]

In early January the KGB brought Emelkina from Siberia
to Lefortovo for questioning and to see Krasin. She had
been involved in the *Chronicle* issues 11, 12, and 13,
processing information and typing some of the first copies.
She admitted as much to the KGB investigators, involving
as well Yakobson and Irina Yakir in *Chronicle* production.
At this point, Krasin, ready to break completely, began to
reveal everything he knew about the *Chronicle* and other
samizdat activities.

It was in November 1972, as Krasin first implicated
others, that dissidents learned that Yakir, too, had been
broken. The stunning revelation came through Yakir's
daughter Irina during the previously noted meeting in
Lefortovo on November 4.

From the late fall of 1972, then, until their trial, Yakir
and Krasin betrayed one after another of their friends and
acquaintances. Moreover, after Irina Belogorodskaya was
arrested on January 3, 1973, she confirmed some KGB
information about persons associated with the *Chronicle* and
other human rights activities. Thus, by extracting
information from a number of persons, most especially Yakir
and Krasin, the KGB was splitting the *Chronicle* group into
demoralized factions. The *Chronicle* itself ultimately reported the methodical procedure as the KGB slowly constructed
its show trial of Yakir and Krasin.

> On 20 January there was a confrontation between
> Emelkina and Pyotr Yakir. At the interrogations,
> Emelkina at first gave details only about her own
> actions. Subsequently she testified about an asso-
> ciation of Irina Yakir and Anatoly Yakobson with the
> *Chronicle*.

> On 16 February there were confrontations between
> Yuly Kim, on the one hand, and Yakir and Krasin,
> on the other.

> Anatoly Yakobson was interrogated about the
> *Chronicle* and documents of the Initiative Group. He
> confirmed his participation in the letters of the Initia-
> tive Group, but did not answer other questions.
> Specimens of handwriting were taken from him for
> graphological analysis.

> In February, Ilya Gabai was interrogated on the basis
> of testimony given by Yakir and Krasin. The greater

part of this testimony was not confirmed by Gabai.

In the course of the spring, testimony by Belogorodskaya began to figure in the interrogations of Irina Yakir, Ludmilla Alexeyeva and others. It became known that in this testimony, the names of Irina Yakir, Gabriel Superfin, Yury Shikhanovich, Ivan Rudakov, Natalya Kravchenko and Ludmilla Alexeyeva were mentioned in a rather "criminal" context.

Vladimir Rokityansky was interrogated [in March] on the basis of testimony given by Krasin. Krasin had stated that Rokityansky had contacts with foreign correspondents, and gave them copies of the *Chronicle*. Rokityansky did not confirm this.

Alexander Alshutov was interrogated [in March] on the basis of testimony given by Pyotr Yakir.

The interrogations of Irina Yakir continued [in April]. "Out of humanitarian concerns" they are conducted in a district police station, so that Irina Yakir can nurse her infant during the breaks. (She has a two month old daughter.)

On 7 May there was a confrontation between Irina Yakir and Pyotr Yakir.

Valentina Savenkova was interrogated on the basis of testimony from Yakir, Krasin and Emelkina about 4,000 rubles which were transmitted from abroad.

The interrogation of Irina Yakir was completed [in June]. Frequent interrogations were conducted over a period of two and a half months, sometimes every day. At first Yakir refused to answer questions. Subsequently she began to confirm testimony which "concerned her personally."

At a confrontation [in June] with Belogorodskaya, Alexeyeva and Kravchenko denied Belogorodskaya's testimony about their part in the preparation of the *Chronicle*. [13]

In this forced march of events, Yakir and Krasin publicly recanted, leaving no doubt among the *Chronicle* circle and others that the two had succumbed to KGB pressure.

Yakir openly confessed in a letter to Andrei Sakharov, responding to Sakharov's public defense of Yakir. The handwritten letter dated April 3, 1973, was delivered to Sakharov in Moscow by a KGB agent. The letter said in part:

> I kept, copied and disseminated anti-Soviet literature and passed on to the west information which was tendentious, was often slanderous in nature, and in certain cases directly appealed for struggle against our existing system. All this has now been appraised by me objectively and is viewed as a violation of Soviet laws. Letters and other documents compiled by me and my circle were immediately praised on reaching the west and used by open and hidden adversaries for purposes of propaganda against our homeland, the Soviet Union. Such mouthpieces of anti-communism as Radio Liberty and NTS . . . have used any negative event in our country to discredit the Soviet system.[14]

About the same time, the KGB permitted Krasin to pass a letter to Yuly Kim, Yakir's son-in-law, addressed to Kim and "friends who are free." Krasin revealed his own change of heart and urged others to do likewise. As later summarized in the *Chronicle*, Krasin concluded:

> The defeat of the "democratic movement" should be acknowledged. The cessation of all opposition activity is not sufficient to save people from repressions. The authorities require guarantees, and these guarantees can be assured only by all-around cooperation with the investigation. Krasin calls upon people to overcome the psychological barrier and testify freely, not only about their own activities, but also about those of others.[15]

By June 1973, the KGB case against Krasin and Yakir was substantially complete. Their defense attorneys were permitted to see the materials, as provided in Soviet law. Ironically, although the long, thorough KGB investigation under Case 24 was directed against the *Chronicle*, neither Yakir nor Krasin had been essential to the *Chronicle*'s existence. As evidence revealed, they had neither edited nor written much for the *Chronicle*. Their roles in the publication mostly concerned its distribution and reproduction. Krasin was involved, as many were, in retyping copies, for example. But Krasin and Yakir were vital in the dissident community and in the *Chronicle* circle specially for their open opposition to Soviet authorities. They were important conduits to the Western press corps, Yakir in particular.

Thus, when the Yakir-Krasin trial opened in the Lyublino district people's court in Moscow on August 27, 1973, the indictment focused on two lines—that both men had been associated with the illegal *Chronicle* and that they were linked with anti-Soviet foreign organizations, chiefly the NTS (People's Labor Union) and Radio Liberty, both of which the Soviet media regularly connected to the U.S. Central Intelligence Agency.[16]

Soviet authorities, in pursuing the *Chronicle*'s foreign connections, sought at once to establish guilt under article 70 of the Russian republic's criminal code to blacken the *Chronicle* group as servants of ever present hostile foreign centers. For Yakir and Krasin to be tried under article 70, the KGB had to present a case showing that their activities not only were "anti-Soviet" but were purposefully conducted to weaken or subvert the Soviet state. Thus, it was important to link Yakir and Krasin with the NTS and Radio Liberty, to emphasize that they had received money from the NTS and that in passing the *Chronicle* and other *samizdat* to Western correspondents, Yakir and Krasin were knowingly part of a larger anti-Soviet conspiracy.

The KGB's political case was helped by the fact that Radio Liberty did routinely broadcast in Russian large segments of *Chronicle* issues as they reached the radio's central offices in Munich, West Germany. Moreover, *Posev*, the monthly Russian emigre journal ideologically connected to the NTS and published in Frankfurt, reprinted whole issues of the *Chronicle*. These reprints were distributed abroad and were also smuggled back into the Soviet Union.[17] The *Chronicle* group instantly realized that a tactical mistake had been made in *Posev*'s and Radio Liberty's use of the *Chronicle* numbers. The group might have been able to prevent that use by private appeal, had it anticipated the KGB tactics. It was too late, however. The KGB script for the trial played amply on the fact that the *Chronicle* to all appearances worked in unison with foreign enemies.

The KGB case was not made from whole cloth. In 1969, Yakir and Krasin did, in fact, receive 4,000 rubles—about $4,000 at the time—from a foreign organization. As both Yakir and Krasin confessed, and Krasin later confirmed, the money came from an Italian organization called Europa

Civita. But it was the head of the NTS who supplied the funds. Also, Krasin and Yakir admitted having contacts with NTS representatives sent into the Soviet Union.

Under other legal circumstances, mere contacts with an organization or even funding by it does not amount to a crime. In the Soviet Union, the KGB easily built a shadow case using the facts just cited. There really was no direct or implicit accusation that Yakir or Krasin sought to overthrow or even change the Soviet political system. The KGB and state prosecutors never went that far. For them, it was sufficient to establish Krasin's and Yakir's link—and the *Chronicle*'s—with anti-Soviet organizations. Anyone in the Soviet Union aware and informed of the trial would be expected to draw the most damaging conclusions.

Yakir and Krasin pleaded guilty. Their trial before a Soviet judge was closed except to those admitted by the KGB. Foreign correspondents and friends of Yakir and Krasin gained information only from a Soviet official who "briefed" reporters, from Soviet TASS accounts, and from his wife, Valentina Yakir, who was allowed in the courtroom. Pyotr Yakir, asking for leniency, pleaded, "I want to die elsewhere than behind barbed wire." The court sentenced both Yakir and Krasin to three years in labor camps and three years in internal exile, despite their cooperation with KGB investigators.

The proceedings proved to be in Russia's "Potemkin village" tradition. The harsh sentences surprised Yakir and Krasin. But the court's actions were for public consumption. So, too, was a dramatic "press conference" staged in Moscow's Journalist Club on September 5, just four days after the trial ended. The Yakir-Krasin trial had earned considerable publicity in the American and West European media, most of it critical of the Soviet Union for what appeared to be a Stalinist show trial. The KGB proposed a Yakir-Krasin "press conference," during which they once more would recant, this time before Soviet and foreign correspondents. The event was meant to counter unfavorable foreign reports. Krasin at first found the idea of a press conference objectionable. The matter was quickly resolved. Krasin has described a meeting with Andropov:

It was just 20 or 30 minutes after the trial, and they had brought me back to Lefortovo prison. A KGB officer came to get me, and as we were walking through the prison, he told me, "You'll be received by the chairman of the KGB." He brought me to the

study of the prison administrator. Andropov was
there. The administrator introduced me and
Andropov told him he could leave. Andropov stood
up from a table, took several steps toward me,
offered me his hand and said, "I'm the chairman of
the KGB."

I said, "I recognize you by your pictures." That
was my first sentence to him!

"Okay," he said, "Sit down, let's talk. They tell
me you have some problems in believing us because of
your sentence. You should now submit an appeal to
the [Russian republic] Supreme Court and they'll
reduce the sentence to just the three years in exile.
And maybe in eight months, we'll release you from
exile, too, and you'll come back to Moscow."

He went on: "Listen, in some of your documents
you say that Stalinism is appearing again in our
country."

"Yes," I said, "That's true. There are some
signs."

He said, "No, no, that's nonsense. No one will
permit Stalinism to come back. We are very firm
about this in the Politburo. Everyone knows what
Stalinism is. I know your father and the father of
Pyotr Yakir were killed during the great purges. I
myself was also almost arrested at the time. I was
second secretary of the Karelo-Finnish republic. The
first secretary was arrested, and I waited for my own
arrest every day. But I was lucky. That's why I
understand the origins of your feelings toward the
Soviet Union. But, listen, we couldn't release you in
the court, because you and Yakir did a lot of things.
But later you'll be back in Moscow and everything
will be okay."

Then he said, "What do you think about participating in the press conference? You know, the
Western press made a big story about your trial. It
will be very helpful if you tell them that what you
said in the trial is true, that nobody pressed you and
so on."

Well, I just had a couple seconds to answer. I
said, "Well, listen, I have told all this during the
trial. I can repeat it once more. It's no problem."

He said, "That's very good. That's the correct
decision."

Well, the meeting was finished. They took me
back to my cell. But everything happened exactly as
Andropov said it would."[18]

In advance of the televised press conference in Moscow's Journalist Club, Krasin rehearsed questions and answers with Major Alexandrovsky for three days. Yakir rehearsed separately with his interrogator. Alexandrovsky told Krasin that the conference would be staged. Only certain of the written questions submitted in advance by journalists would be asked by the foreign ministry's press spokesman, Vsevolod Sofinsky. None, Krasin was told, would raise unfamiliar topics. The press conference received extensive publicity abroad. Some 200 Soviet and foreign correspondents relayed Yakir's and Krasin's restatement of their confessions. Their coaching showed. One American press account referred to the two "reciting rehearsed testimony," and another to a "carefully prepared session."[19]

The Russian republic supreme court took up the Yakir-Krasin sentences within weeks. True to Andropov's word, the court on September 28 wiped out the labor camp terms, banishing both men to exile not far from Moscow. Those terms were later reduced, too, and by the fall of 1974 Yakir and Krasin were back in Moscow.

The pursuit by Andropov's KGB of the *Chronicle* group not only silenced the *Chronicle*. Case 24 destroyed dozens if not hundreds of lives. We know the names of some, but probably not all of the men and women who were sent to labor camps because they worked with the *Chronicle*. Many others who were investigated but not imprisoned would be forever suspect by the KGB, for dossiers grew thick with names of *Chronicle* workers. Many who escaped labor camps lived out dispirited, hopeless lives.

Victor Krasin became an outcast, regarded as a traitor by fellow dissidents. Ostracized by them even in Moscow when he returned from exile, Krasin was spurned also after he emigrated in February 1975. He began a new and lonely life with his wife, Emelkina, in New York City, working as a night watchman while he developed a system to profit from stock investments. None of his old friends from Moscow who immigrated to the United States and Europe would speak with him except Pavel Litvinov. The others would never forgive him for betraying them and other friends.

Pyotr Yakir lived a quiet life in Moscow after he returned to the capital and until his death in November 1982. He, too, was blamed for his betrayal and he never achieved standing again among dissidents. His daughter, Irina, while involved with the *Chronicle*, never was arrested, possibly because she was nursing a child, possibly because she was used by the KGB as a conduit between her father and dissidents.

Irina Belogorodskaya, although arrested, was never put on trial. She was held for investigation on charges of engaging in anti-Soviet agitation and propaganda until after the Yakir-Krasin trial. Then on November 16, 1973, she was pardoned by authorities and released from prison.[20] Two years later she emigrated, moving to Paris. There was no hint from the KGB as to why she was not tried. But it seems evident that she had served her purpose in giving information about *Chronicle* workers. There was never any suggestion of a deal between Belogorodskaya and the KGB. And among fellow dissidents, she was seen as doing nothing more than any of them would do under pressure. It was Litvinov's view, for one, that the KGB sooner or later could break anyone, that everyone would eventually talk.

Ilya Gabai, one of the many persons interrogated or arrested during Case 24, committed suicide in Moscow on October 20, 1973, by jumping off the balcony of his eleventh floor apartment onto the concrete below.[21] He left no note. No one really knows what drove him to take his own life—the years in a labor camp, the constant pressure of KGB harassment and surveillance, the ultimate isolation into which dissidents are forced in the Soviet Union, or personal despair, or some of all.

Anatoly Yakobson and his family, including his ill son, were permitted to leave the Soviet Union for Israel in September 1973. Exactly five years later, he committed suicide there. Personal problems, including the difficulty of making the transition from one culture to another, seem to have pushed him beyond his will to live.

Of others originally connected with the *Chronicle*, Pavel Litvinov was allowed to emigrate from the Soviet Union in 1972, after serving a three-year term of internal exile in a remote Siberian village.

General Pyotr Grigorenko, in 1973, was completing a five-year incarceration in Soviet psychiatric hospitals where he had been committed following his conviction in 1970 on charges of antistate activity. Subjected to cruel treatment during his confinement, the general was later permitted to travel to the United States in 1977. While there, Soviet authorities in Moscow stripped him of his Soviet citizenship.

The fate of those in the *Chronicle* group seemed even in the fall of 1973 to be death, imprisonment, exile, destruction of one's life pattern, not to mention personal, emotional trauma. Moreover, the future looked bleak for the *Chronicle* associates and other dissidents. Two of the most respected and well-known figures in Russia, Andrei Sakharov and Alexander Solzhenitsyn, were being viciously attacked by the official Soviet press for their public opposition to oppressive political and cultural policies. Solzhenitsyn was destined to be forcibly exiled from the Soviet Union in February 1974, as the KGB under Andropov sought to eliminate focal points of dissident opposition.

These, then, were discouraging months for Soviet dissidents. About the time Solzhenitsyn was deported, however, the mood began to change from one of resignation to resistance. Having given in to KGB blackmail, the *Chronicle* group, for one, discovered that political persecution did not cease. Out of a rekindled determination to resist came the decision to revive the *Chronicle*.

NOTES

1. Excerpts from a TASS report in *Izvestia*, August 28, 1973.

2. Much of this information, and throughout this chapter, comes from the author's interview with Victor Krasin on May 12, 1982, in New York. The author's four-hour tape-recorded interview with Krasin was the first time that Krasin discussed his experience at length for publication. The interview drew from Krasin's own unpublished 1,000-page draft manuscript.

3. Boris Shragin, for example, thinks that Yakir and Krasin had somewhat outdated facts about the inner *Chronicle* group, and the KGB as a result used the "hostage" policy because they did not know, from Yakir and Krasin, who exactly produced the *Chronicle*. Shragin interview.

4. Hedrick Smith, *The Russians* (New York: Quadrangle, 1976), p. 461.

5. [*Chronicle/Amnesty*], *A Chronicle of Current Events*, no. 25, p. 228.

6. Krasin interview.

7. Andrei Amalrik, *Notes of a Revolutionary* (New York: Knopf, 1982), p. 230.

8. Krasin interview.

9. *New York Times*, August 30, 1973; and the *Washington Post*, September 6, 1973.

10. Krasin interview.

11. Krasin interview. *Lagernik* is Russian slang derived from the word *lager*, or camp, and meaning "labor camp prisoner."

12. Krasin interview. See also *Chronicle/Amnesty*, no. 28, p. 15.

13. *Chronicle/Amnesty*, no. 29, pp. 61-68. This information was generally known in the dissident community as

events occurred. *Chronicle,* no. 29, itself did not appear until May 1974.

14. *Chronicle/Amnesty,* no. 29, p. 67.

15. *Chronicle/Amnesty,* no. 29, p. 67.

16. *Chronicle/Amnesty,* no. 30, pp. 82-86, reports the trial. This section also draws on the *New York Times,* August 27 and 29 and September 1, 1973; and the *Washington Post,* August 27 and 28, 1973.

17. See the *New York Times,* September 1, 1973.

18. Krasin interview.

19. See Robert Kaiser's account in the *Washington Post,* September 6, 1973; and Theodore Shabad's in the *New York Times,* September 6, 1973.

20. *Chronicle of Human Rights in the Soviet Union,* nos. 5-6, p. 13.

21. *Chronicle/Amnesty,* no. 30, p. 82.

5

NEW TIMES

The *Chronicle* reappeared on May 7, 1974, at a "press conference" in the apartment of Tatyana Khodorovich on Moscow's Prospect Mira 68. Western foreign correspondents crowded into the tiny flat to be told that the *Chronicle*, if not altogether well, was nonetheless alive.

Not only the decision to resume the *Chronicle*, but the way in which the decision was revealed, was a daring move. Tatyana Khodorovich and two close friends, Tatyana Velikanova and Sergei Kovalev, openly announced to foreign correspondents who had made their way to Khodorovich's home that the three would ensure the distribution of the *Chronicle*. In so doing, they were trying to demonstrate that the *Chronicle* was a legal enterprise, that they themselves were doing no more than exercising the right of free press guaranteed in the Soviet constitution. But they also were inviting KGB retaliation, for they were challenging Andropov's authority, deliberately so it seemed.

Three issues had been prepared for the occasion—nos. 28, 29, and 30. Although the *Chronicle* for all intents and purposes had been nonexistent for 18 months, dissidents had assiduously collected information as if to produce new issues. Segments of the *Chronicle* were privately and methodically assembled for the day the *Chronicle* might be revived.

The final production of the three issues, totaling more than 200 single-spaced typewritten pages, was done in a large Moscow apartment, one of those old, sturdy buildings that predate the Bolshevik revolution. The apartment owners were an elderly privileged couple. They were not directly involved with the *Chronicle*, but they were sympathetic with its aims and, like many among Moscow's population, offered what support they could to the *Chronicle* and the democratic movement. Ludmilla Alexeyeva took on the job of typing the three issues. Moving into one room of the three-room apartment, and helped by a friend who dictated from already edited material as she typed on her well-used machine, Alexeyeva pounded out the new *Chronicles* over a period of several days. Her work was complicated by having to fit the *Chronicle* operation to daily needs of the apartment owners. On one night, for example, a dozen of their friends came and went as Alexeyeva, working behind the closed door of the adjoining room, secretly typed one page after another of the three *Chronicle* numbers. On the final day, the apartment owners themselves helped assemble the hundreds of onionskin pages into separate *Chronicle* copies.

Issue 28 carried an editorial note explaining for the record the 18-month silence:

> The reason for the break in the *Chronicle*'s publication was the KGB's repeated and unequivocal threats to respond to each new issue of the *Chronicle* with new arrests—arrests of people suspected by the KGB of publishing or distributing new or past issues (of the material on "Case Number 24" in this issue and the next issue). People faced with the terrible necessity of making decisions which will affect not only themselves are placed in an ethical situation the nature of which requires no comment. But to remain silent would mean to facilitate—even though indirectly and passively—the use of a "tactic of hostages" which is incompatible with justice, morality and human dignity. Therefore, the *Chronicle* is resuming publication and will strive to preserve both the principles and style of previous issues.[1]

There was something new about the *Chronicle*. For the first time, contributors to the *Chronicle* publicly associated themselves with what Soviet authorities bluntly said was an illegal publication. Tatyana Khodorovich was a Russian-language linguist, a cultured woman with origins in Russian aristocracy who deeply believed in the just ends of the blossoming Soviet human rights movement. The other two public sponsors of the new *Chronicle* were equally dedicated. Tatyana Velikanova, a mathematics programer, had long been connected with the *Chronicle* as a source of information. Sergei Kovalev, an internationally known biologist, was a friend of Andrei Sakharov and shared the physicist's concerns about the repressive nature of Soviet society. In a separate statement drafted in Khodorovich's hand, and given to correspondents that May 7 when the *Chronicle* reappeared, Kovalev, Khodorovich, and Velikanova obligated themselves to distribute the *Chronicle*. Others before them had been tried and imprisoned for as much.

"We consider it our duty," they said, "to facilitate the wide distribution to the maximum possible extent. We are convinced of the necessity of making available this very truthful information about infringements of the basic rights of man in the Soviet Union to everyone who is interested."[2]

The statement did not say so, but Kovalev, Velikanova, and Khodorovich were members of the Initiative Group for the Defense of Human Rights. With the decimation of Soviet dissident ranks in the course of Case 24, there was a real problem of reconstructing an editorial organization for the *Chronicle*. The Initiative Group at least had a semblance of organization. Its members not only had been involved in *Chronicle* matters but they had a natural interest in its resumption. The lines of interest were not sharply defined, it should be noted. There were no separate centers of power or territorial claims in the assorted Soviet human rights interests. Although the word "movement" appears often enough in connection with Soviet human rights, dissidents who experienced the years routinely object to the word "movement" as conveying too purposeful and structured a phenomenon. So it was when the idea emerged that the Initiative Group would take responsibility for distributing the *Chronicle*, while others, less well known to the KGB, would actually produce it. It was a vague, undeveloped suggestion. As events turned out, Kovalev became the main editor of the *Chronicle*, although the title was resisted. Then as before, the *Chronicle* was the work of an intimate circle of friends with common objectives who shunned strict and titled functions. But Kovalev assumed the politically dangerous job of selecting and assembling disparate sections of information into a final manuscript that could then be turned over to typists.

When it came to unveiling the new *Chronicle*, experience had taught the dissidents that to identify oneself as a *Chronicle* editor was to invite certain trial and years in a labor camp. Khodorovich recalls that after Anatoly Yakobson and his family, including his seriously ill son, had immigrated to Israel in the fall of 1973, dissidents felt that the *Chronicle* could then be resumed:

> We decided after Anatoly left that people should know that the *Chronicle* was coming out, and that people should know what the *Chronicle* was. And so in 1974, we made that open statement—that we took the responsibility for the distribution of the *Chronicle*. Some people put the wrong interpretation on this statement. They thought we were the authors of the *Chronicle*, that we were continuing the *Chronicle*. That is not what we said. We only said that we thought that in the Soviet Union people should know the truth, and the *Chronicle* was only truth.
>
> There was no identification of editors partly because of modesty, and partly because five minutes after the correspondents would have left, the KGB would have shown up. They listened to everything that was going on. There were facts to prove this. People found listening devices in walls. There was a woman who lived in my apartment with me, who was forced on me as a tenant. My friends said she was my "listening device." She had a KGB-supplied tape recorder in her room, and she probably carried the tapes out of the apartment herself.[3]

The *Chronicle*'s reappearance, unlike its original issue six years before, was a newsworthy event. Foreign correspondents in Moscow correctly interpreted the event as a direct challenge to the KGB as dissidents slowly recovered from the Yakir-Krasin episode. Reporting from Moscow for the *Washington Post*, Robert Kaiser wrote: "Dissidents suggested that the new [*Chronicle*] issues were brought out primarily as a symbolic gesture of defiance to the KGB." In a prophetic statement, Kaiser went on, "Some members of the tiny band of active dissidents believe it was a mistake to bring out new numbers of the *Chronicle* now, since it is likely to infuriate the KGB and prompt a new round of searches, arrests and trials."[4]

The *Chronicle* came back different. The 18-month silence forced the editors and writers who survived Case 24 to rethink their work and methods. The new *Chronicle* was larger, but it was to appear less frequently. It operated with new secrecy. The shattering Yakir-Krasin trial taught the *Chronicle* staff to guard names and details about the publication. In the relatively more open *Chronicle* of the past, Yakir and Krasin had known lots of people who were either connected with the *Chronicle* or other *samizdat*.

Many were now in labor camps because Yakir or Krasin had been able to name them. The lesson drawn from that was simple. Don't ask about what does not concern you. Don't tell others what does not concern them. And most especially don't mention names for the KGB to overhear or gain from interrogations.

The new *Chronicle* came back with a forcefulness that revealed a metamorphosis among dissidents. In a sense, they felt the Soviet authorities had deliberately deceived and outmaneuvered them. They had stopped the *Chronicle*. Still the fear-instilling campaign of political persecutions, interrogations, and trials had continued. KGB threats to arrest friends or relatives of known dissidents persisted. The vitriolic Soviet press campaign against Sakharov and Solzhenitsyn, begun about the time of the Yakir-Krasin trial, continued with ever rising fury. In February 1974, in one of its most desperate acts against dissidents, the Soviet government expelled Solzhenitsyn. He was forcibly seized in Moscow and told that he could either leave the Soviet Union or face trial for treason. When Solzhenitsyn chose exile, he was flown in a Soviet Aeroflot jet to West Germany.

Persistent KGB persecution gradually forced a majority among the *Chronicle* group to recognize that the willingness to halt publication had amounted only to a surrender to the KGB. The overriding Kremlin policy of sharply limiting civil rights, it was clear, was unchanged. Yury Gastev, a Soviet philosopher and son of a Russian poet and revolutionary who was shot in 1937 during Stalin's purges, remembers the dissident attitudes in Moscow in 1974. Now living in exile in Paris, Gastev says he worked with the *Chronicle* for ten years, from 1971 until he was forced to emigrate from Moscow in 1981. He recalled in an interview in the Parisian apartment he shared with Alexander and Arina Ginzburg that the KGB had halted the *Chronicle* by applying the "hostage" tactic and then commencing arrests and trials.

There were two opposite tendencies at work on the *Chronicle* as the KGB pressured. One wanted to stop the *Chronicle*. Another wanted to continue publication. Well, the KGB started threatening arrests. There was the hostage situation. As a result, several people working with the *Chronicle* left the Soviet Union. Several were sent to the camps. As a consequence, people who wanted to continue to put out the *Chronicle* became the majority.

While a lot of people wanted to resume the *Chronicle*, the idea of being responsible for someone else's arrest was hypnotic. Remember that the KGB was calling people in, and telling them that they would personally be held responsible if the *Chronicle* appeared. Could you really, then, take this on your conscience? This was the hostage effect.

What changed? Well, first of all, the Solzhenitsyn and Sakharov cases. Now recall that Yakobson had been one of the hostages. Belogorodskaya was a hostage. Against this background and Case 24, there were two events.

First, there was a serious attempt to repress Sakharov.

Second, the first volume of *Gulag* came out in the West, and Solzhenitsyn was kicked out of the Soviet Union.

That is, right after the Yakir-Krasin trial, a new crackdown began. Everyone began to understand that there was no value in stopping the *Chronicle*. The *Chronicle* was stopped for moral reasons. It was begun again for moral reasons. If it had not been for the Solzhenitsyn and Sakharov cases, the *Chronicle* would not have been resumed.[5]

There were the now familiar dual tendencies in Soviet policy as dissidents resumed the *Chronicle*. KGB chairman Yury Andropov unmistakably carried out a Politburo-dictated policy of repression and political orthodoxy at home, while General Secretary Leonid Brezhnev pursued détente with the West. After Soviet authorities called Andrei Sakharov into the Moscow office of the deputy public prosecutor on August 16, 1973, to warn him against his "anti-Soviet" statements and activities, the official campaign to intimidate Sakharov was stepped up. In November 1973, for example, Sakharov's wife, Yelena Bonner, was called to KGB headquarters six times for questioning.

Meanwhile, the first volume of Solzhenitsyn's *The Gulag Archipelago* appeared in the West in December 1973. Foreign shortwave radio stations broadcast whole excerpts, recalling anew the mass Stalin purges. The damning Solzhenitsyn historical novel, amplified by shortwave broadcasts to millions of Soviet men and women who had never known the Stalinist years or had allowed the horrors to fade from memory, surely enraged KGB chief Andropov. Solzhenitsyn was forcibly exiled seven weeks after *Gulag* was published, making headlines throughout the world.

To add perspective, recall that the Soviet-American détente under Brezhnev's and Nixon's tutelage also dominated international news of the day. A Soviet-American strategic arms limitation agreement—SALT I—had been signed in 1972, along with the antiballistic missile (ABM) treaty. The third Brezhnev-Nixon summit was being prepared for the summer of 1974, this one in the Soviet Union.

Soviet and American negotiators, meanwhile, were among the East and West diplomats locked in ideological battles at the 35-nation talks on the Helsinki agreement. The sharp confrontations in Geneva, where the document was being completed, reflected the Soviet internal struggles. By the time the *Chronicle* reappeared in the spring of 1974, there seemed to be an almost direct correlation between the advance of Soviet-American détente and the intensity of KGB repression inside the Soviet Union. The Nixon administration pressed the Brezhnev leadership to increase the number of emigrating Jews, a political act to gain American domestic support for the White House détente policy. The Nixon administration showed less public concern about the plight of Soviet dissidents in general. In any case, the Soviet leadership by now was extraordinarily defensive on the question of Soviet human rights. Typically, the Kremlin saw in the Helsinki agreement negotiations a Western maneuver to subvert the Communist government. Soviet dissidents, their friends among the Western press corps in Moscow, the *Chronicle*, the Russian-language shortwave broadcasts—these were all regarded by the Soviet leadership as parts of the whole. The KGB persecution of dissidents therefore continued unabated, the KGB marking the cessation of the *Chronicle* simply as an important milestone of an ongoing enterprise.

The new *Chronicle* faced still other changes of circumstance. The news flow to the *Chronicle* had swelled. This was partly the result of the authorities' efforts to contain the human rights movement and partly because of the *Chronicle*'s notoriety as publicist for the aggrieved and persecuted. Yet, even as the news flow enlarged, the risks of producing the *Chronicle* became graver. The KGB quite obviously had both voluminous dossiers on the *Chronicle* group and teams of trained and experienced investigators. If, as before, the KGB did not know who precisely was turning out the Chronicle, it was far better informed of general *Chronicle* operations as a result of the extensive Case 24 investigation.

In these circumstances, the *Chronicle* staff decided to change the frequency of publication. Issues 28, 29, and 30 were made available simultaneously on May 7 in Moscow, although they were dated as far back as 1972. Issue no. 31 was dated May 17 and made available in Moscow a few days later. That issue was unique. Devoted entirely to the tragedy of the hundreds of thousands of Crimean Tatars who continued to fight for their home country all the years after Stalin had them forcibly exiled to Central Asia during World War II, no. 31 was the first time that the *Chronicle* devoted its pages entirely to a single topic.

Thereafter the *Chronicle* began to appear at approximately three-month intervals, and through the year 1980 there were four issues annually. Each issue was far larger than the first numbers of the *Chronicle*. Some were book length, totaling nearly 300 single-spaced typewritten pages.

The very size of the *Chronicle* after it reappeared complicated production. Editors, writers, and typists struggled against exhausting obstacles to produce a single issue by the clandestine procedures that they were compelled to adopt. Compared to the 30- to 50-page issues during the Gorbanevskaya years, the preparation of a single issue of the *Chronicle* in the 1970s was a logistical and organizational triumph. Moreover, the *Chronicle* staff was well aware that the KGB's interest in its activities was intense. They could expect no leniency if they were arrested and brought to trial. Ever numerous, factual accounts of the Siberian camps reminded the *Chronicle* group that harsh, tortuous years of forced labor were potential and real consequences of their news operation. The alternative—exile from the Soviet Union—promised a more comfortable physical life, but wrenching emotional experiences as close families and friends were separated and a homeland left behind for an uncertain future in a foreign country.

Looking broadly at the years from 1974 until the Kovalev-Velikanova-Khodorovich era of the *Chronicle* ended in 1979, the Soviet human rights movement underwent successive assaults by the KGB. The Soviet democratic movement became all the more visible and assertive. And by the end of the decade, Soviet-American relations had decidedly cooled. One new element was the Carter administration's sincere, but sometimes inept and ineffective human rights policy that, when focused on Soviet dissidents, alarmed the Soviet leadership.

To summarize the editorial content of *Chronicle* issues in these years fails to convey the changing character of the publication. To begin with, as a thick quarterly, the *Chronicle* was less an immediate source of news for its Soviet reading audience and foreign correspondents and other foreigners than a reference for or elaboration of events commonly known weeks or months earlier. Even when the *Chronicle* reappeared with issues 28, 29, and 30, foreign press accounts remarked that there was little in their pages that had not already been reported. True, there was far more information in the *Chronicle* about individual trials, other *samizdat* publications, conditions and events in the labor camp system, emigration of Soviet ethnic or nationality groups or gross violations of human rights like the revelation of torture in Georgian prisons. However, even though the *Chronicle*'s reporting network continued to enlarge and improve, foreign correspondents more often than not looked on two- or three-month-old events as history rather than news, even if the *Chronicle* carried new details.

Moreover, other sources of information about Soviet internal events were developing. The *Chronicle*, in 1968, broke ground in publicizing heretofore censored and politically sensitive events in the Soviet Union. Its performance helped nurture other means of bringing pressure to bear on the Soviet government through the tested network of Soviet human rights activists and the foreign press. Thus, besides the earlier Initiative Group and the Human Rights Committee, the 1970s saw the establishment of an equally unofficial Amnesty International chapter in Moscow in 1973. Three years later, following the spectacular signing ceremony of the Helsinki agreement in 1975 by 35 national leaders, including Leonid Brezhnev, Moscow dissidents set up an unofficial Helsinki-monitoring group. Four more unofficial Helsinki groups later were created in other regions of the Soviet Union—in the Ukraine, Lithuania, Georgia, and Armenia. The Moscow group became one important source of immediate information about civil rights in the country. Before its remaining three members suspended the group's work in 1982 under extreme Soviet government pressure, it had issued 195 information documents citing hundreds of specific human rights issues. Many dissidents connected with these organizations had been involved with the *Chronicle* and with foreign correspondents. So the information that once was the special preserve of the *Chronicle* was now more openly available in Moscow and more readily available than ever before. In some ways, the unofficial Soviet human rights activist groups through their own publicist efforts supplanted the *Chronicle*.

Another important extension of the *Chronicle*'s cause developed in these years. With the exile of certain dissidents to Western Europe and the United States, a *Chronicle* network formed to link *Chronicle* supporters in Moscow, London, Munich, and New York. What finally emerged was a redundant system to reproduce facsimiles or approximations of the *Chronicle*. In both forms, the *Chronicle*'s offshoots enlarged the publication's reading audience, particularly among persons with some influence on Western public opinion toward the Soviet Union.

The London involvement began with a translation by Max Hayward of no. 5 of the *Chronicle*, dated December 1968.[6] It appeared in subsequent issue of *Survey*, the British journal dealing with Soviet and East European affairs. Its editor, Leo Labedz, was perhaps the first foreign expert in Soviet affairs to recognize the significance of the *Chronicle*, sufficient in any case to translate into English and reproduce an entire number outside of the Soviet Union. At this point, Peter Reddaway, a Soviet specialist and lecturer at the London School of Economics, became interested in the *Chronicle* and took on the task of translating subsequent issues into English, beginning with no. 7. These he had mimeographed and sent privately to other Sovietologists. At the optimum, about 100 English-language copies of the early *Chronicle* were produced. Asked to do a book, Reddaway collected the first 11 issues of the *Chronicle*—those of the Gorbanevskaya era—to produce an annotated and analytical account of the fledgling Soviet democratic movement that appeared in 1972 as the volume *Uncensored Russia*.

As Reddaway worked on his book, the head of research for the London-based Amnesty International also took an interest in the *Chronicle*. Dr. Zbynek Zeman, a scholar of Czech extraction, recognized that the *Chronicle* published precisely the type of well-documented information about human rights violations with which Amnesty International dealt. Starting in February 1971, then, with issue no. 16, Amnesty International translated each *Chronicle* issue into English. Distribution eventually reached a maximum of 3,000 copies.

As all this was going on in London, other versions of the *Chronicle* were born in New York. Valery Chalidze, the physicist who with fellow scientists Andrei Sakharov and Andrei Tverdokhlebov had formed the Human Rights Committee, had been allowed to travel to the United States for a lecture tour in December 1972. Once Chalidze was there, Soviet authorities promptly deprived him of his Soviet citizenship, thus banishing him from his native country. Within a few months after this, it was clear that the *Chronicle* under KGB pressure had ceased to publish. Chalidze was not directly involved in the *Chronicle*'s production, but he was nonetheless intimately associated with Moscow's dissident community. Once in the United States, and with the *Chronicle* apparently suppressed, Chalidze was urged to fill the void. The stimulus came from Edward Kline, a wealthy New York businessman with a special dedication to Soviet human rights. With Kline's financial backing, Chalidze set up Khronika Press in New York and in mid-1973, as part of Khronika Press, began publishing a facsimile of the Soviet *Chronicle*. The New York version was called *A Chronicle of Human Rights in the USSR*. Printed in both English and Russian, six times a year, its content, style, and format (save for being printed rather than typewritten) mimicked the Soviet *Chronicle*. Originally, the editors were Peter Reddaway and Edward Kline. Subsequently, Pavel Litvinov replaced Reddaway, who became the London correspondent, and Valery Chalidze became editor in chief.

The Kline-Chalidze *Chronicle* drew on a variety of sources in and outside the Soviet Union and ably continued the work of the Soviet *Chronicle* during the latter's 18-month hiatus. Russian-language copies were smuggled into the Soviet Union, and the English-language versions were distributed among Western journalists, government specialists, and scholars specializing in Soviet affairs.

When the original *Chronicle* reappeared in Moscow in May 1974, the question in New York obviously was, What now? The decision was to continue the *Chronicle of Human Rights*, as a backstop to the Soviet *Chronicle* and because it could get information in English about Soviet human rights events to influential readers far more rapidly than the Moscow *Chronicle*. At the same time, it was decided to reproduce the Moscow *Chronicle* itself in Russian as copies arrived in the United States. This amounted to a *Chronicle* printing press in exile. Ultimately as many as 1,200 copies per issue of the Russian-language *Chronicle* were produced in New York, most of them destined for the Soviet Union.

One last facsimile of the Moscow *Chronicle* was conceived in Munich in the late 1970s. Kronid Lyubarsky, the Soviet astronomer who was among the first with *Chronicle* associations to be tried and imprisoned, was allowed to immigrate in October 1977, ultimately to West Germany. Almost immediately, Lyubarsky began canvasing European sources concerning a proposed publication that would rapidly move news of Soviet civil rights issues to the public domain.[7] By the late 1970s, Soviet dissidents were convinced that publicity was a forceful weapon against Soviet authorities. More than one Soviet political prisoner is believed to have received a short sentence or gained early freedom because foreign government and/or public opinion focused on his or her plight. By mid-1978, Lyubarsky had garnered enough support from other Soviet exiles and from West European sources to begin *USSR News Brief: Human Rights*. Its Russian edition was titled *Vesti iz SSSR: Prava Cheloveka*.

Lyubarsky's publication differed from the Moscow *Chronicle* and the Kline-Chalidze periodicals in several respects, the most important being frequency of issue. The *USSR News Brief* appeared routinely every two weeks. Compiled by Lyubarsky from information fed to him directly and indirectly from his sources in the Soviet Union, the small (6 × 8 inches), typewritten newsletter carried the latest reports on KGB investigations, searches, and trials—the very material that made the original *Chronicle* absorbing reading for Soviets and foreigners alike. Lyubarsky benefited from speed of production. An issue dated the first of a month would contain news of Soviet internal political and legal affairs scarcely a week old. Like the New York *Chronicle*'s Russian edition, Lyubarsky's *Vesti iz SSSR* was smuggled into the Soviet Union by various travelers to add to the now varied library of *Chronicle*-type periodicals.

To summarize, the Moscow *Chronicle* after 1974 had to adapt to new circumstances. Other Soviet human rights activists or groups were emerging to take over some of the work of publicizing real or alleged illegal Soviet actions. Other publications had sprung up outside the Soviet Union to duplicate or complement the *Chronicle*. The *Chronicle* staff in Moscow, meanwhile, reached out for more information from more places, while publishing less often. Issue no. 28 drew reports from 28 locales in the Soviet Union. By December 1974, the date on issue no. 34, one could count 71 locales. And issue no. 46, of August 1977, carried news reports from 96 Soviet cities or regions, among them labor camps.[8]

The *Chronicle*'s news reports had already moved beyond the immediate Moscow scene before the 18-month break in publication. There had been items about the Crimean Tatars and about Lithuanian events, some of the latter drawn from the *Chronicle of the Lithuanian Catholic Church*, an underground publication modeled on the Moscow *Chronicle*. These first attempts at broader reporting of Soviet civil rights and related issues led to news about other national and religious groups. An information channel was set up with the Georgian republic in southern Soviet Union, and beginning with issue no. 32, in July 1974, there were more or less regular *Chronicle* reports from the Georgian scene. Issue no. 36 carried a particularly sensational report of alleged use of torture on Georgian political prisoners.[9] *Chronicle* contributors had information earlier about KGB investigators in Georgia beating prisoners, in some cases torturing one man with lighted cigarettes. The *Chronicle* withheld a news report, however, until the information could be verified. The capacity to confirm information and the hesitation in publishing rumors or speculation reflected an unprecedented maturity among *Chronicle* editorial staff. The *Chronicle* group was also acutely aware by this time that the KGB was looking for factual mistakes to document that the *Chronicle* published "fabrications" harmful to the Soviet Union. Prove that, the KGB reasoned, and those associated with the *Chronicle* violated article 70 of the Russian republic's criminal code. That would be all the KGB needed.

Over the months, the *Chronicle* also set up information channels with Soviet Baptists, Pentecostalists, and Adventists. All minority religious groups in the Soviet Union, they suffered official persecution. Men and women who had refused to accept required state registration of their religious denominations especially had been targets for harassment and sometimes severe suppression. The Russian Orthodox church, the major religious concentration in the Soviet Union, has been a persistent object of government opposition. By December 1974, the new *Chronicle* was drawing enough information that editors could establish a "Persecution of Believers" section. It carried news about trials of church members, closing of churches, banning or confiscation of Bibles and other religious literature, appeals by believers to Soviet or foreign authorities, and persecutions of parents who attempted to give their children religious instruction.

The *Chronicle* started to include news about Soviet Jews at the end of 1969. As more and more Jews sought to leave the Soviet Union in the 1970s, the *Chronicle* reportage of the Jewish emigration issue, closely connected to Soviet-American trade and political relations, became a regular section.

Along with its standard information on interrogations and trials of those involved with *samizdat*, the *Chronicle* of the 1970s expanded to deal with civil rights in broader terms. The *Chronicle* carried a report of an unofficial open-air art exhibit in Moscow in 1974 that was broken up by Soviet police using water trucks.[10] The *Chronicle* took up the political case of an Austrian teacher prevented from marrying a Soviet writer, a 1975 case involving the practice and interpretation of Soviet laws concerning marriages to foreigners.[11] The *Chronicle* began to report routinely on all emigration controversies, placing these in the context of Soviet civil rights guarantees. It gave its own account of a mysterious explosion in January 1977 in a Moscow subway that killed a number of people and led to suspicions of a KGB provocation.[12] The *Chronicle* delved further into allegations and eyewitness reports of political prisoners being abused in psychiatric clinics. It reported on attempts by dissatisfied workers to establish a free trade union, independent of state control.[13]

Equally conspicuous as the *Chronicle*'s news reports encompassed other areas of civil rights was the sheer volume of facts pouring out of this crude underground press. Long accustomed to Soviet mass media, which avoid concrete facts often enough when dealing with sensitive issues, Soviet readers of the new and larger *Chronicle* were deluged with names, addresses, titles, dates, places, times, and numbers. The *Chronicle* prided itself on piling fact on top of fact, in place of generalizations and cliches found in the official Soviet press about the taboo subjects. Although the *Chronicle*'s editors' and contributors' choices of information reflected a certain point of view, news items and reports themselves were written in a studiously detached style. One seldom found editorial judgments creeping into the *Chronicle*'s pages.

The *Chronicle* under Kovalev reestablished itself in 1974 as an important symbol of the Soviet human rights movement, even though groups like the unofficial Helsinki-monitoring group in Moscow quickly had become a main source of dissident news in Moscow. Tatyana Khodorovich, who worked in the Institute of Russian Language of the prestigious Soviet Academy of Sciences, remembers vividly a well-known professor and doctor of philosophy approaching her quietly one day along an institute corridor to ask if a new *Chronicle* issue was available. He confided in Khodorovich:

> The important thing is that the *Chronicle* continues to come out. If it exists, free thought exists. And thus people exist, too, who consider it their duty and obligation to stand against lies and violence. But not by violence. That is extremely important. Our single salvation for our closed, right wing society is publicity. That is why I always wait with trepidation to see if the *Chronicle of Current Events* appears. If we'd had no tragic events in our country, the *Chronicle* would not exist. But there have been these events. And so there will be a *Chronicle*.[14]

It was not surprising, of course, that the KGB's Yury Andropov viewed the reappearance of the *Chronicle* precisely as an important symbol and, from the KGB's perspective, intolerable. Before 1974 was out, just eight months after the *Chronicle* was resumed, Sergei Kovalev had been arrested and charged with editing the *Chronicle*. In November 1977, Tatyana Khodorovich was pressured to emigrate. In December 1979, Tatanya Velikanova was arrested and later tried.

The trials of Kovalev and Velikanova served to contest the Soviet government's stamp of illegality on the *Chronicle*. Their proceedings challenged in an ostensibly public forum the nature of Soviet freedom of press and speech—both guaranteed by the Soviet constitution.

Before dealing with the trials, note should be made of concurrent KGB investigations into other underground news publications that had sprung up after the *Chronicle*. For as the *Chronicle* established itself and as it gained notoriety in Moscow and other Soviet cities or regions, it nurtured similar typewritten periodicals. The KGB regarded them as offensive as the *Chronicle*, even if they did not share the same stature.

The best known of the other newsletters was the *Chronicle of the Lithuanian Catholic Church*. It figured into the Kovalev trial, for the Moscow *Chronicle* had close contacts through Kovalev with the Lithuanian offshoot. Much that the Lithuanian *Chronicle* gathered about violations of religious and political rights in the Lithuanian republic was summarized in the Moscow *Chronicle*. News from the small Baltic republic thus went to a far larger audience than might be expected.

The first Lithuanian *Chronicle* was dated March 19, 1972. Typewritten and then retyped countless times, the underground publication appeared about five times a year after that. Each issue carried the words: "When You Have Read It, Pass It On."[15] The Lithuanian *Chronicle* focused especially on official persecution of the Catholic church, but it was also notable for raising issues of Lithuanian national rights. Like the Moscow *Chronicle*, the Lithuanian publication adopted a dispassionate tone, factually recording persistent arrests, trials, and related human rights violations arising from Soviet government actions to control the Lithuanian population and the Catholic church.

Like the Moscow *Chronicle*, the Lithuanian *Chronicle* also drew KGB attention almost immediately. Lithuanian editors themselves believed the KGB investigation began early in June 1972, less than three months after the first issue.[16] The KGB probe became known as Case 345. The first major trial, of five persons connected with the Lithuanian *Chronicle*, was staged December 2-24, 1974, before the

Lithuanian republic supreme court. They were charged with disseminating the *Chronicle* and reproducing it on a homemade duplicating machine. All five were found guilty and, despite recanting, were sentenced variously to prison or labor camps for anywhere from a year to five years.[17]

This was only the first of successive trials involving the Lithuanian *Chronicle* throughout the 1970s. Ordinarily, the defendants were accused of circulating or reproducing the *Chronicle* along with other *samizdat*. Despite extensive investigations, including searches and interrogations in Moscow, the KGB was unable to silence the Lithuanian *Chronicle*.

Another notable unofficial *samizdat* periodical of the times was *Veche*. It first appeared in January 1971, and became Case 38 of the KGB in Vladimir, a city near Moscow. *Veche*–an ancient word referring to town meetings in old Russia–was a journal that promoted a distinctly Russian nationalist cause. *Veche* lasted until July 1974, when its editorial board publicly announced that the journal was closed down. The statement followed a series of KGB apartment searches and interrogations and disputes within the *Veche* editorial group itself.[18] Its first editor, Vladimir Osipov, publicly requested permission in 1972 to publish *Veche,* and he made no effort to conceal his identity as editor or the publication. Osipov was arrested in November 1974 and tried. In September 1975, he was convicted of engaging in antistate propaganda, under article 70.[19]

The underground bulletin *Jews in the USSR* first appeared in 1972. By this time, the Soviet government under American pressure had begun to take a more lenient view toward Jewish emigration. But with more Jews leaving the Soviet Union, greater numbers also applied for permission to emigrate, and bitter disputes broke out over so-called "refusniks"–Jews denied exit papers for one reason or another. *Jews in the USSR* dealt with these matters and with Jewish culture in general. The KGB began probing *Jews in the USSR* in May 1975, with coordinated apartment searches and questioning in Moscow, Leningrad, Odessa, Kharkov, and Vladimir. KGB investigators persisted through the 1970s in what appeared to be a campaign of harassment, for the KGB failed to bring anyone to trial despite interrogation of hundreds of people.[20]

The *Ukrainian Herald* was begun in 1970 and, along with the Moscow *Chronicle* and the Lithuanian *Chronicle*, ranked high on the KGB's list of typewritten underground publications to be suppressed. The *Ukrainian Herald* was all the more suspect because it reflected what the central Soviet leadership regarded as Ukrainian nationalism. The *Herald* was caught up in a general police crackdown in the Ukraine. In 1973, three men were tried in Kiev for a number of political acts, among them taking part in two issues of the *Herald*. They were given variously from four- to seven-year sentences in labor camps.[21] In December 1980, three more were sentenced in a Lvov court to equally severe labor camp terms for editing the *Herald*.[22]

These descriptions of *samizdat* periodicals are by no means a complete account, nor do they pretend to suggest the full array of Soviet underground publishing. *Samizdat* periodicals in the Soviet Union have included everything from the *Chronicle* category to literary journals to political essays. They all shared the tendency, necessary in Soviet circumstances, toward clandestine operation. They were all produced by some inefficient, time-consuming means—the typewriter, home photography, homemade hectographs or mimeographs. Because of the foregoing, they all had small audiences. And they all drew special attention of the KGB because they functioned outside of the Soviet state machinery.

That was why, of course, Sergei Kovalev was arrested in December 1974. The KGB had needed but a few months after the *Chronicle* reappeared to assemble enough information on Kovalev to bring him to trial. It was the beginning of a new KGB campaign against the *Chronicle*.

NOTES

1. *A Chronicle of Current Events,* no. 28, p. 8, [*Chronicle/Amnesty*].
2. See the *Washington Post,* May 13, 1974.
3. Khodorovich interview.
4. *Washington Post,* May 13, 1974. See also Christopher Wren's report in the *New York Times,* May 13, 1974.
5. Gastev interview.
6. Much of this section draws from Reddaway interview and from Chalidze interview.
7. Lyubarsky interview.
8. *A Chronicle of Human Rights in the USSR,* no. 29, p. 60, [*Chronicle/Rights*]. These statistics and others in this section were compiled by Ludmilla Alexeyeva.
9. *Chronicle/Amnesty,* no. 36, pp. 183–85.
10. *Chronicle/Amnesty,* no. 34, pp. 64–65.
11. *Chronicle/Amnesty,* no. 37, pp. 44–46.
12. *Chronicle/Amnesty,* no. 44, pp. 127–31.
13. *Chronicle/Amnesty,* no. 48, pp. 83–91, 164–66.

14. Khodorovich interview.

15. For a brief history of the Lithuanian *Chronicle* until 1978, see *Chronicle/Rights*, no. 30, pp. 36-40. The article "The Chronicle of the Lithuanian Catholic Church" is by Tomas Venclova, a Lithuanian who emigrated in 1977.

16. *Chronicle/Amnesty*, no. 36, p. 188.

17. *Chronicle/Amnesty*, no. 34, pp. 19-22.

18. See *Chronicle/Amnesty*, no. 32, pp. 68-69, for some of the details.

19. See *Chronicle/Amnesty*, no. 34, pp. 28-30; no. 37, pp. 5-8; and no. 38, pp. 97-98, for accounts of Osipov's arrest, trial, and appeal of his sentence.

20. See, for example, *Chronicle/Amnesty*, no. 37, pp. 20-21; no. 56, pp. 135-37; and *Chronicle/Rights*, no. 16, p. 50.

21. *Chronicle/Amnesty*, no. 30, pp. 90-91.

22. *Chronicle/Rights*, no. 40, p. 9.

6
TRIALS

Sergei Kovalev, an eminent Soviet biologist by profession and editor of the *Chronicle* on principle, was brought to trial in December 1975, found guilty of libeling the Soviet state, and sentenced to seven years in a labor camp and three years in internal exile. Five years later, in August 1980, Tatyana Velikanova, a mathematician and a *Chronicle* editor, was tried for precisely the same political crime, also judged guilty, and confined to a strict regime labor camp for four years and exile for five more years.

These were deliberately harsh sentences, intended to show the *Chronicle* group that KGB chief Yury Andropov would deal severely with them and other dissidents, regardless of East-West détente. Kovalev was 45 years old at the time of his trial. Velikanova was 48. Life in a Siberian strict regime labor camp was hard enough for younger, stronger people, let alone those who were not conditioned to manual labor, plus the cold and hunger of camp existence.

Operating according to political guidelines, Soviet courts went through elaborate procedures, as did the KGB in pretrial investigations, to "prove" in the Kovalev and Velikanova trials that the *Chronicle* had libeled the Soviet Union under article 70 of the Russian republic. The specific accusation in this regard centered on the *Chronicle*'s publication of alleged deliberate fabrications that damaged the Soviet state.

The legal controversy over the *Chronicle* dominated one facet of the Kovalev and Velikanova trials. The other reflected Soviet political times one way or another. There is still serious question as to how cycles of favorable and unfavorable East-West relations bear on Soviet domestic events. But it can be documented that a general line of orthodox domestic policy accompanied Soviet efforts at détente with the West in the 1970s. Indeed, whether relations warmed or cooled, depending on particular foreign policy disputes, the Kremlin's approach to dissidents remained consistently repressive.

Thus, it was not surprising that during the Kovalev and Velikanova arrests and investigations, when there were numerous foreign appeals for leniency, Soviet authorities ignored the entreaties. They did so, one concludes, because domestic politics demanded that Kovalev, Velikanova, and others who basically were challenging the Soviet government system should be strictly called to account. To sample the Kremlin mood, note September 9, 1977, when Andropov spoke at a Moscow Bolshoi Theater celebration of the one-hundredth anniversary of the birth of Felix Dzerzhinsky, founder of the *Cheka,* the original Soviet secret police. A segment of Andropov's speech dealt directly with dissidents:

> We try to help those who have erred, to change their minds, to dispel their misconceptions. But we must proceed otherwise in those cases when certain so-called dissidents begin to violate Soviet laws. We still have a very small number of such people, just as unfortunately we still have thieves, grafters, speculators and other common criminals. Both categories of people do damage to our society and hence must be punished in full conformity with the requirements of Soviet laws. [1]

Andropov's grouping of dissidents with "common criminals" conveyed both the Kremlin's view of people like Kovalev and Velikanova and the likely treatment such would receive at the hands of the KGB and Soviet courts. It was entirely expected that once arrested, Kovalev and Velikanova would be judged guilty and sentenced, as were so many other dissidents before them. The basic facts of the proceedings are these:

Arrested in December 1974, Kovalev was brought to trial December 9-12, 1975, in Vilnius, the Lithuanian capital. [2] There were two reasons for the choice of venue. One, as Sakharov and other dissidents contended, Soviet authorities, sought to screen the Kovalev trial from unwanted observers, Soviet or foreign. That was easier to accomplish in Vilnius, distant from Moscow. Two, the KGB meant to link Kovalev with the *Chronicle of the Lithuanian Catholic Church* from whose pages the Moscow *Chronicle* freely took information for reprint. Under the rubric of Case 345, the KGB was pursuing the Lithuanian *Chronicle* as it simultaneously attempted to break up the Moscow *Chronicle*. In the Kovalev trial, the KGB struck at both.

Kovalev was charged under the Russian republic, not the Lithuanian, criminal code. A long list of accusations was brought, including "restarting the publication of the *Chronicle of Current Events,* collecting material for it, and assembling, editing and transmitting abroad issues 28-34."[3] Moreover, Kovalev was accused of possessing three issues of the Lithuanian *Chronicle* and using its material in the Moscow *Chronicle,* of signing statements backing the Initiative Group for the Defense of Human Rights, and of signing a number of statements in support of other dissidents. To prove in open court that Kovalev edited the *Chronicle,* the KGB and state prosecutors submitted documents, some with Kovalev's handwritten notes in the margins, that appeared in similar form in the *Chronicle.* Also, the KGB took Kovalev's announced intention to disseminate the *Chronicle,* put that together with the fact that the Kline-Chalidze Khronika Press in New York had reproduced issues 28-34, and argued that Kovalev was demonstrably guilty of disseminating anti-Soviet materials abroad.

The Velikanova trial, although occurring five years later, was remarkably similar to Kovalev's. Arrested November 1, 1979, she was tried August 27-29, 1980, in a Moscow district court where several other dissidents previously had been sentenced and which was physically easy for police to block off. Velikanova fell under Case 26012, a new file on the *Chronicle.*[4] The KGB assembled 12 volumes of material, some of it confiscated from Velikanova herself in KGB house searches. Investigators had prepared about 40 witnesses. They had drawn testimony from previous *Chronicle*-related trials and had assembled transcripts of foreign shortwave radiobroadcasts dealing with the *Chronicle.*

Like Kovalev, Velikanova was charged with resuming the publication and circulation of a "libelous, anti-Soviet illegal journal, the *Chronicle of Current Events*"—a crime under article 70. Reference was made to the May 1974, press conference, when she, Kovalev, and Khodorovich publicly had taken up the *Chronicle* cause. Velikanova specifically was accused of preparing and distributing 25 issues of the *Chronicle* in all, nos. 28 through 52, and with collecting and possessing materials for issue no. 53. She was said to have maintained "criminal links" with the Khronika Press, providing it with anti-Soviet materials. In addition, state prosecutors charged Velikanova with signing Initiative Group statements and with composing or signing Group documents said to be anti-Soviet. Her activities going back as early as 1969 were alleged to have "facilitated acts of ideological diversion" against the Soviet Union.

One after another witness was brought into the courtroom to support the state case against Velikanova. Some did; others, at the crucial moment, refused to testify against Velikanova. She herself, considering the whole procedure a sham, would not take part in the trial. She did attempt to read a statement explaining her position, but the judge would not permit her to do so. Velikanova's only words during the three-day trial were uttered after the labor camp sentence was read. "The farce is ended," she said.

The Kovalev and Velikanova cases rested largely on the Soviet authorities' contention that the *Chronicle* itself was libelous under article 70 and thus illegal. Therefore, anyone connected with the *Chronicle* was automatically guilty of a crime under Soviet law. Although the outcome of both trials was predictable, Soviet authorities committed substantial untold funds to contrive a legal-sounding case against Kovalev and Velikanova—hence, the months devoted by KGB agents to apartment searches, interrogations, analyzing documents and handwriting, and assembling witnesses. Clearly, it was important to Soviet authorities to produce evidence for libel accusations.

The editors of the *Chronicle* had become aware as early as the Yakir-Krasin investigation in 1973 that the KGB was pursuing the matter of libel. It should be said at the outset that neither article 70 nor other Russian republic laws concerned with libel have ever been tested to elicit legal definitions. The same holds true for concepts like "anti-Soviet," "subversion," or "discrediting" the Soviet system. There is no precise understanding or elaboration of these terms. In practice, in the Soviet Union, an act of libel is defined merely by the case materials the KGB and prosecutors submit to individual courts. If a given writing is said to be anti-Soviet and thus libelous, that is what it is.

In 1973, KGB interrogations led dissidents to suspect that the KGB was trying to prove that published *Chronicle* information was deliberately inaccurate and consequently illegal. Thus it was that one day in the spring of 1973 in New York a statement abruptly arrived at the office of newly established Khronika Press. A barely legible Russian text recalled that a factual error had been made in *Chronicle* issue no. 14, dated June 30, 1970. The statement, smuggled out of Moscow, said that while it had been reported that a certain prisoner Baranov had been killed as he tried to flee a penal psychiatric, the truth was he had only been wounded. The statement went on:

> The *Chronicle* sincerely apologizes to its readers for this unintentional error which resulted from the extraordinarily complicated conditions of receiving information from penal camps. The *Chronicle* requests that this belated correction be published on the pages of those independent organs of the press which earlier published the erroneous statement. [5]

Thus did the outside world learn in 1973 that while the *Chronicle* had ceased publication, its editors were still active. And thus began the legal shadow boxing between the *Chronicle* and the Soviet authorities. The clandestinely written *Chronicle* statement carried an attached note warning that the item on prisoner Baranov was being used by the KGB to buttress an accusation that the *Chronicle* published "deliberately false and slanderous" information. Although foreign media reporting the item from the *Chronicle* probably could not have understood the situation, the editors were asking them to join in a legal defense against the Soviet KGB.

In September 1973, just a few months after the *Chronicle*'s editors had issued their correction, Krasin and Yakir were sentenced. The Moscow court verdict finding them guilty also declared the *Chronicle of Current Events* per se to be illegal. This ruling later was used as an established precedent in the indictment of Sergei Pirogov, who was convicted in 1974 in the northern city of Arkhangelsk for distributing the *Chronicle*. That indictment, referring to the Moscow court ruling, said the *Chronicle* contained "deliberately false fabrications which defame the Soviet political and social system."[6] It is true that the indictment was drawn up in one remote region of the Soviet Union by authorities quoting from a Moscow court verdict whose legality is open to question. The point, however, is that the authorities, with noticeable frequency, were pressing the libel charge against the *Chronicle*. In his own defense against this charge, Pirogov maintained that any factual errors in the *Chronicle* were unintentional. These errors, he argued, could not be considered libelous under Soviet law, since article 190-1 refers to "deliberately" false information, and article 70 refers to "slanderous fabrications." "Deliberately" became an important word.[7] Gabriel Superfin, whose trial on *Chronicle*-related charges had been held a few months before, in May in Orel, had also used that defense. He contended that the *Chronicle* contained truthful, authentic information.[8]

By the spring of 1974, as the *Chronicle* was resumed after its 18-month break, the "libel" stamp was causing serious concern. Andrei Sakharov, Andrei Tverdokhlebov, and Vladimir Albrekht issued a statement that denounced recent harsh prison sentences for dissidents and raised the libel matter. The statement was sent to several international organizations, including Amnesty International. In defense of the *Chronicle* the signers said in part:

> Both abroad and in our country, the *Chronicle of Current Events* is well known as the anonymous information bulletin which publishes news about the persecution of individuals for their beliefs or for the dissemination of information. In numerous judgments of Soviet courts and in statements by representatives of the official point of view, the *Chronicle* has been declared libelous. We believe that the information in the *Chronicle* is factually correct with the possible exception of a few accidental inaccuracies. . . . We consider that labeling the *Chronicle* as libelous is based on the mistaken identification of any negative information about Soviet life with libel.[9]

By the time Sergei Kovalev was brought to trial in December 1975, the authorities were prepared to once and for all establish the libel charge against the *Chronicle*. Twenty-two witnesses were called, some to testify to the inaccuracy of *Chronicle* information. A doctor at the Dnepropetrovsk special psychiatric hospital maintained that the medical staff properly administered drugs and rules, in contradiction to *Chronicle* reports of mistreatment of imprisoned mathematician Leonid Plyushch. Another doctor testified that details about a Kirov region psychiatric prison and treatment of a political prisoner were factually incorrect. There were other instances cited by Soviet prosecutors to argue that the *Chronicle* issues edited by Kovalev contained "deliberately false" information.

The argument came down to a battle of statistics, as Andrei Sakharov later recounted. By then a Nobel Peace Price laureate, Sakharov had gone to Vilnius in support of his friend Kovalev. He was barred from the courtroom by police. At a "press conference" after the trial, Sakharov noted that Kovalev, too, had prepared for the trial,

knowing full well from the investigation that authorities
intended to document the libel charge. Sakharov summarized:

> In the seven issues of the *Chronicle* which figured in
> the charges, there are 694 separate items. The
> investigators investigated 172 of these. In 11 cases
> Kovalev does not exclude the possibility of a mistake.
> He was preparing to prove that none of these mis-
> takes was premeditated or libelous. 89 items were
> acknowledged to be accurate even by the investi-
> gators, and in 72 cases Kovalev intended to prove the
> absence of error in the reports of the *Chronicle*.
> However, he was not given the opportunity to even
> begin on this task. . . . In court, only seven items
> were examined, through which the prosecution wanted
> to prove the libelous nature of the *Chronicle*. Today
> we are in a position to assert that only in one or two
> cases of little significance did the prosecution manage
> to cast doubt on the accuracy of the reports in the
> *Chronicle*. [10]

The libel argument in the Kovalev case came down, then,
to the accuracy of seven news items or references, and
even those, Kovalev claimed, were open to dispute. The
Chronicle group regarded this statistical battle with authorities as a victory. Given hundreds of pages of typewritten news reports, drawing on information often passed
by word of mouth, most of it beyond the reach of accuracy
checks, the KGB, it turned out, really could not document
its accusation that the *Chronicle* was "deliberately" inaccurate or carried "fabrications." Indeed, the *Chronicle* was
not shown to be regularly inaccurate, let alone deliberately
so.

If a victory in some terms, the *Chronicle*'s passing of an
accuracy test did nothing to spare Kovalev a labor camp
sentence. The court, blithely ignoring evidence or at least
arguments to the contrary, followed political dictate and
convicted Kovalev of dealing in libelous information harmful
to Soviet state interests. He was ordered to the labor
camps for seven years, plus three years of exile.

The KGB persisted. When Velikanova was indicted, in
August 1980, authorities once more raised the accusation of
libel. Velikanova, in her written statement rejected by the
court, admitted that "any objective and impartial analysis . . . would reveal no small number of mistakes [in the
Chronicle]. But such an analysis would also reveal other
facts: that the journal the *Chronicle of Current Events* is

in no way libelous and has as its aim the most objective and conscientious disclosure possible of material concerning the violation of laws by official bodies and their individual representatives, and of material on opposition to these violations."[11]

Velikanova argued that the KGB had meticulously avoided assessing the accuracy of *Chronicle* news. Certainly, state prosecutors failed to show a consistent pattern of willfully mistaken and damaging reports in the *Chronicle*—ostensibly the legal test of articles 70 and 190-1. Witnesses were called up, as they had been in the Kovalev trial, to testify that whatever the *Chronicle* had reported, it was not true. But there was no convincing evidence. In his summary, the state prosecutor mainly argued that Velikanova's activities linked her to anti-Soviet emigres and foreign "reactionary groups."[12]

There is a fantasy-like air about the repeated confrontations between Soviet dissidents and authorities over the libelous nature of the *Chronicle*. Even when the KGB assiduously matched *Chronicle* information to witnesses, sometimes flying prisoners to Moscow from remote labor camps to testify at trials, the state prosecutors failed to press successfully their libel case. And it is apparent from the history of the *Chronicle*, that whether or not the publication was legal or illegal under any interpretation of articles 70 and 190-1, those associated with it were destined to be persecuted. Yet the KGB and the state prosecutors and courts went through painstaking legal-appearing procedures, as if authentically weighing the guilt or innocence of the accused.

One can easily conclude that this was done for public consumption, particularly abroad, to demonstrate the Soviet Union's just legal system. That conclusion does not really hold up, for with one or two exceptions, the trials of dissidents associated with the *Chronicle* were effectively closed. Courtrooms were packed with KGB agents or their families, a standard KGB technique for filling a courtroom with the "public" and denying entrance to others. Even had the trials been open to Western diplomats and journalists, the legal sham involved would have been transparent. Defense attorneys, named by the state, some engaged by dissidents, never were allowed to develop their own cases fully, to challenge the interpretation of libel, to summon legal experts, or to question the legality of pretrial investigations.

This is to suggest that the *Chronicle* proceedings were not really show trials, not in the unambiguous way that Krasin and Yakir were put on display. They seemed more like experiments, to determine how far authorities might move toward a "legal" solution to political dissent. After all, at one extreme, the KGB could simply seize dissidents and put them in labor camps. For reasons that delve into the Stalin legacy, that solution to political problems is little tolerated in the Soviet Union, first and foremost by the political leadership. The tendency has been to at least go through the motions of legal proceedings, and, as we have seen, some very elaborate ones.

From the perspective of the *Chronicle* and its editors and staff, the ultimate result has been about the same. Exile, labor camps, psychiatric clinics, isolation cells, and interrogations awaited the dissidents as surely as during Stalin's time. Yet their conflict with the state was moved gradually from secret rooms of Lubyanka prison to a court-room where at least there was a pretense of rule of law. That gave the *Chronicle* supporters a first, tenuous opportunity to defend the *Chronicle* under provisions of the Soviet criminal code. Dissidents at least put the questions: Is publication of facts reflecting unfavorably on the Soviet Union a libelous act? What constitutes "deliberately false fabrications"? Are unintentional inaccuracies appearing in Soviet publications proof of guilt under articles 70 and 190-1 of the Russian republic criminal code? Is it a crime for Soviet citizens to reproduce information from Soviet official records of legal proceedings?

These questions and scores of others were explicit in KGB prosecutions of the *Chronicle*. They concerned basic issues of free speech and press in the Soviet Union. They had not been aired to this degree in the Soviet Union since the late 1950s, during the years immediately after Khrushchev's de-Stalinization speech, or perhaps more accurately since the 1920s, before Stalin consolidated power. It was of little immediate comfort to the *Chronicle* staff that the issues were raised, for they proved to be immaterial to final court verdicts. Yet the very fact that Soviet authorities explored the technicalities of libel in *Chronicle* cases opened a door to continuing discussion of provisions of articles 70 and 190-1 and other laws limiting civil rights, chief among them freedom of the press.

With Velikanova's arrest and subsequent trial, others had taken up the *Chronicle* editorship in what was by then an informally established succession. There were always new *Chronicle* editors, writers, and typists ready to replace those arrested or intimidated by the KGB. Three men took over from Velikanova. One was Leonid Vul, who in 1980 was 31 years old. Another was Yury Shikhanovich, then 47.[13] The third was Alexander Daniel, 30.

A graduate of Moscow University's philological faculty, Vul could trace his family history to Stalin's terror. His grandfather, Yefim Vul, was a labor camp commandant for the NKVD. Arrested in 1942, the grandfather served eight years in a labor camp. Released in 1950, he was arrested the next year, and exiled to Soviet central Asia where within months he died. The grandfather's older brother, also named Leonid Vul, worked for the *Cheka* and in the 1930s was chief of police in Moscow. In 1939, as Stalin's purges claimed thousands of victims, he was arrested and shot.

The young Leonid Vul, trained in Russian language and literature, was unable to find a position after leaving Moscow University and turned to odd jobs. From 1977 to 1981, he sharpened knives in a Moscow cafeteria to support his wife and daughter. He was later to edit the *Chronicle* with Yury Shikhanovich and Alexander Daniel, a fact that KGB soon learned.

Shikhanovich was already publicly identified with the Moscow dissident community by the late 1960s. A mathematician by training and doctor of education, he taught at Moscow University until 1968. In that year he signed a letter protesting the confinement of Alexander Yesenin-Volpin in a psychiatric hospital, and for that he was fired from his teaching post. In 1972, Shikhanovich was arrested and charged under article 70, in part for his connections with the *Chronicle*. Sent to a psychiatric clinic, he was released two years later and got a job on the editorial board of a popular science journal in Moscow called *Quantum*.

One trail followed by the KGB to Vul, Shikhanovich, and Daniel led through Alexander Lavut. A mathematician, Lavut was a member of the Initiative Group for the Defense of Human Rights, and, like many of his friends—Kovalev, Khodorovich, Velikanova, to name three—contributed information to the *Chronicle*. He attracted KGB attention in 1975, when he took a parcel from Moscow to Vilnius to Kovalev, then under arrest and awaiting trial. Questioned in Vilnius by the KGB, Lavut was asked purposely if no. 34 had been issued, that Kovalev himself was interesting in knowing this. Lavut refused to answer, but clearly by then the KGB placed Lavut in the *Chronicle* group.[14]

The KGB moved against Lavut again shortly after they arrested Velikanova in November 1979. Lavut was put under continuous KGB surveillance several weeks later, his telephone was cut off in January 1980, the KGB pressured his wife the next month to persuade Lavut to halt his "antisocial activity," and in mid-February, KGB agents searched Lavut's Moscow apartment.[15] Lavut, like many of his friends, handled considerable *samizdat* material, including, of course, the *Chronicle*. Among the collection, agents found *Chronicle* issue no. 55 with "editorial notes and insertions" in the handwriting of Shikhanovich.[16]

Lavut subsequently was arrested, on April 29, 1980, after a second search of his home. Held for nine months, he was tried December 24-26, 1980, in a Moscow court under article 190-1 of the Russian republic criminal code. Similar to article 70 outlawing anti-Soviet agitation and propaganda, 190-1 provided a maximum sentence of three years' imprisonment. The indictment against Lavut contained the familiar charges—possessing, writing, and circulating various *samizdat*, the *Chronicle* included, that damaged the Soviet state. Lavut's case, No. 46616, stretched back to 1968. He refused to plead guilty, choosing to admit that he had been involved with *samizdat* and arguing that there was nothing illegal in doing so. He was sentenced to three years in prison, and then at the end of that term, three years more.[17]

By the time of Lavut's trial, the KGB had begun closing in on Vul, Shikhanovich, and Daniel, as KGB agents worked again to shut down the *Chronicle*. In June 1980, Shikhanovich was called in for a "talk" with the Moscow KGB. Reproached for failing to keep promises made in 1973 in Lefortovo prison when previously arrested, a KGB investigator asked Shikhanovich directly: "Yury Aleksandrovich, when are you finally going to stop working on the *Chronicle*?"[18] A *Chronicle* news item parenthetically remarked that the question apparently arose from the discovery in Lavut's apartment of a *Chronicle* issue containing editorial notes in Shikhanovich's handwriting.

Shikhanovich admitted nothing. Nonetheless, there was no mistaking that the KGB was increasingly informed about production of the *Chronicle* under its present editors. The proof came early in 1981, when KGB agents in a swift and unprecedented action seized an issue of the *Chronicle* in final manuscript form in Vul's apartment. Never in the years of contest between the KGB and the *Chronicle* staff had authorities managed to disrupt production of an issue.

News of the KGB's confiscation of issue no. 59 spread quickly in Moscow among dissidents. It was instantly clear to them that the KGB had gotten more than a final draft of a *Chronicle* issue. Incriminating papers in various handwritings were seized to lead the KGB to the wider network that produced the *Chronicle*. New editors took over the

Chronicle, and in issue no. 60, dated December 31, 1980, and circulated in Moscow in August 1981, there was this blunt four-paragraph editorial note:

ISSUE 59 CONFISCATED

On 20 February 1981 officers of the State Committee for Security [KGB] for Moscow and the Moscow region confiscated the manuscript of the *Chronicle of Current Events* No. 59 and all the materials for its preparation during a search of Leonid Vul's apartment.

Most of the texts were written by L. Vul and Yu. Shikhanovich. The KGB will apparently have no trouble identifying other handwritings as well.

Since future involvement in the *Chronicle* of persons now known to the State Committee for Security would threaten its publication, they consider it necessary to cease their work on the *Chronicle.*

The resignation of those who were preparing issue No. 59 and the absence of material for it have made its publication impossible. For the same reason, the period of August to November 1980 is not fully covered in this issue [No. 60].[19]

The search of Vul's apartment also yielded some printed issues of the *Chronicle* produced in New York by the Kline-Chalidze Khronika Press. Vul was fired from his menial cafeteria job in early April 1981. A few days later his wife was called to KGB offices. There she was pressed to "influence her husband's attitude." Vul himself was called in separately by the KGB on April 10 for questioning about his connection with the *Chronicle.* KGB investigators by their remarks indicated they had already established the connection to their satisfaction, and that Vul was a suspect in what was revealed as Case No. 538.[20] As of this writing, neither Vul, Shikhanovich, nor Daniel had been charged.

The KGB discovery and confiscation of issue no. 59, along with an undisclosed number of handwriting samples, broke up the entire Vul-Shikhanovich-Daniel editorial network. New editors, their identities secret, continued the *Chronicle* but with noticeable disruptions. Issue no. 60 was dated December 31, 1980, fully a year following issue no. 58. Moreover, no. 60 did not actually begin appearing in Moscow until several months later, the result of increasing lag time between the closing date of a *Chronicle* issue and completion of final typewritten copies. The thickness of the *Chronicle*—issue no. 60 ran more than 100 pages—had tended to delay production once information was collected. But so too had KGB harassment. Issue no. 61 was dated March 16, 1981, and issue no. 62 carried the date July 14, 1981. Totaling more than 160 typewritten pages, issue no. 62 did not appear in Moscow until the spring of 1982, some nine months after the editorial closing of the issue. Following still another interval, issue no. 63, dated December 31, 1981, appeared in Moscow in March 1983, a thick volume of 230 typewritten pages. Thus there had been a 15-month break in publication, clear evidence that the most recent KGB investigation into the *Chronicle*, dramatized by the confiscation of issue no. 59, had caused serious problems in producing the *Chronicle*. At the very least, quarterly publication had twice been prevented since 1979, and at the worst for the dissidents, the KGB was forcing longer silences.

To review the 1970s, giving the *Chronicle* a context, the Soviet KGB under Andropov's direction was unrelenting in its campaign to control what was frequently called the "democratic movement" and to silence all unofficial publications in the Soviet Union. There was little doubt that the Carter administration's human rights policy in the United States added to what Soviet authorities already saw as a threatening internal problem. Hardly had Jimmy Carter taken office in 1977 in Washington than he replied to a letter from Andrei Sakharov. A photograph taken of Sakharov at this time in his Moscow apartment shows him displaying a piece of stationery with the words "The White House" clearly visible.

The 35-nation Helsinki agreement, rather than merely codifying post-World War II European frontiers as the Soviets had wanted, was turning into a Western ideological triumph. Not only were international organizations and governments calling the Soviet Union to account for failing to observe human rights provisions of the Helsinki accord, but Soviet dissidents themselves were using the document to their ends. Reflecting the Kremlin concern, General Secretary Leonid Brezhnev warned in a speech on March 21, 1977, that Moscow would tolerate no American interference in Soviet internal affairs.

In the years following, dozens of publicized Soviet dissidents were either imprisoned or pressured to leave the country. By the end of 1981, virtually all members of the unofficial Moscow Helsinki-monitoring group and the four other Helsinki-monitoring organizations had been sentenced to labor camps. Their numbers included Anatoly Shcharansky, Yury Orlov, as well as Ivan Kovalev, son of

Chronicle editor Sergei, plus Tatyana Osipova, his wife, and Anatoly Marchenko and Victor Nekipelov.[21] Further, Soviet authorities decimated the ranks of the Initiative Group and the Moscow chapter of Amnesty International. The chairman of the latter, Valentin Turchin, emigrated. The secretary, Andrei Tverdokhlebov, was tried and imprisoned at about the same time as Sergei Kovalev. Not least in the KGB's campaign to crush dissent, Andrei Sakharov was banished from Moscow, where he was the most visible symbol of the "democratic movement" and served as a conduit for information to the outside world. He was exiled in January 1980 to the eastern Soviet city of Gorky and virtually cut off from all human contact.

The *Chronicle* nonetheless survived, although the price in human terms was increasingly high. Dozens of men and women—no precise count is possible—went to Soviet labor camps because they worked for the *Chronicle*. Yet, by the end of the Brezhnev era, in November 1982, the *Chronicle* had survived successive KGB campaigns. One can document at least five major KGB investigations into the *Chronicle* since 1968 involving hundreds of agents. Those investigations *did* have an effect, in addition to closing down the *Chronicle* for 18 months. Fewer issues were produced in successive years as apprehension and fear spread among those willing to risk their careers and futures by associating with the *Chronicle*. Yet each issue of the *Chronicle* also represented another small victory for Soviet dissidents in their resistance to authoritarian practices, even as the victories were less frequent.

The *Chronicle*'s content and style remained impressively constant, given the numbers of hands material passed through and given the frequent changes of editors and writers. The *Chronicle* regularly carried partial transcripts of trials, some compiled from clandestinely made tape recordings. There were news notes from labor camps, gained from established and tested underground channels of information with the help of relatives, camp guards, or freed political prisoners. News routinely came from several Soviet republics, notably Lithuania, the Ukraine, Latvia, Estonia, Georgia, and Armenia. Statements of dissident groups, foreign documents bearing on Soviet civil rights, and official Soviet documents not generally known to the Soviet public continued to appear in the *Chronicle*.

All of this was gotten together in ways that over the years had become a *Chronicle* reporting system. It was a system that the KGB continued to find frustratingly immune to detection and destruction.

NOTES

1. *Izvestia,* September 10, 1977, carried the text of Andropov's speech.
2. For the *Chronicle* reports of the Kovalev case, see *A Chronicle of Current Events,* no. 34, pp. 2-4; no. 35, pp. 117-18; no. 37, pp. 18-19; no. 38, pp. 78-91, [*Chronicle/Amnesty*].
3. *Chronicle/Amnesty,* no. 38, p. 81.
4. For the main account of the case, see *Chronicle/Amnesty,* no. 58, pp. 2-11.
5. *A Chronicle of Human Rights in the USSR,* no. 2, p. 5, [*Chronicle/Rights*].
6. *Chronicle/Amnesty,* no. 32, p. 23.
7. Ibid., p. 24.
8. Ibid., p. 15.
9. *Chronicle/Rights,* no. 9, pp. 13-14. The statement is dated May 28, 1974.
10. *Chronicle/Amnesty,* no. 38, p. 90.
11. *Chronicle/Amnesty,* no. 58, p. 4.
12. Ibid., pp. 6-10.
13. Information on Leonid Vul and Yury Shikhanovich comes from *USSR News Brief,* no. 11, 1981, p. 3, on Daniel, Alexeyeva interview.
14. *Chronicle/Amnesty,* no. 35, p. 119.
15. *Chronicle/Amnesty,* no. 56, pp. 112-14, contains details on Lavut and his arrest.
16. *Chronicle/Amnesty,* no. 57, p. 37.
17. For materials on the Lavut trial, see *Khronika Tekushchikh Sobytii,* no. 60, pp. 7-20; and *USSR News Brief,* no. 16/17, 1980, p. 1.
18. *Chronicle/Amnesty,* no. 57, p. 37.
19. *Khronika Tekushchikh Sobytii,* no. 60, cover page; and *USSR News Brief,* no. 16, 1981, p. 3.
20. *USSR News Brief,* no. 11, 1981, p. 3.
21. The U.S. government's commission on the Helsinki accord, known officially as the Final Act on Security and Cooperation in Europe, maintains careful records on the fates of Soviet Helsinki group members. See, for example, the commission's report dated January 15, 1982.

7
THE NETWORK

A huge shadow staff has sustained the *Chronicle of Current Events*, funneling information from the most secretive of Soviet institutions, filtering and refining masses of facts, and providing contact with the foreign press corps and foreign shortwave radiobroadcasters. Over the years, the *Chronicle*'s editors have known scarcely a fraction of the hundreds of men and women who, quietly and sometimes at the risk of their own and their families' futures, have formed a *Chronicle* network that now covers most of the Soviet Union. Yet, by all accounts of those who have worked within the *Chronicle* group, it is this undefined but nonetheless real network that explains the editorial success and stubborn persistence of the *Chronicle*, despite extraordinary attempts of the Soviet secret police to root it out.

To use the term "editors" is a necessary but imprecise shorthand for discussing those who produce the underground publication. Persons once involved in final stages of *Chronicle* issues repeatedly have said in interviews that there really have been no *Chronicle* "editors" in the larger sense of persons who plan and direct *Chronicle* coverage. "Compiler" seems the more accurate description of *Chronicle* editors' actual functions, for they usually have had little say about what information reached them and most frequently have been responsible only for assembling what information they did receive into readable, coherent form.

Outside of the small group in Moscow that has provided continuity for overall production responsibility, there has been a larger corps of correspondents, informants, messengers, writers, typists, couriers, and distributors without which the *Chronicle* would have remained the narrowly focused, brief bulletin it was in 1968. Now a periodical of 100 pages and more per issue, the *Chronicle* probably ranks in numbers of people producing it with a large newspaper. That the *Chronicle* staff cannot be reduced to an organizational chart or to a list of names reflects its essential voluntary nature, as well as the clandestine cast that years of resisting the KGB have given it.

Recall that Yakir and Krasin between them were able to give the KGB names of more than 200 people whom they believed were connected with the *Chronicle*. And that was only five years after the *Chronicle* had begun. Persons then working with the *Chronicle* estimate that the real figure would be some 400.[1] By the late 1970s and early 1980s, the nationwide network of *Chronicle* correspondents and informants was believed to be greater still. All but a handful of those associated with the *Chronicle* have been so in an informal way, offering information, for example, or arranging to reproduce the *Chronicle* as they became acquainted with it through friends or foreign radiobroadcasts.

What would be called the "news flow" in an American periodical has developed in the *Chronicle* case with remarkable efficiency. It has improved over the years as the network spread, connecting not only the sources of news but readers and users of *Chronicle* information both inside the Soviet Union and abroad. The KGB seems to have been unable to halt the *Chronicle* news flow, and indeed may have decided that the most difficult task in attempts to silence the publication. For *Chronicle* information moves through successive hands to typed pages in a private world of special and close peripheral relationships. It may be remembered that in the first months of the infant *Chronicle*, Natalia Gorbanevskaya advised in an unsigned editorial note that anyone could pass information to the *Chronicle*: "Simply tell it to the person from whom you received the *Chronicle*, and he will tell the person from whom *he* received the *Chronicle*, and so on. But do not try to trace back the whole chain of communication yourself, or else you will be taken for a police informer."[2] This system has functioned for years with impressive reliability and accuracy, while also protecting the *Chronicle*. Even persons who lived in Moscow and knew active dissidents and who themselves were involved in the democratic movement usually did not know who compiled the *Chronicle*. As importantly, neither did they seek to know, according to the principle that the less one knew about the *Chronicle*'s operations the better. The reason was obvious, given frequent KGB interrogations about the *Chronicle*. Especially after the Krasin-Yakir trial in 1973, information about the internal *Chronicle* was little discussed for fear that someone would be broken by the KGB and reveal names once more.

To discuss the organization of the *Chronicle* is virtually a contradiction in terms. Those who have worked on the *Chronicle* describe an amorphous, undisciplined process in which participants pass slips of paper with handwritten notes brought from Siberia or carry a few sheets of type-written paper across Moscow to another apartment.[3] Trust in one another and deep commitment to promoting the practice of civil rights nurtured voluntary and self-disciplined work on the *Chronicle*. It has been a system devoid of directives and commands, as well editorial assignments.

Given the genesis of *Chronicle* reportage, starting with Litvinov's careful notes of the Galanskov-Ginzburg trial in 1968, it was natural that successive contributors to the *Chronicle* would report especially about trials or KGB investigations. News from labor camps also flowed naturally to the *Chronicle*, as wives and friends of dissidents returned from remote Siberian prisons to pass information. The Soviet labor camps eventually became something of a sieve for information. Alexander Ginzburg, who managed a "Solzhenitsyn fund" to supply money to help political prisoners' families, spent years in labor camps. He was exiled in 1979, and now lives with his wife, Arina, in Paris. Interviewed there, the kinetic, articulate Ginzburg recalled how information got from labor camps to the *Chronicle*.

The basic thing is that there are lots of political prisoners. Each one is sentenced to a certain period of time, so no month passes when someone is not released. Naturally, he can carry a good deal of information from the camps. When you leave the camp you feel like a "stuffed duck," we'd say. For three months before you are scheduled for release, people are giving you information to pass on. After I got out, I'd remember things in my sleep and I'd wake up and write them down.

Then you would write down things in the camps and smuggle those out. It's hard, but not impossible. I managed to get a copy of the labor camp rules smuggled out. In 1969, we made a tape recording inside a camp and smuggled that out and Voice of

America broadcast it. We thought about smuggling for 24 hours a day.[4]

Soviet authorities soon realized, of course, that damaging information was coming from the camps—they had only to read the *Chronicle*—and they tried to stem the information flow. Vladimir Bukovsky also spent years in the labor camps for protesting Soviet violations of civil liberties. He, too, was exiled, and joined other Russians in the Paris community of exiles. One spring day, sitting in a Paris café, an incredulous setting compared to a Soviet labor camp, the perceptive, witty Bukovsky also recounted in accomplished English how information got from the camps:

The information comes by devious routes. Some is carried when a fellow is released from the camps. There would be a contact somewhere along the line after he left. Or you could bribe prison guards so that when you met with relatives, you could pass written information or verbal information. Then the relatives might stop in Moscow and pass on what you said.

You could bribe guards, for example in Mordovia [labor camp network]. These were all new camps, organized in 1972, and there were all new guards. They would pass notes sometimes when they became sympathetic to our situation. There was a mass hunger strike in the camps in 1974, and when they saw that, the guards were sympathetic.

You can also corrupt the guards. They don't earn much. They don't have much. They come from provincial areas. You might, for example, get something from Moscow—a cigarette lighter—and bribe a guard. Or he would give you an address. The bribe—the goods or the money—would be sent there in exchange for passing information.[5]

Arina Ginzburg, one of the many wives and mothers of Soviet political prisoners who sustained their husbands and sons during years of imprisonment, made the arduous trips to the labor camps, knowing the humiliations the women were subjected to. Body searches, she remembers, were especially severe. Moreover, prison authorities would threaten relatives. If they passed on information to the *Chronicle*, the relatives were warned, life would be made harder for the husbands or the sons in the camps. Sometimes authorities bluffed, sometimes not, and there would be retaliations. Not only were there strip searches of the women. Packages were ripped apart and closely examined. Guards sat within sight and earshot of visitors at the camps. But there were always secret ways to get information out. Sometimes, as Bukovsky recalls, guards or civilians working in the Soviet camp system would carry information, adding to that brought by prisoners themselves. Through these channels, then, came news of hunger strikes, of mistreatment of prisoners, of inadequate medical care, of transfers of prisoners from one camp to another, and of the organization and staffing of the labor camp network itself. The *Chronicle* thus became a rare reference for previously unobtainable information about the entire Soviet penal system.

Trials of dissidents are an obvious source of news for the *Chronicle*. Although ostensibly public, the trials usually have been held in courtrooms packed with KGB-arranged crowds. But when friends of dissidents could argue their way into the courts, they would make careful notes of procedures. It was risky business, for the notetaker was automatically identified to the KGB and he or she invited arrest or questioning. In later years, friends of dissidents smuggled small tape recorders into courtrooms. From these recordings have come the unusual transcripts of trials published by the *Chronicle*. The Sony recorders, provided by foreign friends, were small enough to be concealed under a coat. A small microphone with an on/off switch was grasped in the hand, the wire to the recorder running up the wearer's inside sleeve. Because it was impossible to change batteries inside the courtroom without attracting attention, the *Chronicle* reporter recording a dissident trial was per force selective about what went onto tape. Soviet-manufactured batteries powered a recorder for only about two hours, enough for one 120-minute cassette. Thus, closing arguments or particularly significant testimony might be recorded, but never a whole trial.

As one reads through the *Chronicle* chronologically, one increasingly comes upon long sections of trial transcripts. By the mid-1970s it was commonplace for the *Chronicle* to publish verbatim question-and-answer segments from restricted Soviet court proceedings.[6] As unvarnished reporting, there was little in the official, government-censored press to match these revelations of the Soviet legal system in action. Time and again, as Soviet authorities attempted to stage political trials in the form of authentic proceedings, the *Chronicle* published embarrassing verbatim texts showing judges refusing to hear dissidents' evidence, or prosecutors and investigators distorting facts and of judges handing down sentences against all rational consideration of original charges. The *Chronicle*'s trial accounts revealed the persistence and skills of any good investigative reporting.

The *Chronicle* tended to include longer and longer reports as the frequency of publication declined and the size of *Chronicle* issues increased. And information more frequently came from within closed Soviet institutions, like the KGB and Glavlit, the Soviet censorship organization.[6] The *Chronicle* attracted sources of information not just among publicly known Soviet dissidents, but from scores of men and women working within the Soviet Communist party, government, police, and military agencies. Thus the *Chronicle* has revealed internal Glavlit documents banning certain books, ordering libraries to withdraw specific volumes, and instructing state bookstores to halt sales of some titles or even recall them. A transcript of segments of a secretly tape-recorded conversation between Soviet Jewish *refusniks*–applicants refused emigration visas–and an official of the party central committee apparatus is an absorbing account of the views of both sides in what had become an international controversy over Soviet Jewish emigration. A *Chronicle* source has been able to obtain and report regulations of the Soviet interior police, the MVD, which is responsible for operations of the Soviet prison system.[7]

The *Chronicle*, in another instance, was able to report details of a private briefing containing state statistics on religious belief and places of worship in the Soviet Union, a sensitive issue with a history of violent official actions. The briefing, given to staff members working on the *Large Soviet Encyclopedia*, got to the *Chronicle* in a way that is revealing of how confidential information reaches the *Chronicle*. The now exiled Ludmilla Alexeyeva by chance was the conduit for the report supplied by another informant. In an interview in her Tarrytown, N.Y., home, she recounted how the secret report was "leaked" to the *Chronicle*:

> Vasily Furov was the deputy chairman of the Council for Religious Affairs [under the USSR Council of Ministers]. He prepared this confidential report that was not supposed to be for publication. In this report he was talking about how many churches in the Soviet Union were still functioning and how many were closed. It was statistical information that was secret in the Soviet Union. We could only suspect, we did not know the specific numbers.
>
> I got the report this way. There was a lady in Moscow whom I knew and who like me, though she

had no interest in dissident affairs. A Russian Orthodox believer, she knew that I was a dissident, and she told me that one of her friends wanted to meet a *Chronicle* reporter to tell him about the statistics. I didn't want to tell her that I was working for the *Chronicle*. I was afraid, you know. I thought they [the KGB] might be trying to trap me.

Two weeks passed, and this man came to my place of work. He was afraid to come to my apartment. He was probably afraid it was monitored by the KGB. He didn't tell me his name, but he looked the way very high-level officials looked in the Soviet Union. He wore a good dark gray suit and had a Parker pen, something most Russians don't have. He was scared and he looked at me with fear and repulsion. But he told me everything. He would not write it himself. He would dictate the information and I put it in my handwriting.

He told me that he decided to do this because he was a believer himself. He understood, he said, how important it was that it become known in what a terrible state religion was kept in the Soviet Union. He had thought about this for a long time, and he wanted to pass the information on to the West. The only way he could think of was using the *Chronicle*.[8]

The secret government report on the status of religious practices in the Soviet Union appeared in the *Chronicle*, no. 41, dated August 1976. It subsequently became a reference for Western news accounts because official statistics had simply been unavailable. The confidential Furov briefing noted, for example, that of 77,676 Russian Orthodox churches existing before the 1917 Bolshevik revolution, only 7,500 were functioning by the mid-1970s. There were, by official count, only 200 synagogues out of a prerevolutionary total of 5,000 and 1,000 mosques out of 24,000.

Other *Chronicle* information revealed similar eyewitness reporting. Large-scale disturbances in October 1977, in the Lithuanian capital of Vilnius, involving 10,000 or more persons, were described a few weeks later in no. 47. Members of religious minorities contributed information to the *Chronicle* describing police persecution as they attempted to worship or perform baptismal rituals. Baptists, of whom there are hundreds of thousands in the Soviet Union who refuse official registration, became a plentiful source of *Chronicle* news.[9]

As information for the *Chronicle* made its way to Moscow, and then within Moscow to the final editors, the dangers of carrying news reports increased. Not only were couriers vulnerable to search and possible arrest by the KGB, but because they often possessed handwritten notes they were responsible for the fates of *Chronicle* informants. While the huge network channeling news to the *Chronicle* has remained largely unidentified to the KGB, the persons immediately surrounding the *Chronicle* have, reasonably, feared police action. Imagine, if you will, concentric circles, the ones closer to the center being the relative handful of men and women who have assembled whole sections of the *Chronicle* ready for final editing. These have been the *Chronicle* staff who have lived in daily apprehension of being seized by the KGB literally while walking down a street, or of being arrested after sudden KGB apartment searches. When one was carrying *Chronicle* news or other *samizdat* around Moscow, anxiety always heightened and tension built as one constantly watched the street crowd for signs of KGB surveillance agents.

Yefrem Yankelevich, a mathematician and son-in-law of Andrei Sakharov, compiled summaries of *samizdat* for the *Chronicle*, drawing from various *samizdat* journals, essays, and documents that circulated in Moscow and from persons who came to the Sakharov apartment with information. Now in exile and living with his wife, Tatyana, and two children in Boston, the quiet-spoken Yankelevich has described how information was passed and communications maintained in Moscow among persons connected with the *Chronicle*:

> When we passed information, we tried not to use the telephone, but rather simply go to the house of the person getting the information. We assumed that the telephones were tapped in the apartments. Sometimes we'd use pay telephones along the street.
>
> You would take information to the editors when you knew a deadline was near, when the next issue of the *Chronicle* was about to appear. That was once every two months at first, then four times a year.
>
> Was it dangerous? Yes, for the people you were contacting. When I saw I was being followed by the KGB, for instance, I would turn around and go back home. Of course, I might have been followed more often than I knew. They could have followed me to my contacts without my knowing it.
>
> Here's how I would do it. I would travel by trolley, bus, or subway. I might have five or ten pages of material with me in a briefcase. I would try

to be cautious. I would never tell anyone when or where I was going. I would try to leave home inconspicuously, and then I'd try to remember the faces of the people around me on the street or in the subway. When I'd change trolleys or subways, I would check to see if any of the same passengers did the same. My obvious objective was not to escape the KGB surveillance. That was impossible. My objective was just to see if I was being followed.

I believe I was followed many times when I didn't know about it. Sometimes I dound out too late. Once, for example, I met a family friend in the subway and we talked for a bit. It was half a year later that I found out that this same person was stopped by the KGB after we had talked and warned not to see me again.[10]

It was common knowledge in Moscow that the mere possession of *samizdat* was not enough to send a person to the labor camps. Kronid Lyubarsky has commented: "The KGB does not punish the crime. It punishes the person."[11] A number of dissidents actively involved in the *Chronicle* were never arrested. Some were exiled abroad. Others were tried and committed to brutal years in Soviet labor camps or psychiatric clinics. No one has discovered the pattern, but dissidents in Moscow did know that if the KGB did decide to arrest you, they wanted evidence of one's involvement with the *Chronicle* or other political activities in the form of documents—hence the particular apprehension among persons who carried *samizdat*. Lyubarsky, who worked for the *Chronicle* in the late 1070s, has recalled moments in Moscow:

There's always a psychological stress. I remember a case at a subway stop. It was Mayakovsky Square. I had a briefcase full of *samizdat*, and as I started up the escalator, I turned to wave to a person I was leaving. Just at that moment, I felt a hand on my shoulder. Someone said, "You're arrested." In that split second, I began to think what I had with me. Not only the *samizdat*, but also a notebook with names and addresses. It was just a joke. But that impact of hearing "You're arrested." It's so strong. Everything blurred.[12]

Lyubarsky has estimated that between 20 and 40 persons have been involved in the final stages of a *Chronicle* issue to prepare it for typing. In the early years, Gorbanevskaya could alone collect, read and edit, and produce the master manuscript from which typists would work. But as the *Chronicle* grew thicker and its content more varied, another system necessarily developed. Individual persons would put together segments of the *Chronicle*, as Yankelevich has described, and deliver those already prepared sections to *Chronicle* editors. Entire documents or trial proceedings, including verbatim transcripts, would be readied by *Chronicle* contributors. These pages, either typed or written in longhand, would be delivered to *Chronicle* intermediaries, individuals personally known to contributors, or to editors themselves.

In the years following the Yakir-Krasin trial, when the *Chronicle* developed gradually to a thick periodical, the sheer volume of information posed production problems. For in the last weeks before an issue was scheduled for completion, sections needed to be brought together, checked for what errors could be detected, read for simple spelling, grammatical, and punctuation mistakes, and then edited for consistency with the *Chronicle*'s detached style. The whole then was arranged according to the established format and a master manuscript was readied for typing. (The production and distribution of the *Chronicle*, challenging problems in themselves, will be dealt with in the next chapter.) It was a critical moment, just before the master *Chronicle* issue moved along for production. This was the moment, recall, that the KGB seized *Chronicle* issue no. 59, edited by Leonid Vul, Yury Shikhanovich, and Alexander Daniel. All editors feared as much, for despite extraordinary care in concealing their work places and contacts, they could never be certain what the KGB knew. Editors necessarily wondered if the KGB simply was waiting for that moment when the *Chronicle* staff had brought all the material together in one room in one Moscow apartment, before the knock on the door.

That more master manuscripts or segments have not been confiscated can be traced to the way information has been passed in the *Chronicle* network. The KGB, although successful in pinpointing editors after long months of investigation, has not proved very effective in the short term. This may only reflect the obvious point that the KGB Fifth Directorate, responsible for internal political security, has limits to the number of agents and money it can invest to stop the *Chronicle*. In any case, the *Chronicle* reporting system advocated by Gorbanevskaya has passed the test of time with high marks for reliability and security.

The system has its flaws, however. Essentially passive, the *Chronicle*'s news flow works only in one direction—from the bottom up. For the most part, the editors have had to rely on natural instincts of contributors for supplying news. They have generally not been able to direct what events or trends should be reported. The result has been uneven reportage of large areas of *Chronicle* editorial fare. Civil rights issues in the Ukraine have been routinely covered. The Lithuanian republic has received considerable attention, for example, while the other two Baltic states of Estonia and Latvia have received far less space in the *Chronicle*. The same can be said for Byelorussia. The Soviet central Asian republics have received scant coverage, partly because Soviet central Asian minority nationalities have separate prison camps. Russian political prisoners have had little contact with central Asian Muslims, this also being reflected in lack of *Chronicle* coverage.

The geographic imbalance in *Chronicle* reportage is mostly the result of the passive news flow system. Individuals with particular interests or contacts outside Moscow tended to become a channel of information, without a *Chronicle* editor much able to develop new channels or broaden coverage to include all Soviet areas.

One can find similar imbalances in the early years of the *Chronicle* regarding religious affairs, or the vast Soviet rural population, or workers' grievances, or women's rights. The *Chronicle* was the child of Moscow intellectuals concerned with rights of speech and press. Successive issues of the *Chronicle* attracted readers with like attitudes, ready to contribute like information. Grigorenko's special interest in the Crimean Tatars, Alexeyeva's contacts with the Ukrainians, and Kovalev's connections with the Lithuanians likewise accounted for some earlier editorial themes.

Only later were there deliberate attempts to include news that did not per chance flow to the *Chronicle*. A regular section on Soviet Jews was consciously established, as the editors recognized the significance of the Soviet Jewish emigration issue. The same held true for Volga Germans. News of the Jewish community began to appear regularly in the *Chronicle* in 1970, and of the Volga Germans in 1974. The reason lies in a recognized identity of interests that developed between the *Chronicle* group and other Soviet groups concerned with violations of civil rights. That same identity of interests lead to reportage of abuses in Soviet psychiatric clinics, of seedling efforts at a Soviet free trade union, of rights of disabled persons, and of women's rights.

However, even a cursory reading of the *Chronicle* will show it to be consistently and heavily weighted to the original topics of Soviet political trials, conditions in labor camps, and KGB attempts to suppress free speech and press. This may be another way of saying, of course, that the *Chronicle* never pretended to be or to become a mass audience newspaper or periodical, even if conditions had permitted. It is also to say that the *Chronicle*, operating under clandestine circumstances, has generally used what it received from sympathetic contributors, rather than forge an editorial balance.

The surrogate *Chronicles* in London, New York, and Munich have become important in their own right as outlets for Soviet internal news. Their circumstances allowed editors leeway in shaping publications, although the Kline-Chalidze *Chronicle of Human Rights in the USSR* or the Lyubarsky *USSR News Brief* found themselves limited, too, by the available channels of information from the Soviet Union.

The *Chronicle of Current Events* that is translated and printed by Amnesty International has become an unequaled source of photographs of Soviet human rights activists. Smuggled from the Soviet Union and reproduced beginning in the volume containing *Chronicle* nos. 28-31, the rare photographs also show Soviet labor camps and psychiatric clinics, along with graphic pictures of KGB agents harassing Baptist worshipers, for example, or protesting Jewish *refusniks*. The cumulative Amnesty photograph collection is unique for portraying another dimension of *Chronicle* editorial concerns.

News reports that have reached New York and Munich from Moscow have come through many channels. Recall that the Kline-Chalidze *Chronicle* was started in the spring of 1973, after it seemed that the Moscow *Chronicle* had been silenced. With that Moscow outlet closed, information flowed to New York. Peter Reddaway, who worked with the New York *Chronicle* from its inception, recalled in a 1974 radio interview:

> We were amazed at the volume of material forwarded
> to us: it was really enormous, so much so that we
> were never able to fit all the available material in
> one issue. The sources are many: for instance, we
> have received a great deal from the so-called demo-
> cratic circles, the humanists, as it were, of the
> Soviet movement for human rights. We have receiv-
> ed, and still receiving, a lot of material from labor

camps, psychiatric institutions, and from the activists of the Jewish exodus movement. Much material comes from Lithuania—especially that excellent publication, the *Chronicle of the Lithuanian Catholic Church*. . . . Furthermore, we receive much from Baptists and other religious groups as well as from the republics, such as the Ukraine, Armenia and so on.[13]

The *samizdat* coming from the Soviet Union was already considerable even before the Kline-Chalidze *Chronicle* was established. This underground stream of documents from the Soviet Union to Western Europe and the United States began as a trickle in the mid-1960s. The volume had become so great by 1972 that the Munich-based Radio Liberty assembled enough *samizdat* to produce four volumes averaging more than 600 pages each. These formed the basis of a *samizdat* archive, directed initially by Albert Boiter, that grew to tens of thousands of pages of material. In 1973 and 1974, when the New York *Chronicle* was getting underway, the Radio Liberty *Arkhiv Samizdata* averaged more than 3,500 pages of documents from the Soviet Union each year.[14]

This material was being smuggled or simply carried out of the Soviet Union by Western correspondents, by tourists, and by diplomats. Some was being sent in diplomatic pouches. The early issues of the *Chronicle* itself were slipped into the sealed diplomatic mail of the Moscow embassies of Italy, the United States, France, and Canada, although not necessarily with the ambassadors' knowledge.[15] Letters sent to Vienna and Helsinki from Moscow successfully carried *samizdat*. Addressed to these "neutral" capitals, they seemed to pass Soviet surveillance of international mail more readily than letters going elsewhere in Western Europe.

There was very little risk in these enterprises, and so the *samizdat* flow surged by the year. At worst, a foreigner carrying *samizdat* out of the Soviet Union would be searched and the material confiscated. This happened, for example, to a British actor who agreed to carry a copy of the *Chronicle*, no. 19, from Moscow back to London. He apparently aroused KGB suspicions when he had dinner in a Moscow restaurant with a well-known dissident. An unexpected KGB search at Moscow's Sheremetyevo International Airport turned up the *Chronicle*.[16] But for every piece of *samizdat* the KGB found, hundreds of other documents streamed out of the Soviet Union. Thus, the New York *Chronicle* has been richly supplied with information.

The same can be said of Lyubarsky's *USSR News Brief*. Moreover, both this publication and the New York *Chronicle* have made valuable use of the telephone to gather information from the Soviet Union. International telephone communications as a connecting link of Soviet dissidents and their foreign sympathizers have never attracted public notice equal to their importance. Both Valery Chalidze, in New York, and Kronid Lyubarsky, in Munich, have routinely gotten information indirectly by telephone from the Soviet Union. Lyubarsky has recalled in an interview how his information network developed for the *USSR News Brief*:

> The first issue listed political prisoners and that attracted attention. It showed that this was serious work. Still the first issues remained small. But then in a few months channels of information developed. People trusted the *News Brief* and contributed news. As well, the *Chronicle* people in Moscow recognized the importance of the *News Brief* and agreed to give me information. I also get information indirectly from Moscow by telephone. About 70 percent of the information is my own . . . through my own channels.[17]

The *News Brief* also draws reports from the Estonian Relief Center for Political Prisoners in Stockholm; the Free Latvian Union in Muenster, West Germany; the Elta Press in New York, a Lithuanian organization; the Society of Human Rights in Frankfurt; the International Center for Baptists in Gummersbach, West Germany; and from Radio Liberty in Munich.[18] These sources are specifically mentioned to illustrate how diversified channels of *samizdat* information from the Soviet Union have become. Each of these and dozens of other organizations outside the Soviet Union have special contacts inside the country. Combined with foreign journalists, businessmen, and diplomats, their representatives have become valuable reservoirs of immediate *samizdat* news about the Soviet Union.

The *News Brief* and the *Chronicle of Human Rights in the USSR* thus enjoy a certain advantage over the Moscow *Chronicle*. They can tap many sources of information beyond the reach of the Moscow publication and, moreover, do so quite freely and rapidly. At the same time, they enjoy an ease and speed of editorial production that the Moscow *Chronicle* can never hope to experience.

The surrogate *Chronicles* have been directed to two large audiences. One is abroad, largely in the United States and Western Europe, and composed of journalists, government officials, human rights advocates attached to various civic organizations, and scholars. The other audience is the Soviet population itself. Some 2,000 copies of the Russian translation of each issue of the *Chronicle of Human Rights in the Soviet Union* are printed and most of those are intended for the Soviet Union. In addition, Khronika Press has reprinted Russian copies of the Moscow *Chronicle* as issues have been received in New York. The pressrun has gotten up to as many as 1,200 and these, too, are meant to be smuggled into the Soviet Union.[19] As many as 200 of Lyubarsky's Russian version of the *USSR News Brief* are printed for an internal Soviet readership, although only half perhaps slip through Soviet security. At times, the foreign-produced *Chronicles* are believed to have rivaled the Moscow production in circulation. Numbers are necessarily approximate.

Soviet authorities have had little tolerance for the surrogate *Chronicles* produced abroad. In recent years, officials have subjected visiting foreigners to more careful screening, trying to stem the flow of printed matter being smuggled into the country. Scores of copies of the New York *Chronicle* and Munich *News Brief* have been confiscated by KGB agents at Soviet entry ports, Moscow first among them. Lyubarsky has heard indirectly of KGB threats against his life. More concretely, in the summer and fall of 1982, Soviet authorities precipitously restricted international telephone communications between Moscow and the United States. This was done by sharply reducing the number of lines between the Soviet Union and the United States and Western Europe and eliminating direct dial service altogether. Instead, calls had to be made through Moscow operators. As negligible as this seems, the effect was to make it easier for Soviet security agencies to monitor conversations of all sorts between Soviet citizens and foreigners and to prevent those the KGB found objectionable. This would include, of course, discussions involving political, civil rights, and legal matters.[20]

Because of the considerable resources of the surrogate *Chronicles*—especially the *USSR News Brief* and the *Chronicle of Human Rights in the USSR*—the Moscow *Chronicle* can no longer be viewed in isolation. It remains the center for processing and recording information about the democratic movement in the Soviet Union. Yet the others so substantially supplement the Moscow *Chronicle* that something like an unofficial and uncensored information network has evolved. The *USSR News Brief* now functions as the news wire for Soviet *samizdat* civil rights and political information. Its pithy, timely reports usually contain the first available news of trials, KGB activities, underground political movements, strikes, social disturbances, and the like in the Soviet Union. The *Chronicle of Human Rights in the USSR* combines some of this same information with news in the United States. Thus, it provides a larger context for the human rights movement dealing with Soviet civil rights matters.

The Moscow *Chronicle* itself now contains the fuller, detailed, and perhaps more authoritative accounts of events. Because the *Chronicle*'s appearance in Moscow often trails by months the events it reports, the *Chronicle* has become a hybrid periodical—part newsmagazine, part scholarly journal, part archive. It seldom now is an original news source for the international press corps in Moscow, for most of its information has in the main become known by the time it appears. Yet it remains a periodical, attempting to report news under extraordinarily difficult conditions. Some of those involve its production, a feat that few appreciate and that is accomplished with unheralded dedication.

NOTES

1. Alexeyeva interview.
2. Peter Reddaway, ed. and trans., *Uncensored Russia: Protest and Dissent in the Soviet Union* (New York: American Heritage Press, 1972), p. 54.
3. I am indebted to many sources for information in this chapter. While it is difficult to credit each and every detail, the interviews with the following were especially helpful: Alexeyeva, Lyubarsky, Salova, Yankelevich, Alexander Ginzburg, Arina Ginzburg, and Gastev.
4. Ginzburg interview.
5. Bukovsky interview.
6. See, for example, *A Chronicle of Current Events*, no. 40, pp. 4-33, [*Chronicle/Amnesty*], for detailed accounts of the 1976 trials of Andrei Tverdokhlebov in Moscow and Mustafa Dzhemilev in Omsk.
7. See, for example, *Chronicle/Amnesty*, no. 51, p. 187, for a directive of the Lithuanian republic Glavlit. *Chronicle/Amnesty*, no. 40, pp. 86-90, contains the transcript dealing with Soviet Jewish emigration. *Chronicle/Amnesty*, no. 57, pp. 57-59, gives information on MVD directives.
8. Alexeyeva interview.
9. See, for example, *Chronicle/Amnesty*, no. 55, dated December 31, 1979, for representative *Chronicle* news sections on Orthodox Christians, Adventists, Baptists,

Pentacostalists, and Catholics.

10. Yankelevich interview.

11. Lyubarsky interview.

12. Ibid.

13. The interview with Radio Liberty in London is available in transcript as Radio Liberty Special Report, May 22, 1974.

14. For background, see Albert Boiter, "Samizdat: Primary Source Material in the Study of Current Soviet Affairs," *Russian Review*, no. 3 (July 1972); and Radio Liberty Research Report, October 25, 1974.

15. Corti interview and Reddaway interview. Corti personally sent *samizdat* material in the Italian diplomatic pouch, unbeknown to the Italian staff, when he worked in Moscow in the Italian embassy in the 1970s. The Soviet authorities eventually compelled the Italian government to sever the relationship.

16. Reddaway interview.

17. Lyubarsky interview.

18. Ibid.

19. Chalidze interview.

20. For comment and interpretations, see the *Los Angeles Times* and the *Economist*, both for September 11, 1982; *CSCE Digest*, September 24, 1982, published by the U.S. Commission on Security and Cooperation in Europe; and *USSR News Brief*, no. 13, 1982.

8
UNKNOWN, UNSUNG

In his memoirs of years surviving in Soviet labor camps and fighting for Soviet human rights, Vladimir Bukovsky says he would erect monuments to two things: one, the political anecdote, because in Communist countries it reveals authentic public opinion, and the other, the typewriter, because it has been the machine of a free press in the Soviet Union.[1]   While no match for the printing press, the typewriter, it is true, has made Soviet *samizdat* possible, not least the *Chronicle*.

In regard to the *Chronicle*, recognition must go, too, to the scores of men and women who for more than a decade and a half have produced it, and largely with typewriters. They ultimately account for the *Chronicle* becoming more than a private record.   It is a truism, but nonetheless worth keeping in mind, that the original *Chronicle* produced by Gorbanevskaya in a Moscow apartment in April 1968, would have been a different sort of communication if it had been only in handwritten form.   The typewriter, and the dozens of people willing to retype the *Chronicle*, transformed it into an approximation of a printed periodical instead of a private newsletter.   The *Chronicle* owes its fame, one can reasonably argue, to the fact that it functioned as a printed publication, albeit in crude form.

In modern industrial societies like the United States and countries of Western Europe, where free access to printing presses and photocopiers is taken for granted, it is difficult to imagine the exhausting complexity of producing the

Chronicle in the Soviet Union. First, recall that all printing presses, duplicating machines, and photocopiers in the Soviet Union are state-owned and -controlled. That is, the KGB oversees their use. There are known cases of dissident groups establishing illegal underground presses, but these have been rare. Moreover, officially printed material in the Soviet Union is censored by the government agency Glavlit. There is, in short, no conceivable, practical way for a Soviet citizens' group to mass-produce thousands or tens of thousands of copies of a newspaper, periodical, or newsletter without state permission. Indeed, in 1977, the Soviet government tightened up already close surveillance of some 4,000 state-controlled printing presses and other reproduction equipment. While the reason for the new regulations was not explained, the KGB and other security forces were given additional authority to account for use of not only printing presses but for type and matrices as well. [2]

Photocopiers, whose widespread availability in the United States has revolutionized industry, business, education, and the average person's daily life, are both rare and restricted in the Soviet Union. It has been estimated that there are a few more than 20,000 photocopiers in the whole country. Installed in Soviet government offices, they often are available only to senior officials and their staffs. [3]

Thus, only with great difficulty, if at all, can Soviet citizens gain access to the technical equipment of the printed or reproduced mass media. The task of producing the *Chronicle* has from its beginning challenged the imagination, daring, and endurance of the *Chronicle*'s network. Each step of the process—from acquiring paper and typewriters, to arranging persons and places to write, to assembling and distributing the *Chronicle*—invites KGB intervention. The same has held true for other forms of producing the *Chronicle*, homemade photocopying or mimeograph. The persons who have physically reproduced the *Chronicle*, either for pay or as volunteer labor, have routinely subjected themselves and their families and friends to KGB suspicion, if not interrogation or worse.

Those men and women who have produced the *Chronicle* are known, if at all, only to an immediate circle of relatives and friends. Over the years, Soviet civil rights activists learned that anonymity best protected them from the KGB, at least up to the moment of arrest. Thereafter, the more publicity, the better, especially in the foreign media, where specific mention of individuals might spark foreign government or public outcry and bring pressure to bear on Soviet authorities. The *Chronicle*'s typists, however, never graduated to international celebrity rank. There are reliable reports of several women sentenced to labor camps for typing the *Chronicle* and of others interrogated. For the most part, the names of those who did produce the *Chronicle*–and most of them have been women–have disappeared in that anonymous mass that forms the private Soviet world.

Often the first master copies of the *Chronicle* were produced by persons also involved in its editorial process. That was the convenient, fast way. In the early years, one person could turn out a whole issue of 30, 40, or 50 typewritten pages in two or three days of hard work. As the *Chronicle* became thicker, however, the sheer number of pages immensely complicated production. No longer could one person manage alone an entire issue of 100 to 200 closely spaced pages. Alexander Ginzburg, who worked with the *Chronicle* between terms in labor camps, still vividly recalls returning to Moscow in 1974 after one five-year sentence and witnessing in a Moscow apartment a whole team of typists secretly turning out an issue.[4]

The first problem a staffer faced in producing an issue was obtaining a typewriter. In the early 1960s, typewriters for private purchase were scarce in the Soviet Union, as were many consumer goods. Even as production of Soviet models and foreign imports later increased, however, typewriters could leave a trail for the KGB to follow. Sometimes a purchaser of a new or used machine would be required to give a name and address. Moreover, it was believed among Soviet dissidents that the KGB routinely took samples of type imprints from each machine. Typed *samizdat* material would be matched against these samples to incriminate the writer.

Ludmilla Alexeyeva, who typed many *Chronicle* issues, recalls buying her first, used typewriter at a Soviet *kommission* store–the network of state-operated used goods outlets–for 50 rubles in 1963. That was about two-thirds of an average monthly wage. The machine was a Mercedes, old and badly maintained. She next bought an East German Erika typewriter in 1974 for 240 rubles —then about twice an average wage. The machines were scarce, and Alexeyeva acquired the Erika only because a woman sympathetic to the unofficial Moscow Helsinki-monitoring group donated her place on a purchaser's waiting list to Alexeyeva. Foreign-manufactured typewriters were preferred over the lower quality Soviet machines, which frequently broke down. Kronid Lyubarsky, also involved in the *Chronicle* and *samizdat*, bought a Yugoslav typewriter in the late 1970s for 220 rubles. Others found used machines or inherited them from friends. When Pavel Litvinov emigrated, he passed on his typewriter to Tatyana Khodorovich. Still others surreptiously used typewriters at their jobs to produce the *Chronicle* and similar *samizdat*.

There is an unmistakable attachment of *Chronicle* workers to the typewriters. It is borne out by the fact that even with the passing of a decade or more they can still recall in interviews precisely the manufacture of their typewriters, the price, and where the machines were purchased.

Those who worked with the *Chronicle* and also typed individual issues faced the problem of work space. They only aroused suspicion by typing at home. The constant noise of the machine carried through thin walls of Soviet apartments, possibly spurring a hostile or suspicious neighbor to inform the KGB. KGB-implanted listening devices in apartments could pick up continuous typewriter sounds. The prudent choice, then, was to type the *Chronicle* in apartments not readily identified by the KGB as those of dissidents or their friends. Using such apartments meant, however, carrying a 20-pound typewriter hidden in a satchel from one's home to another address, pushing onto crowded buses or the subway, and then trudging blocks with the heavy load to the final destination.

Production of the first master copies of the *Chronicle* usually was entrusted to *Chronicle* workers. They copied from a final manuscript assembled by an editor or editors and secretly brought to what one may imagine as a jerry-built print shop, a "safe" Moscow apartment. The first copies were produced, necessarily, at high speed, for as master copies were being produced, the fear of a KGB search was ever present. Typists thus worked at a feverish pitch. Kronid Lyubarsky's wife, Galina Salova, for years wrote for, reproduced, and distributed the *Chronicle*. "I would look at people after they had put out an issue of the *Chronicle*," she remembers. "Their eyes were red. They obviously had had no sleep. You had to do this fast. And it had to be done in secret, because the KGB could show up anytime."[5]

The initial master *Chronicle* copies were typed single-spaced, to put as much information as possible on one, thin page. Between 6 and 12 or so carbon copies were produced at the same time as the original. It was physically hard work. Typists would pound keys, of old, manual typewriters, trying to give clarity to carbon copies. There was a premium on accuracy, for mistakes usually were not erased, but simply "x-ed" out. So typing for the

Chronicle meant tense, exhausting hours closeted in a safe apartment, feeling anxiety rise as fatigue set in and wondering if the KGB was preparing a search.

The first *Chronicle* issues in the late 1960s were produced on thick, coarse paper. It was so heavy that only six carbon copies were legible. Later, typists used onionskin as it became available. That has always been in short supply, however, in the Soviet Union. Moreover, onionskin is as often used in the Soviet Union to roll cigarettes. Thus, anyone who purchased onionskin in large quantities was automatically suspected by the KGB. Even though professional typists routinely bought that type of paper, KGB investigators well knew that dissidents also produced *samizdat* with onionskin.

The trick was first to find Moscow stores that by chance had received some onionskin paper. There was little available. *Chronicle* typists would go from store to store, buying as much paper as they thought would appear acceptable. They knew, of course, that salesclerks monitored sales for the KGB. Carbon sheets have been equally difficult to obtain, and purchasing quantities of carbon paper also triggers KGB suspicion. Keep in mind that to produce 20 copies of a 100-page issue of the *Chronicle* required 2,000 sheets of onionskin and possibly 100 pieces of carbon paper. In Moscow, then, where onionskin paper is sold a few pieces at a time to make cigarettes, it has been no mean feat to gather the paper for an issue without drawing the KGB.

Once the first master copies of the *Chronicle* were typed, they were distributed to a small group within Moscow. One copy always went to a Western correspondent to share with colleagues in Moscow. Another was smuggled abroad for reproduction and distribution to various sources, among them Amnesty International and Khronika Press in New York. The remaining copies were intended for retyping, for the *Chronicle* achieves what circulation it does by the chain-letter process. The reproduction of the *Chronicle* has always been done voluntarily and with no particular organization. Individuals have on their own arranged for typists, sometimes paying them, sometimes not. Sometimes the condition for obtaining a master issue of the *Chronicle* was to return that copy plus perhaps as many as four other reproductions.

Galina Salova, who took over the task of reproducing *Chronicle* issues from her husband after he was arrested in 1972, was intimately involved in the process. The daughter of a KGB officer, she had acquired other convictions.

Interviewed in Munich, where she worked for Radio Liberty, Salova remembered what it was like to reproduce the *Chronicle*:

> I paid typists 20 kopecks a page. It was difficult to find thin paper and carbons. You had to buy it at special stores. And people who worked there watched who bought the paper. A woman friend of mine found a professional typist to buy the paper, since she had reason to do so because of her work. How did we find the paper? Someone would call and tell me that there is carbon paper at such and such a store. I'd tell friends to go buy what they could. You could only buy a limited amount—say 50 or 100 pieces.
>
> There were other problems. At work, I typed on an electric machine. It was hard to make the switch to a manual typewriter and work with any speed. Besides, I was always nervous when the *Chronicle* was being retyped.
>
> For one thing, there was the problem of getting a *Chronicle* copy for retyping. Here's the scene: I'm sitting at my desk at work. A friend calls. Would I like to drop by for a cup of tea? In dissident circles, you never ask questions. You never say, why? Maybe we meet in a third house. If we meet in an apartment, they would openly give me the *Chronicle* issue. But we would not talk out loud about it—apartments were monitored. We'd write notes to each other if we had to exchange information. Like how many copies of the *Chronicle* I had to give back.
>
> If we arranged to meet, say, in the subway to pass the *Chronicle*, the person might give me a book. Inside would be a copy of the *Chronicle*.
>
> That same night after work, I would try to take the *Chronicle* to the home of an intermediary, so it would not be in my apartment. I normally often would visit friends after work. And either in someone's apartment or along the street, I'd meet the intermediary and pass the *Chronicle* for retyping.[6]

Although many women have retyped the *Chronicle* without charge, professional typists have also been engaged. There have been advantages. They can own and use typewriters in their homes without arousing suspicion. Normally, they produce book manuscripts, student theses, or officially sanctioned materials. Moreover, they are good typists and work fast. They risk the confiscation of their typewriters if caught producing the *Chronicle*, and, probably as important, the KGB opens a file on them. In extreme instances, the professional typists of the *Chronicle* face more severe penalties—loss of their jobs, for instance. A labor camp term awaited some if they were actively involved in *samizdat*. Retyping the *Chronicle* might then be one more item in the list of state accusations.

The professional typists of the *Chronicle* have come from all ranks. They have worked for all reasons. And they have had their own systems. Some have produced the *Chronicle* voluntarily, out of idealism. Some have taken pay, usually less than the normal charge for typing in Moscow. Often professional typists have been married and worked at home in their small apartments. But one woman produced the *Chronicle* in her Moscow office on an imported IBM Selectric, working whenever co-workers were absent. She could type an entire copy of the *Chronicle* with carbons in one day under the best circumstances. Others took longer if they combined work at home with their normal daily jobs. Galina Salova paints the portrait of the typist in Moscow:

First, you should know that typing is generally a low paying job in the Soviet Union. One typical professional typist lives in a communal apartment [sharing kitchens and bathrooms]. We usually tried to avoid these typists for the *Chronicle* except in urgent cases because of the risk of her being found out. She typically would live in an old building in Moscow or in the distant edges of the city. Some of the places they lived in should have been destroyed long ago.

They weren't dissidents, but the typists would cry, I remember, when they would read some of the things in the *Chronicle*. These were women 35 or 40 years old. Some younger. One was 65 years old. They usually were married and had children. Husbands of two of my typists did not know they were working on the *Chronicle*. Other husbands did.

The typists would work after their own jobs were finished. They had families and all, so they could work maybe two hours a night. If we were busy, they could manage four hours. Figure that she finishes her job at 6 P.M. She would have to shop for her family and fix a meal. So maybe she would start typing the *Chronicle* at 9 P.M. and work until 1 A.M. They could have made more money typing for,

> say, a writer. But they worked on the *Chronicle*. These women were very respected by us. They didn't have to risk so much for so little money.
>
> Not all would work for the *Chronicle*. I had contact with three of four typists at a time. I asked many more to do work, but they refused. Some would start working for us, and then stop.
>
> Or we'd see that a typist had, say, three children and no husband. We'd give her a less risky job than typing the *Chronicle*. She could be fired you know, and then be without money. There was always the question of being responsible for others' suffering.[7]

Tension, fear, and uncertainty were companions to the production of the *Chronicle*. Salova vividly remembers one October night in Moscow when she became aware of blatant surveillance. The KGB had assigned marked police cars that night to follow her slowly as she walked along Moscow streets. By then her husband, Kronid Lyubarsky, had been in the labor camps for years. She felt alone and frightened. That cold, fall night, she carried smuggled notes from a political prisoner, intending to go to a friend's house to transfer minute handwriting from cigarette paper to more readable form.

> I went to a bus stop finally. I was terrified. There were two police cars at the bus stop. No one knew where I was. My purse was filled with letters from the prisoners. My daughter, 16 years old, was out of town. In two months, my husband was due to be released, and I thought, "Then I'll be in prison." Suddenly, I don't know what happened, I started running along the street. It was stupid, I know. Maybe it was some kind of mental attack. But it was nighttime. It was pitch dark. I felt alone. I just panicked. It happens to everyone.[8]

It was not that so many *Chronicle* people were finally discovered and punished by the KGB. The percentage of the possibly thousands of Soviet men and women connected one way or another to the *Chronicle* who were actually imprisoned has been relatively small. But the KGB has been unpredictable. One never knew if finally one had become a KGB candidate for arrest. The uncertainty created an atmosphere of elementary terror among the *Chronicle* people, and it became their daily existence.

A seemingly mundane problem of producing the *Chronicle* was the financing. A representative issue, done by a professional typist at 20 kopecks a page (100 kopecks to the ruble) would total about 20 rubles. Even that price was half the going rate for professional work. But 20 rubles amounts to 10 to 15 percent of a monthly wage. Many of those reproducing the *Chronicle* have had no other money to live on aside from their pay. They could not always accept the extra financial burden of the *Chronicle*. The logical choice for some, then, was to sell it. Prices per copy varied. Figures of 2 to 5 rubles a *Chronicle* copy are mentioned. Some people sold other *samizdat*-reproductions of Solzhenitsyn's novels, for example—to help subsidize production of the *Chronicle*. Others accepted contributions from friends and sympathizers. Still others simply paid from their own pockets for reproduction of *Chronicle* issues, necessarily giving up something for themselves.

Photocopying became the second most favored technique to reproduce the *Chronicle* in the early 1970s and thereafter. Cameras have always been readily available in the Soviet Union, even when basic consumer goods have been in short supply. The assembly of cameras, like wristwatches, also plentiful in the Soviet Union, maintains a defense-related work force skilled in precision manufacture. The home photocopying technique was simple. Pages of the *Chronicle*, or other *samizdat*, were photographed, using a mounted 35 millimeter camera and lights. From the negatives, page prints were made. Although this technique was reasonably fast, it was expensive, for photographic printing paper is costly in the Soviet Union and often difficult to obtain. Nonetheless, as KGB records and *Chronicle* reports have revealed, photocopying of *samizdat* has become widespread.

One former Soviet citizen, a professional photographer and now living in the United States, recalled various means by which *samizdat* was produced. In one case, printing paper was sometimes obtained in a government office that produced geological maps. The office used yard-wide rolls of photographic printing paper 30 yards long. For a bribe of some cognac and rubles, a roll of the paper would be diverted. It was enough for hundreds of prints. Many professional photographers in Moscow produced not only *samizdat* as a private occupation but also pornographic literature, the latter sometimes paying for the former. Copies of the *Chronicle* were produced in the same home photo studios in Moscow that also turned out illicit issues of *Playboy*.

There have been attempts to manufacture duplicating or mimeograph machines to reproduce the *Chronicle*. On the whole, the efforts have been unsuccessful. The basic parts are difficult to find in the Soviet Union. Ready-made duplicating machines are controlled by the secret police along with printing presses.

As electronic photocopying machines became more prevalent in the Soviet Union, persons with access to them produced the *Chronicle* in limited numbers. There is a known instance of a young soldier working in the Moscow office of the Soviet defense ministry's chief of staff who produced *samizdat*. The machine was a Soviet-made Era photocopier. For a year the young soldier secretly turned out *samizdat*. The material given to him to reproduce was mild in content, for the intent was to test this particular channel for reproduction. The soldier was caught, however, and assigned to the Soviet far east.[9] In another instance, *Chronicle* people had contact with a man who, having access to a photocopier, simply sold a clandestine service. But it proved difficult to produce the *Chronicle* in significant numbers through this contact.

Finally it can be asked why the *Chronicle* group did not establish an underground printing press. The unregistered Soviet Baptists for years have turned out whole volumes of religious literature and Bibles on secret printing presses. In February 1982, a group of Baptists was arrested in the Kirghiz republic after the KGB uncovered a clandestine press. KGB agents seized 600 printed Bibles in the raid. The press had been operating for more than ten years, turning out Bibles in Russian, Ukrainian, and several other languages.[10]

Chronicle workers have only tentatively considered establishing a printing press, for several reasons. First, an unregistered printing press is unequivocally illegal in the Soviet Union. In its struggle to be a public, legal publication, the *Chronicle* has shunned as best as possible openly illegal actions. Establishing an underground press would only serve KGB purposes, the argument went, in portraying the *Chronicle* as a conspiratorial organization.

Second, it is no easy matter to operate an underground press in the Soviet Union. Baptist groups that have done so with some success have been located in remote regions of the Soviet Union. They have been able to hide a printing press in towns or villages where the KGB is not so prevalent. Moscow is another story altogether. Running a secret printing press in a Moscow apartment building chal-·lenges the imagination. The risks of being detected have seemed to the *Chronicle* staff extraordinarily high.

Third, to obtain a printing press, type, ink, and paper in the Soviet Union without KGB knowledge is a major undertaking. Kronid Lyubarsky recounts that he was offered a small printing press located in the Soviet Caucasus for use by the *Chronicle*. He decided, however, that to transport the press in pieces to Moscow and set it up, undetected by the KGB, was probably impossible.[11]

Once the *Chronicle* was produced, the next task was to distribute issues. Keeping in mind that issues were turned out like chain letters, the distribution process logically mimicked that system. A given *Chronicle* number would continue to be reproduced for weeks and months after the first master copies became available in Moscow, as successive individuals acquired a copy in Moscow or elsewhere in the Soviet Union and arranged for retyping. The lag time tended to increase as issues became larger. For example, *Chronicle* issue no. 62, dated July 14, 1981, appeared in Moscow in December of that same year, fully six months later. Additional copies thus were not in the hands of readers for a year or more after the date marking the editorial closing of a *Chronicle* issue.

The *Chronicle* has always shared the hazards of handling any *samizdat*. Few want to possess a *Chronicle* copy any longer than necessary, for fear of the KGB. Lyubarsky remembers some of the problems in passing copies of the *Chronicle*:

After the typists were finished, I would pick up [*Chronicle*] copies and carry them in a large briefcase. Everyone carries a briefcase or large bag in Moscow. For books, or food, or whatever one buys. This was my most worrisome point. I was afraid I'd forget the briefcase somewhere, that I'd stop and absently leave it, with all the material inside.

We found that as far as passing the *Chronicle*, the less complicated the better. Once, for instance, we decided to pass a copy like this. There was an old barrel at a spot in Moscow that I'd seen. It had been there a couple years. So it was decided to use this like a mail box. I'd leave the *Chronicle*—in this case for retyping—and the woman typist would pick it up from the barrel. So what happened? The first time I put a *Chronicle* issue in there, some one found it and took it. It just disappeared.

Well, I'd pick up the *Chronicles*. I'd try to lose the KGB surveillance, but that was naive. They are professionals. We're just dilettantes. Distributing the *Chronicle* was the most unpleasant task. People are lazy, they wouldn't want to come and get their

> copy. But I wanted to get rid of them. It was dangerous to hold on to the copies. I would call people to get their issue, or even deliver it myself. So it took about a week to get the *Chronicle* to my regular clients. I'd have 12 copies, and they would go to the first 12 on the list. The next 12 copies went to the next 12 and so on. There were cases when if someone was going from Moscow to another city, you would send some or all 12 copies with them. [12]

The *Chronicle* has gained national circulation in the Soviet Union since its inception. Once distributed only in Moscow, then in Leningrad and Kiev, the *Chronicle* now reaches most major Soviet cities. It is believed that the *Chronicle* routinely has been distributed to these Soviet cities in large numbers: Leningrad, Vilnius, Riga, and perhaps Tallin in the Baltic states region; Kiev, Odessa, Kishinev, Kharkov, and Erevan in the southern and southwestern regions; and Novosibirsk, Sverdlovsk, Krasnoyarsk, Irkutsk, Volgograd, Tomsk, and Tashkent in the Soviet Siberian and central Asian areas. The *Chronicle* has found its way elsewhere, to remote Siberian villages to political prisoners in exile, for example. But given the reproduction and distribution system, there is no reliable method to document where each issue of the *Chronicle* moves or how many copies.

The total circulation of the *Chronicle* generally is estimated in the thousands, not many in a country of 270 million people. In successive reproductions by typewriter or photocopying, a single *Chronicle* number might total between 1,000 and 10,000 individual copies. Each number might, in fact, vary in total copies, depending, for example, on the extent of KGB harassment at the time or availability of paper. Multiply by ten for the number of readers per issue, and the total reading audience in the Soviet Union of a *Chronicle* issue might be 10,000 to 100,000. These are only approximations. The truth is that no one really knows either the readership or the circulation of the *Chronicle*.

The *Chronicle*'s audience has been magnified, however, by foreign radiobroadcasts. Especially in the earlier years, when the *Chronicle* was almost the sole source of uncensored and reliable news of political affairs in the Soviet Union, the foreign press corps routinely extracted information from the *Chronicle*. In turn, Radio Liberty, Voice of America, BBC, Deutsche Welle, and other foreign radio stations broadcast the information back to the Soviet

Union in Russian-language programs. Radio Liberty, the American-financed radio station transmitting in Russian and other languages of the Soviet Union, eventually broadcast whole issues of the *Chronicle*. The programs have been recorded in the Soviet Union for transcription and *samizdat* circulation. Thus, the entire state Glavlit censorship system has been circumvented, and *Chronicle* reports have reached millions of Soviet listeners.

Several conditional facts must be kept in mind in assessing the *Chronicle*'s network. First, Soviet authorities reinstituted jamming of foreign radiobroadcasts in August 1968, coincident with the invasion of Czechoslovakia. The jamming was not halted until 1973, the year the Brezhnev leadership searched for a conciliatory gesture to spur the Helsinki agreement negotiations. From 1973 until late 1980, Soviet audiences for foreign broadcasts blossomed. It became politically acceptable in the Soviet Union to quote from BBC or Voice of America. The "radios," as Western shortwave broadcasters were called, became the conduit for a vast amount of information previously unavailable to the Soviet population. In turn, the Soviet state press routinely denounced the broadcasts, the criticism intensifying as East-West relations deteriorated in the late 1970s and early 1980s. Soviet authorities once again began jamming the "radios" in August 1980, as the Polish free trade union Solidarity formed. Certainly, the cumulative popularity of foreign broadcasts in the 1970s was the basic reason leading Soviet authorities again to disrupt this source of troublesome—to them—information.

An essential element in the *Chronicle*'s network has been the foreign press corps in Moscow, first and foremost the American correspondents. Soviet dissidents interviewed about the *Chronicle* often mention individual reporters who took special interest in the struggle between Soviet authorities and dissidents. To mention some is to risk slighting other correspondents who were equally involved, but these names come up: George Krimsky and Roger Leddington of the Associated Press; Ray Anderson, Hedrick Smith, and Henry Kamm of the *New York Times;* Anatole Shub and Robert Kaiser of the *Washington Post;* James Yuenger and Frank Starr of the *Chicago Tribune;* Robert Toth of the *Los Angeles Times;* and Jay Alexbank and Alfred Friendly, Jr., of *Newsweek*. Other correspondents have been mentioned: Robert Evans of Reuters; David Satter, *Financial Times;* and David Bonovia, *The Times* of London. A number of correspondents from Agence France Presse and Deutsche Presse Agent and from Dutch and Swiss news agencies were also involved with dissidents.

Soviet authorities recognized the importance of foreign correspondents in the *Chronicle* and other *samizdat* information network. Some of the best informed Western reporters were routinely harassed, and some were expelled. David Bonovia and George Krimsky, for example, were ordered out of the Soviet Union in the early 1970s. The KGB interrogated Robert Toth for three days before he was permitted to leave Moscow in 1978. There was no doubt that their contracts among Soviet dissidents, and their reporting of what Soviet authorities considered highly objectionable information, led to their expulsions.

Official Soviet pressure on Western correspondents flowed from the détente-initiated policy of suppressing internal dissent, as the Soviet Union opened its frontiers to Western trade, financial assistance, and technological transfer. Soviet authorities early recognized that without knowledgeable, interested Western correspondents in Moscow, Soviet dissidents had fewer means to amplify their grievances against Soviet government violations of civil rights.

A combination of events in recent years has reduced both the flow of *Chronicle* information and its immediate influence. KGB campaigns against the *Chronicle* have unmistakably contributed to its less frequent appearance, to difficulties in reproduction, and to more limited distribution with the Soviet Union. It is rare now when the *Chronicle* prompts a news story either in Moscow or elsewhere. *Chronicle* information, six months or more old, has lost its urgency. Moreover, as it has become a large volume, a given *Chronicle* issue is more difficult to handle, from the initial editing, to typing, to distribution. It has become a physically difficult task to deliver 10 or 15 copies of a 100- or 200-page *Chronicle* manuscript to readers in Moscow or in other Soviet cities. Those experienced with the *Chronicle* further reflect that KGB intimidation has frightened away persons who in earlier years might have assisted the *Chronicle*. The prospect of KGB interrogrations, let alone years in labor camps, has taken its toll in the network.

The *Chronicle*, however, remains a symbol of a movement for civil rights in the Soviet as a source of information about the movement. Its very survival in the Soviet Union, despite repeated KGB efforts to eliminate it, has already earned the *Chronicle* a place in contemporary Soviet history. Why the KGB has failed to achieve its objective deserves separate consideration.

NOTES

1. Vladimir Bukovsky, *To Build a Castle: My Life as a Dissident* (New York: Viking Press, 1979), pp. 140-42.

2. Radio Liberty Research Report, January 9, 1978.

3. Associated Press dispatch from Moscow, September 3, 1981.

4. Ginzburg interview.

5. Salova interview.

6. Ibid.

7. Ibid.

8. Ibid.

9. Lyubarsky interview.

10. *USSR News Brief*, no. 5, 1982, pp. 1-2.

11. Tatyana Khodorovich, Alexander Ginzburg, Ludmilla Alexeyeva, and Kronid Lyubarsky have discussed the problems of reproducing the *Chronicle* other than by typewriter and agree that under current circumstances in the Soviet Union other techniques remain inefficient.

12. Lyubarsky interview.

9
KGB vs. CHRONICLE

The Soviet State Committee for Security, the KGB, has hunted the *Chronicle* for more than a decade and a half, assigning hundreds of agents and investing untold millions of rubles to destroy the *Chronicle*'s network and silence the most important surviving symbol of the Soviet movement for rule of law and a democratic society. In campaigns marked by periodic success, the KGB has nonetheless failed to achieve its ultimate objective. Why this is so must remain speculative until, if ever, KGB records become available, or until former KGB agents reveal secret deliberations of the most secret and feared Soviet state agency.

We do know that Yury Andropov, during his 15 years as chairman of the State Committee for Security, took a personal interest in the *Chronicle*. Victor Krasin's testimony, revealing Andropov's involvement in the Yakir-Krasin's case, suggests that other major trials of *Chronicle* editors or participants cleared through Andropov's office. Because these trials often had both domestic and international ramifications, there is all the more reason to believe that the *Chronicle* ranked high on the list of Andropov's and the KGB's concerns.

That translates really into concern of the Soviet political leadership. The Soviet secret police is just one branch of the Soviet political organization. Recall that Andropov, who was named KGB chairman in 1967, was also a nonvoting member at that time of the ruling Communist party Politburo. He was made a full member in 1973. Through this system of interlocking directorates, the senior Soviet leadership thus ensures lines of control through all Soviet party, government, military, and police bureaucracies. With Andropov attending deliberations of the Politburo, the KGB, of course, carried out policies of the Soviet leadership in suppressing dissidents.

It has not, therefore, been for lack of authority, concentrated effort, or determination that the KGB has been unable to stop the *Chronicle*. Rather, Soviet dissidents connected with the *Chronicle* over the years suggest other reasons. The opinions break down into three categories.

First, some dissidents contend that the KGB has simply been outwitted by the *Chronicle*. True, successive editors, writers, and distributors have been imprisoned. But the fact is that others have moved immediately to take up *Chronicle* responsibilities. With very few exceptions, the *Chronicle* always has appeared according to schedule. The main exceptions, of course, have been the 18-month hiatus in 1973-74, when nos. 28, 29, and 30 were delayed, the suppression of no. 59 in November 1980, the one confiscated by the KGB, and the delay of no. 63. The persistent and otherwise regular appearance of the *Chronicle* is a remarkable record, given that the *Chronicle* group faced a professional, experienced Soviet security agency equipped with all the contemporary electronic devices for surveillance, monitoring, and analysis of evidence. It may be, as Vladimir Bukovsky proposes, that the KGB is too narrowly focused. "The KGB believes in the theory of the center," Bukovsky says. "They look for a mastermind. But these people on the *Chronicle* never worked in a centralized manner."[1] In fact, contends Yury Gastev, who wrote and reported for the *Chronicle* almost from the start until his exile to France in 1981, the *Chronicle* operated along multiple and parallel lines. Thus, even when one channel was blocked, information continued to flow along other channels, and other editors assembled and produced the information as a *Chronicle* issue.[2]

The KGB, an offshoot of the highly centralized and structured Soviet bureaucracy, operates more as a military organization. Although the KGB chief carries the title of chairman, he also has military rank. His immediate deputies are generals. Andropov himself was a general of the army, second highest grade in the Soviet armed forces after marshal. Subordinates hold ranks of colonel, lieutenant colonel, major, and so on. The KGB, however, hunted a *Chronicle* that was more akin to partisans or a guerilla army. The *Chronicle* has been made up of small groups whose individual members were well known to one another and who could act spontaneously and freely, unencumbered by bureaucratic regulation and order.

Dissidents like Bukovsky and Gastev argue that the KGB has really been ill-equipped with tactical experience to crush the *Chronicle*, no less than structured military units have routinely failed against mobile partisans. There has been no single director of the *Chronicle*, no editorial board, no physical structure to destroy and hence destroy the *Chronicle*. Yet the one view goes, the KGB has consistently sought out individuals for punishment or exile, on the apparent theory that once its leadership was eliminated, so too would be the *Chronicle*.

This leads to a second possible explanation. Yefrem Yankelevich, among others with long association with the *Chronicle*, suggests that although Soviet authorities could in fact silence the *Chronicle*, the cost would be out of proportion to the return. On any given date, the KGB could arrest 200, 500, or 1,000 known or suspected Soviet dissidents—the men and women who, according to KGB records, have been regularly engaged in *samizdat*. Arrests on this scale, Yankelevich contends, would almost surely include the core group responsible for the *Chronicle*.[3] In practice, however, the political costs of reinstituting Stalinist mass terror in the Soviet Union would surely far outweigh whatever benefits Soviet authorities might gain in silencing activist dissidents.

Indeed, the commonplace view is that Soviet dissent in the sense of popularly expressed complaints about civil rights has become so widespread in the Soviet Union that *only* mass terror on a grand scale could generate the fear and intimidation necessary to cow the Soviet population.

Yet, to revive the practices of Stalinism, to give the KGB that unrestricted power possessed by the NKVD of the 1930s, to generate the stark fear in all echelons of Soviet society that Stalin's mass purges did—to undertake these actions would require a radical change in the Soviet power structure. To order mass arrests for the sake of quieting the *Chronicle* means to loose the most totalitarian, brutal forces in Soviet society—the real criminal element, if you will. Once this is done, of course, the number and types of victims are unpredictable. No one recalls more vividly than Soviet political leaders, Andropov among them, that Stalin's purges took a heavy toll among the Communist party, government, and eventually the ranks of the secret police itself.

It is no less true that a concentrated mass purging of Soviet dissidents, even if contained, which is unlikely, would nurture both opposition and demoralization in the

Soviet Union and an outcry abroad. The foreign reaction might well be weathered by the Kremlin, as it
has weathered the temporary Western outcry against the
invasion of Czechoslovakia, the occupation of Afghan-
istan, or Soviet pressure against Poland. But widespread opposition within Soviet intellectual, technological, managerial, and academic ranks has not been
and cannot be ignored by the Soviet leadership. These
groups provide the expertise for the operation of the
Soviet leadership. In sum, the argument goes, the
arrest of a few hundred active dissidents, including the
Chronicle group, could start a chain reaction. It might
be the first act threatening release of such oppressive
forces that Soviet society would turn in a direction
benefiting neither the leaders nor the led.

As a consequence, the KGB finds itself bound by
unwritten Soviet convention within which it must
operat—hence, the persistent attempts of KGB investigators to pursue a "legal" elimination of the *Chronicle*.
The laborious, detailed investigations, requiring
months, if not years, and demanding hundreds of
agents to stage trials of the *Chronicle*'s editors are the
evidence that the Soviet secret police cannot, in fact,
pursue the more drastic, Stalinist course to silence the
Chronicle.

The *Chronicle* therefore exists because it is, indeed,
representative of popular opinion in the Soviet Union,
persuasive enough that the KGB must tread warily.
For if the *Chronicle* equated with merely a handful of
Moscow intellectuals concerned with censorship of their
poetry or novels, it surely would not have resisted the
KGB this long. As with several lesser underground
Soviet periodicals, the *Chronicle* could have been
broken up with little fanfare.

A third theory as to why the *Chronicle* survives
posits KGB complicity. This theory has no support
among those who have been involved with the
Chronicle. Nor is there evidence from KGB actions or
from information gained by dissidents during KGB
interrogations to suggest that there is any official
tolerance for the *Chronicle*. The policy may possibly
have dictated constant harassment of the *Chronicle*
group, cyclical arrests and trials of editors, exile for
some, labor camps for others, all to contain *Chronicle*
activities, but not with the intention to silence the
Chronicle. Not at least since it resumed publication in
1974.

This theory holds some credence. There is no doubt

that the KGB possesses thorough files on the *Chronicle*'s operation. Pavel Litvinov, Kronid Lyubarsky, and Ludmilla Alexeyeva, among others, have reflected that the KGB knew of their involvement with the *Chronicle* long before any action was taken against them. If the KGB has yet to perfect its surveillance of the *Chronicle*'s operation, its agents nonetheless know enough to make production far more difficult than they do. The confiscation of no. 59 in its last stages of preparation is a sharp reminder of KGB potential. The question, then, is why, short of mass arrests, does not the KGB apply more pressure? And the answer may be that for good reason there has been no intention to do so.

The reason may be that the *Chronicle* as it exists serves to attract the most active Soviet dissidents, thereby grouping them for ease of KGB identification and control. Valery Chalidze suggests that the KGB thereby knows the most troublesome—from the Soviet authorities' perspective—men and women. To destroy the *Chronicle*, the rallying point, Chalidze says, would mean that when the inevitable successor appeared, the KGB would face a whole new network of Soviet dissidents. It may be more manageable for the KGB simply to allow the *Chronicle* to survive as a quarterly periodical under KGB surveillance.

There is no evidence to support this interpretation. Nor is there any evidence that the KGB has ever tried to manipulate the *Chronicle*. To the knowledge of participants in *Chronicle* work—Gorbanevskaya, Alexeyeva, Khodorovich, for example—there has been no KGB attempt even to infiltrate the *Chronicle* group. This may be because the staff has been so closely knit that infiltration is practically impossible. In any case, the notion that the *Chronicle* has functioned as long as it has because of deliberate decision of the Soviet leadership cannot be dismissed out of hand, not if one is realistic about the strengths as well as the weaknesses of the Soviet secret police.

There is sometimes a tendency to view the Soviet KGB as an impersonal, precisely functioning robot, tramping cruelly and heartlessly over the Soviet man or woman who dares raise a voice in protest. Successive accounts of Soviet dissidents temper this picture. The KGB seems truly to be representative of Soviet society, as any government institution seems to reflect its own culture. The KGB, although infamous for violating basic human rights, also is famous for incompetence, sluggish bureaucracy, human greed, and stupidity, among other qualities that mark the Soviet state machinery. Some Soviet dissidents believe, Vladimir Bukovsky among them, that domestic KGB agents are generally less qualified than those chosen for the more glamorous, risky, and important foreign assignments. The KGB staff dealing with internal dissent is, in this view, composed of those rejected for international work and are, accordingly, less educated, cultured, intelligent, and sophisticated.

Such generalizations by Soviet exiles are drawn, of course, from personal experiences with the KGB. Various men and women associated with the *Chronicle* have provided disparate portraits of KGB investigators and agents. In long months of interrogation, the staff often became closely acquainted with their KGB case officers. Galina Gabai, who worked with the *Chronicle* almost from the start and edited no. 10, was questioned several times by the KGB. She recalls being taken to Lefortovo prison. It boasts, among other things, one of the best libraries in Moscow, for it includes politically illicit books confiscated from dissidents and generally unavailable to the Soviet population. Gabai's husband, Ilya Gabai, used the library when he was held in Lefortovo in the late 1960s. Galina remembers her KGB interrogators:

> They were usually very smart, and they were always polite. This was my experience, and my husband's. The agents, of whatever rank, never raised their voices. They always used your name and patronymic. They would offer you tea and exchange pleasantries. I do remember they were rude when I was pregnant, when they couldn't question me at the KGB offices. Instead, they would question me while I lay in bed in the hospital. This was in the spring of 1973, when they were investigating Case 24 against the *Chronicle*.
>
> Later when I felt better, they would send a car for me and bring me to Lefortovo and question me all day long. I was six or seven months' pregnant by then. I remember one KGB agent for example. He was educated, polite, a human being. There was no petty harassment. He would permit me to bring flowers to my husband in prison. Sometimes he would wear his KGB uniform. His rank was major. He could discuss literature and so on. The best educated never talked politics.[4]

The KGB began summoning Ludmilla Alexeyeva for questioning in 1972, also in connection with Case 24 and the *Chronicle*. Her interrogator was Vladimir Pavlovich—his first name and patronymic. Alexeyeva never learned his family name. Recollecting the past as she was interviewed in her house in Tarrytown, N.Y., Alexeyeva described the encounter this way:

He was older than I. At the time I was 43, he was 47. He was good looking, with wavy hair, quite gray. The KGB interrogators always dressed well. He wore foreign-made suits, with matching shirts and socks. He was well groomed. He spoke absolutely perfect Russian.

But there is a certain difference between those who in childhood are not members of the intelligentsia. He learned well from the non-intelligentsia. He wrote perfectly, but from the selection of phrases, from his intonation, you knew he was not one of our circle. He had a family and lived in Moscow. He told me once that thieves had gotten into his dacha outside of the city. It must have been fully furnished, because he said the thieves had stolen a television set among other things. He was kind, I think. But of course as a KGB officer, he was honest in his obligations and could do mean things. He would say, "We are all Chekists."

He seemed to have been with the KGB a long time. He had a personal office on Peschanaya Square. It was a normal Moscow building, seven or eight floors, with a normal door to a normal apartment house. But he also had an office on Dzerzhinsky Square, the KGB headquarters. It was fairly large, maybe 20 by 25 feet. It was furnished with a rug, modern desk, shelves, books, a safe. His desk had a lamp, pen set, calendar, and a typewriter to one side. You can tell the rank by the office.

I was questioned by another KGB officer—Alexander Mikhailovich. He was a chief of one of six divisions. And when I was taken to him, even Vladimir Pavlovich did not dare to enter his office, but instead backed away from the door. Alexander Mikhailovich was a big boss. He had a certain style that was not mass produced. He was the only one I knew in the KGB who was from the intelligentsia. The others all felt insecure next to us. They knew the difference in the cultural level.[5]

The typical experience of the *Chronicle* staff in Moscow with the KGB was not all that frightening. True, the ultimate consequences of interrogations, arrests, and then trial and imprisonment could be devastating. But they were not physically threatened during preliminary questioning in Lefortovo, and none was physically abused. The standard KGB interrogation technique relied more on wearing down a person, isolating him or her physically, spiritually breaking a person to the point that it seemed in one's best interest to confide in the KGB, to at least confirm information possessed by interrogators. A curious relationship seems to have developed. The KGB as an organization has been feared and hated by the *Chronicle* group, among others, in Soviet society. But those involved with the *Chronicle* seldom speak bitterly about individual KGB case officers.

The *Chronicle*'s network knew the KGB to be a fundamentally corrupt institution. Whatever personal niceties were shown to men and women summoned for interrogations, there was no forgetting that the KGB functioned outside of legal or ethical restraints commonly accepted in modern Western societies. Like other powerful centers in the Soviet Union, the KGB enjoyed privileges accordingly. Access to apartments, automobiles, dachas, and shops with plentiful supplies of domestic and foreign foods and durables are the common rewards in Soviet society for high-level ranks of the Communist party, government, military, and the KGB. Kronid Lyubarsky notes that internal rules allow KGB officers a share of any items they confiscate. Hence, the typewriters taken in large numbers from *Chronicle* staff, along with diamonds, gold, jewelry, and other valuables seized from speculators or theives, are turned over to the state resale shops—the *kommission* stores—where KGB officers have first pick. Because the KGB also sets the prices, they acquire expensive or rare items inexpensively.[6] The corruption in the KGB then extends from the petty to the grandiose. The *Chronicle*, seeking to expose violations of rule of law, with all that connotes, has necessarily been looked on by the KGB as a natural enemy.

That fundamental antagonism between the *Chronicle* and the KGB—if not Andropov personally—surely has intensified over the past decade. The KGB has poured such huge resources into its war against the *Chronicle* that it has amassed a considerable vested interest in pursuing its object. Victor Krasin says that he counted about 400 different KGB agents assigned to watch his movements during several months in 1969, the surveillance teams being changed every time he identified them.[7] Other accounts suggest that if one considers KGB techniques—24-hour, 7 days-a-week surveillance, full-time electronic eavesdropping and tape transcribing, extensive interrogations, coordinated and nationwide probes—the manpower alone devoted to the *Chronicle* cases over the years must run into thousands of persons. The cost in rubles cannot be publicly known and because investigations of the *Chronicle* always involved other political and *samizdat* activities.

It can be said with certainty, however, that the *Chronicle* has ranked among the leading half-dozen political cases in the Soviet Union since the famed Sinyavsky-Daniel trial of 1966. The *Chronicle* has interested the KGB, it is fair to say, with the same intensity as the cases of Andrei Sakharov, Alexander Solzhenitsyn, Anatoly Shcharansky, and the unofficial Helsinki groups. Like these cases, the investigation of the *Chronicle* has crossed frontiers. The KGB has routinely alleged that the *Chronicle* group is the vehicle of foreign subversive agencies. The *Chronicle* has been portrayed by the KGB as the center of Soviet traitors, of the ideological opposition, of the politically innocent, of morally corrupt, parasitic renegades.

Reading the official Soviet calumny heaped on the *Chronicle* and its associates, it is difficult to select the true official assessment. The official smearing of the *Chronicle* is meant as much to warn off the Soviet public as it is to blacken the *Chronicle* and make it distasteful to the Soviet rank and file. The assessments that many *Chronicle* staff have given probably are more accurate measures of the significance and role of the *Chronicle*, no matter whether one is for or against the publication.

By now, the *Chronicle* is probably first and foremost a symbol of resistance to capricious rule. As Alexander Ginzburg notes, the persistence of the *Chronicle* shows what can be done by people who shed or surmount their fear—"who will accept five years."[8] Kronid Lyubarsky, in the same vein, suggests that the "mere existence of the *Chronicle*—regardless of arrests—proves the indestructibility of the democratic movement. Like a flag," he says, "the longer the *Chronicle* lasts, the more important it becomes."[9]

As a symbol, the *Chronicle* says, then, that the overwhelming power of the Soviet state can and has been resisted by a faction of the citizenry, that no matter the punishments meted out by the Soviet leadership, there remains a dedicated element among the Soviet population openly championing rule of law. That is a rare accomplishment in Soviet history. The Soviet record is filled with instances of the slightest loyal opposition being crushed by the central leadership, let alone an opposition seeking political change.

That the *Chronicle* survived KGB efforts to eliminate it could not be much appreciated in the Soviet leadership. The rise of former KGB chief Yury Andropov to the pinnacle of Soviet power especially did not augur well for the

Chronicle. The statements of Andropov, while he directed the secret police from 1967 to 1982, and KGB actions left no doubt that the *Chronicle* and Soviet dissidents have been regarded as intolerable. There was no reason to believe that the official view would alter while Andropov filled the post of party general secretary, or after.

The *Chronicle* has remained also a valuable source of information in the Soviet Union. From its small beginnings it has expanded to a publication with some 20 sections, covering events of broad interest. The information may not be all that timely, now that the *Chronicle* has been forced to quarterly or even biannual publication. Yet, in a country where authorities censor the slightest damaging information, timeliness of information is not always that important. What is important is access to otherwise concealed facts. Valery Chalidze credits the *Chronicle* after even its first years with forming a cumulative portrait of an authentic Soviet life hidden from the general public but known by officials and by their victims, those brutalized by the secret police and the Soviet legal system working in concert.[10]

It is true that the *Chronicle* still has had only a small audience among the Soviet population. Unquestionably, millions of Soviet workers, peasants, government functionaries, and students have never heard of the *Chronicle of Current Events*. But it is also true that the *Chronicle* has circulated among those in the Soviet Union who enjoy moral authority and influence, if not political power. It can reasonably be argued that the *Chronicle* has affected important opinion in the Soviet Union far beyond its physical circulation, much as does the American journal *Foreign Affairs*.

At the very least, the *Chronicle* is a reminder that censorship is not all-inclusive in the Soviet Union. At the most, the *Chronicle* provides hard facts about a range of Soviet matters-functioning of the courts, the secret police, the penal system-against which to measure official statements. When that is done, the result is to show official Soviet mass communications for what they are, the company voice, the corporate house organ willing to engage in generalization to justify the regime. The *Chronicle*'s expose of official manipulation of information has certainly been a dominant reason behind the Kremlin's desire to crush the *Chronicle*.

The *Chronicle* has in many ways served as a political center. It is a role that the original *Chronicle* group meeting in the late winter of 1968 never sought. It is a role that many Soviet dissidents associated with the

Chronicle reject to this day. Yet Pavel Litvinov, for one, believes that the *Chronicle* did develop into a center, drawing like-minded individuals into a common enterprise. He distinguishes this *Chronicle* role from that of a political center, for in fact the *Chronicle* has never proposed a political program or defined its activity in a political form.[11] In the Soviet Union, where both the manufacture of children's toys and the compilation of the annual economic plan are political acts, it is perhaps a difficult distinction to say that the *Chronicle* is a center, but not a political center; for propagation of rule of law is necessarily a political act in the Soviet system, inasmuch as the legal network ultimately and directly responds to political judgments.

Another controversial question is whether the *Chronicle* is an underground or clandestine publication. The *Chronicle*'s editors and staff have resisted this description, for in Russian the word "underground" historically carries conspiratorial, illegal connotations. The *Chronicle* group, if anything, has sought legal, open operation, and the editors have persistently opposed official efforts to make the *Chronicle* out to be some sort of secret and subversive center.

Yet the *Chronicle*'s manner of functioning fits the common definition of an underground publication. Editors, writers, and distributors have been forced to work in secrecy, for fear of KGB punishment. The longer the *Chronicle* survived, the more persons arrested and imprisoned or exiled; the more clandestine the *Chronicle*'s production, the greater the secrecy among informants and the more surreptitious the reproduction and circulation of the *Chronicle*. These procedures have been the price for a free press in the Soviet Union.

The *Chronicle*, more than any other underground publication or unofficial group in the Soviet Union, merged group interests in the Soviet population that otherwise would have had little contact. The grievances, experiences, and aspirations of Moscow intellectuals, Baptist believers, Jewish *refusniks*, and political prisoners, to name a few, came together under the aegis of the *Chronicle*. In this sense, the *Chronicle* did become a political center and symbol, and on a national scale.

The *Chronicle* under successive editors and staffs has demonstrated how a free and responsible press might operate in the Soviet Union. It has studiously hewed to factual reporting and just as arduously avoided direct editorial judgment. The *Chronicle* consistently has tried to present unbiased accounts, presenting the official position in dissident trial, for example, as dispassionately as the defendant's. That is a remarkable record, given the atmosphere of contrived and manipulated information created by the Soviet mass media.

This is not to glorify the *Chronicle* or to present it greater than life size. *Chronicle* writers have made mistakes in fact. Editors have let questionable rumor into issues. And its content cumulatively shows a distinct bias toward what have become known as dissidents. The *Chronicle* is unmistakably the voice of the oppressed, the victimized, the powerless in Soviet society.

As a journalistic enterprise, under the given conditions, it still must earn superlatives. The *Chronicle* has never deliberately attempted to mislead or misinform its readers. Its staff has instead sought to build trust and respect between the *Chronicle* and its public. That alone has been no minor feat in Soviet society, ridden as it is with suspicion and apprehension, the legacy still of the Stalinist era. Most importantly, the *Chronicle* says that the search for the truth remains a noble, human yearning.

NOTES

1. Bukovsky interview.
2. Gastev interview.
3. Yankelevich interview.
4. Gabai interview.
5. Alexeyeva interview.
6. Lyubarsky interview.
7. Krasin interview.
8. Ginzburg interview.
9. Lyubarsky interview.
10. Valery Chalidze, *To Defend These Rights: Human Rights and the Soviet Union* (New York: Random House, 1974), p. 55.
11. Litvinov interview.

Appendix A

1953

    March 5 — Stalin dies.

1956

    February 14-25 — Twentieth Party Congress; Khrushchev makes his "secret speech" against Stalin.

1964

    October 14 — Khrushchev is dismissed.

1965

    September 8 — Sinyavsky and Daniel are arrested for publication of their books in the West under the pseudonyms of Abram Tertz and Nikolai Arzhak.

    December 5 — Dissidents stage the first Soviet Constitution Day demonstration to protest the arrests and forthcoming trials of Sinyavsky and Daniel.

1966

    February 10-14 — Sinyavsky and Daniel trial. Sinyavsky is sentenced to seven years in labor camps, Daniel to five.

1967

    January 21-22 — Galanskov and Ginzburg are arrested for producing the *samizdat* journals *Phoenix-61* and *Phoenix-66* and *Syntax*.

    January 22 — Bukovsky and friends organize the Pushkin Square demonstration to protest the arrests. Bukovsky is arrested later in the day.

    May 18 — Andropov named KGB chairman.

1968

    January 8 — Galanskov, Ginzburg, Dobrovolsky and Lashkova trial begins. Galanskov is sentenced to seven years in prison, Ginzburg to five years, Dobrovolsky to two years and Lashkova to one year.

April 30 — The first issue of *Chronicle* is completed by Gorbanevskaya.

August 21-22 — The Warsaw pact countries invade Czechoslovakia.

August 25 — Seven dissidents stage protest demonstration against the invasion in Red Square. Six of them are arrested.

October 9-11 — Participants of the Red Square demonstration are sentenced to various prison and exile terms.

1969
May 7 — Grigorenko is arrested in Tashkent.

May 19 — Ilya Gabai is arrested in Moscow and transferred to Tashkent.

May 20 — Initiative Group for the Defense of Human Rights announces its formation in Moscow.

December 24 — Gorbanevskaya arrested.

1970
c. January — KGB's Fifth Chief Directorate created in Moscow.

July 7 — Gorbanevskaya sentenced to an indefinite term in a special psychiatric hospital.

1971
Case 24 — the KGB's probe of the *Chronicle* — begins sometime this year.

December 30 — Party central committee reportedly approves plan to suppress the *Chronicle*.

1972
January 11-15 — KGB agents search homes of more than 30 persons in eight Soviet cities in coordinated investigation into *Chronicle*. Lyubarsky arrested, January 14.

June 21 — Yakir arrested.

September 12 – Krasin arrested.

October 15 – Date of 27th issue of *Chronicle*. This is the last issue until the *Chronicle* reappears in 1974.

November 2 – Galanskov dies in the Mordovian camp complex.

March 9 – First issue of the *Chronicle of the Lithuanian Catholic Church* appears.

1973

February 28 – Dissidents tell foreign correspondents in Moscow that *Chronicle* no. 28 would not be published for fear of KGB reprisals.

April 27 – Andropov named full member of the Politburo.

August 27-September 1 – Yakir and Krasin trial. They are sentenced to prison and exile. Prison terms are later commuted by Russian republic supreme court.

1974

May 7 – *Chronicle* reappears after 18 month silence. Khodorovich, Velikanova and Kovalev announce their responsibility for distributing the publication.

December 27 – Sergei Kovalev arrested in Moscow.

1975

December 9-12 – Sergei Kovalev tried and sentenced to seven years in a labor camp and three years in internal exile.

1979

November 1 – Velikanova arrested.

1980

April 19 – Lavut arrested in Moscow.

August 27-29 – Velikanova tried and sentenced to a strict regime labor camp for four years and exile for five more years.

December 24-26 – Lavut tried and sentenced to three years in prison.

1981

February 20 — KGB seizes the manuscript and the source materials for *Chronicle* no. 59 while conducting a search of Vul's apartment.

1983

Chronicle no. 63 appears in Moscow. Dated December 31, 1981 (sic), *Chronicle* had not been published for more than one year.

Appendix B

CHRONICLE CONTENTS

Chronicle editors beginning with the first issue in 1968 have listed the contents of each issue on the first page. A reading of these contents through successive issues reveals both the constant themes of the *Chronicle* and the increasing breadth of its reporting as it gained readers and support among the Soviet population. The content list below has been compiled from Amnesty International English translations and from Russian language editions of the *Chronicle*. The date of each issue is that affixed by editors in Moscow. It generally can be considered an "editorial closing" date, but not the date that the *Chronicle* issue necessarily appeared in Moscow.

No. 1   April 30, 1968
The trial of Galanskov, Ginzburg, Dobrovolsky and Lashkova • Protests of the trial • Repressions following the protests • Protests in connection with the trial • Repressions in connection with the protests • Statement to the Budapest Conference of Communist and Workers Parties • Political prisoners • Leningrad trial • Arrest of Valentin Prussakov.

No. 2   June 30, 1968
Extra-judicial political repressions of 1968 • Several episodes from the campaign condemning those who signed the letter • Leaflet of the group "Cherch" on Mayakovsky Square • Appeal of representatives of the Crimean Tatar people to world opinion • About Alexander Solzhenitsyn • Letter from Anatoly Marchenko • News in brief • Addenda and corrigenda.

No. 3   August 30, 1968
(Irregular issue, no content headings.)

No. 4   October 31, 1968
Court proceedings in the case of the Red Square Demonstration of August 25, 1968 • Soviet press about the trial of

the participants in the demonstration • *Samizdat* documents about the demonstration • About political prisoners sentenced for "high treason" • "New method" of conducting house searches • Supplement material on the case of Sinyavsky and Daniel, known as "The White Book" • News in brief.

No. 5   December 31, 1968
Survey of the *samizdat* publications for 1968 • Trial in Leningrad on December 17-26, 1968 • Supplement to the list of extra-judicial political repressions in 1968 • News in brief • Corrigenda • The Year of the Human Rights continues in the Soviet Union.

No. 6   February 28, 1969
The trial of Irina Belogorodskaya • The case of Boris Kochubiyevsky • The case of Ivan Yakhimovich • Political prisoners' ultimatum • Extra-judicial political repressions in 1968-1969 • Explanation of the national policy • Followers of Lysenko raise heads • *Samizdat* news • News in brief • Corrigenda.

No. 7   April 30, 1969
The trial of Gomer Bayev • The arrest of Ivan Yakhimovich • The arrest of Victor Kuznetsov • Political prisoners and exile • New repressions of Uniat priests • The movement of the people of Meskhetia for return to the homeland • "Relocation" of the Crimean Tatars in Crimea • Fetisov's Group • Brief biography of Andrei Sverdlov • Concerning the family of A. E. Kosterin • *Samizdat* news • Extra-judicial political repressions in 1968-1969 • News in brief • About the trustworthiness and accuracy of the information published in *Chronicle*.

No. 8   June 30, 1969
The trial of Boris Kochubiyevsky • The trial of Ilya Burmistrovich • The arrest of Pyotr Grigorenko • The arrest of Ilya Gabai • The June 6, 1969 Crimean Tatar demonstration at the Mayakovsky Square • Second attempt of self-immolation in the Ukraine • The fate of the dissidents proclaimed mentally ill • Alexander Ginzburg's hunger strike • Anatoly Marchenko is being investigated again • Appeal to the UN Human Rights Commission • The Union of the Independent Youth • Extra-judicial political persecution in 1968-1969 • *Samizdat* news • News in brief • Addenda.

No. 9   August 31, 1969
On the anniversary of the invasion of Czechoslovakia • The

trial of ten Crimean Tatars · Two trials of persons sentenced to forced medical treatment · The arrest of Genrykh Altunyan · The case of Yury Levin · The case of Ilya Gabai and Pyotr Grigorenko · New persecutions of Meskhs · Extra-judicial political persecutions · *Samizdat* news · News in brief · Addenda and corrigenda.

No. 10   October 31, 1969
The trial of Anatoly Marchenko · The trial of B. V. Talantov · The case of M. S. Ryzhyka · Persecutions of the Initiative Group in Defense of Human Rights in the USSR · The arrests of Baltic fleet officers · Arrests and persecutions in Gorky · The demonstration of the Scandinavian students · The case of the M. P. Yakubovich · The fate of Yury Ivanov · Kazan Special Psychiatric Hospital · On the forthcoming Stalin jubilee · Customs procedures at the Sheremetyevo airport · *Samizdat* news · Book review · News in brief · Addenda · Answers to the readers of *Chronicle*.

No. 11   December 31, 1969
Solzhenitsyn's expulsion from the Writer's Union · Pyotr Grigorenko · About the Special Psychiatric Hospitals · Political prisoners in Vladimir Prison · Hunger strikes in the Mordovian camps · The investigations of the case of naval officer Gavrilov and others continues · The arrest of Vladimir Gershuni · The arrests of Moscow students · Detention, arrest and trial of Victor Krasin · The arrest of Natalia Gorbanevskaya · The trial of Vladimir Borisov (Leningrad) · The trial of Genrykh Altunyan · The repressions of the members of the Initiative Group · Extra-judicial political repressions · *Samizdat* news · Addenda and corrigenda · Repressions in 1969.

No. 12   February 28, 1970
Prison diary of Pyotr Grigorenko · The trial of Pyotr Grigorenko · The trial of Ilya Gabai and Mustafa Dzhemilev · Political trials in Soviet cities · News from the Mordovian political camps · Letters from the Soviet Jews · Supplementary material on the Solzhenitsyn's expulsion from the Writer's Union · Foreigners speak in defense of Soviet political prisoners · News in brief · *Samizdat* news · Addenda and corrigenda.

No. 13   April 30, 1970
Moscow: The trial of Vladimir Gershuni · Moscow: The trial of Valeriya Novodvorskaya · Gorky: Political trials under article 70 and article 72 of the USSR criminal code ·

Kharkov: The trial of Nedobora and Ponomarev • Kharkov:
The trial of Levin • Extra-judicial actions around Kharkov
trials • Once again about Karavansky • The trial of
Yakhimovich and others • *Samizdat* news • News in brief.

No. 14   June 30, 1970
The arrest of Andrei Amalrik • About the fate of Pyotr
Grigorenko • The imprisonment of Zhores Medvedev in a
psychiatric hospital • Statements by Vladimir Bukovsky •
Soviet press on repressions of dissidents in the USSR •
Stalin's pictures are protected • Details of the Ryazan trial
• Persecutions of the believers • From the history of the
Soviet censorship • Extra-judicial persecutions • News in
brief • *Samizdat* news • Addenda and corrigenda.

No. 15   August 31, 1970
The trial of Natalia Gorbanevskaya • The trial of Olga Ioffe
• The arrest of R. Pimenov • Political trials in various
Soviet cities • The case of Levitin-Krasnov • Searches and
arrests of Jews desiring to emigrate to Israel • In
Mordovian labor camps • Extra-judicial persecutions • News
in brief • *Samizdat* news • Addenda and corrigenda.

No. 16   October 31, 1970
The friends and foes of Solzhenitsyn • The trial of Pimenov
and Vail • In defense of Andrei Amalrik • The trials in
Yerevan • The trials in the past • Persecution of the
believers • Following the newspaper statements • Ex-
tra-judicial persecutions • About the fate of Pyotr
Grigorenko • News in brief • *Samizdat* news • Obituary •
Addenda and corrigenda.

No. 17   December 31, 1970
The trial of Amalrik and Ubozhko • Andrei Amalrik's final
address • The trial of Valentin Moroz • Solzhenitsyn's letter
to the Nobel Foundation • The Committee for Human Rights
in the USSR • Public statements regarding the trial of
Pimenov, Vail and Zinoveva • The Leningrad trial of the
"hi-jackers" • Trials of recent years: the case of the UNF
[Ukrainian National Front] • Persecution of Jews wishing to
emigrate to Israel • Rigerman, American citizenship and the
Soviet police • The fate of Fritz Mender • Political prisoners
in the Mordovian camps • News in brief • *Samizdat* news.

No. 18   March 5, 1971
Political prisoners in psychiatric hospitals • The hunger
strike in Vladimir Prison • Political prisoners in the
Mordovian camps • A survey of events in the Ukraine • The

Jewish movement for emigration to Israel • The Crimean Tatar movement • The warning to the Committee for Human Rights • Trials of recent years • News in brief • *Samizdat* news • Obituaries • Letters and statements • Corrigenda to several issues of the *Chronicle*.

No. 19   April 30, 1971
The arrest of Vladimir Bukovsky • Vladimir Gershuni's notes from the special psychiatric hospital in Oryol • The hunger strike of Borisov and Fainberg • The fate of members of the All-Russian Social-Christian Union for the Liberation of the People • An appeal by the Crimean Tatar people • The movement of the Meskhetians for a return to their homeland • The Jewish movement to leave for Israel • Extra-judicial persecution • Banned films • Items from the Soviet press • News in brief • *Samizdat* news.

No. 20   July 2, 1971
Political trials (May-June 1971) • The movement of the Meskhetians for a return to their homeland • Extra-judicial persecution • News in brief • *Samizdat* news • Obituary • Addendum.

No. 21   September 11, 1971
Political trials • The Dnepropetrovsk psychiatric hospital of special type • Open letters from A. I. Solzhenitsyn to Andropov, USSR Minister of State Security, and Kosygin, Chairman of the USSR Council of Ministers • Materials of the Committee for Human Rights • The investigation into the case of V. Bukovsky • The Jewish movement to leave for Israel • The Meskhetian movement • Religious persecution • News in brief • *Samizdat* news.

No. 22   November 10, 1971
On the presentation of the Nobel prize to A. I. Solzhenitsyn • The case of Vladimir Bukovsky • Material concerning the forthcoming International Congress of Psychiatrists • News from the Mordovian camps and Vladimir Prison • Material from the regional press • The movement to leave for Israel • Appeals in defense of human rights • News in brief • *Samizdat* news • Letters and statements.

No. 23   January 5, 1972
The case of Vladimir Bukovsky • The final speech of Bukovsky • The trial of Nadezhda Emelkina • Hunger strikes by political prisoners • Concerning the anniversary of the "airplane" trial • The movement to leave for Israel •

The persecution of believers in Lithuania • News in brief • *Samizdat* news • Obituary.

No. 24   March 5, 1972
The case of Vladimir Bukovsky • Searches and arrests in January • The hunger strike of Fainberg and Borisov • Political prisoners in the Mordovian camps • Religious persecution in Lithuania • Document of the World Federation for Mental Health • The Jewish movement to leave for Israel • Material from newspaper articles • Extra-judicial persecution • News in brief • *Samizdat* news.

No. 25   May 20, 1972
Political trials • Searches, interrogations, arrests • An interview with A. I. Solzhenitsyn • On presentation of the Nobel prize to A. I. Solzhenitsyn • The letter of A. I. Solzhenitsyn to Pimen, and S. Zheludkov's reply • Political prisoners in the Mordovian camps • The persecution of believers in Lithuania • Outside the Moscow synagogue on 29 March • Extra-judicial persecutions • News in brief • *Samizdat* news.

No. 26   July 5, 1972
The arrest of Pyotr Yakir • Political trials • Searches, interrogations, arrests • Pre-trial investigations • Political prisoners in psychiatric hospitals • Expulsion of a correspondent • "In honour of Nixon" • Shevchenko Day in the Ukraine • The press conference of J. Dobosch • New functions for the [security] organs • The events in Lithuania • Materials from newspaper articles • Extra-judicial persecution • News in brief • Letters and documents • *Samizdat* news • The "Memorandum" of A. D. Sakharov • Corrigenda to previous issues • Additional corrections.

No. 27   October 15, 1972
Activities of the Human Rights Committee • New information on the Leningrad "airplane" trial • Materials from newspaper articles • The end of school No. 2 • News in brief • *Samizdat* news • Addenda and corrigenda • Repressions in the Ukraine • Searches, interrogations, arrests • The Events in Lithuania • Persecution of the Crimean Tatars • In prisons and camps • In the psychiatric hospitals • Letters and statements.

No. 28   December 31, 1972
The death of Yury Galanskov • A chronicle of Case No. 24 • The trial of Dandaron • Repressions in the Ukraine • The

Presidium of the USSR Supreme Soviet answers a letter from 273 Jews • The directives on urgent hospitalization • News in brief.

No. 29   July 31, 1973
A Chronicle of Human Rights in the USSR • The trial of Davydov and Petrov • The case of Bolonkin, Balakirev and Yukhnovets • Repression in Oryol • Trials in the Ukraine • The case of Leonid Plyushch • The trial of Andrei Amalrik • A chronicle of Case No. 24 • Events in Lithuania • Biographies • News in brief.

No. 30   December 31, 1973
The trial of P. Yakir and V. Krasin • The trial of Yury Shikhanovich • The trial of Bolonkin and Balakirev • A. Feldman tried • The trial of V. Lisovoi, E. Pronyuk and I. Semanyuk • The investigation of G. Superfin's case • In the prisons and camps • In psychiatric hospitals • Events in Lithuania • Materials on Sakharov • Activities of Soviet Jews • An unpublished decree of the Presidium of the USSR Supreme Soviet • News in brief • *Samizdat* news • Material from the Soviet press.

No. 31   May 17, 1974
The trial of Dzheppar Akimov • The trial of Reshat Dzhemilev • The position of the Crimean Tatars in the Crimea • Letters from the Crimea • Documents of the Crimean Tatar movement: Appeals, statements, information sheets • Letter to Kurt Waldheim • Documents from official correspondence.

No. 32   July 17, 1974
The deportation of Solzhenitsyn • The trials of Khaustov, Superfin, Nekipelov, Pirogov • Case No. 15 in Leningrad • Pentecostalists intend to leave the USSR • Soviet Germans want to leave for West Germany • The persecution of Crimean Tatars • Events in Lithuania • The case of Pailodze • In the prisons and camps • In the psychiatric hospitals • An unpublished decree • The unofficial international scientific seminar in Moscow • About the journal *Veche* • In the Moscow Writers' Organization • Extra-judicial persecution • From the Soviet press • News in brief • *Samizdat* news • V. Nekrasov, 'Who Needs This?' • Letters and statements • Addenda and corrigenda.

No. 33   December 10, 1974
Political Prisoners' Day in the USSR • Food norms • Order number 020 • In the Mordovian camps • In the Perm camps

• A list of prisoners in the Perm camps • V. Moroz's hunger strike • Letters and Statements • News in brief • Trials of recent years.

No. 34   December 31, 1974
The arrest of Sergei Kovalyov • The trial of Kheifets • The trial of Ladyzhensky and Korovin • Trials in Armenia • The trial of Shtern • A trial in Vilnius • Arrests, searches, interrogations • In the camps and prisons • In the psychiatric hospitals • Persecution of Soviet Germans • Persecution of Crimean Tatars • Persecution of religious believers • Georgian *samizdat* on the situation in the Georgian patriarchate • Surveillance of Ginzburg and Marchenko • Extra-judicial persecution • An exhibition by independent artists • Biographies • News in brief • Letters and statements • *Samizdat* news • Official documents • Trials of recent years • Corrigenda and addenda.

No. 35   March 31, 1975
The situation of Leonid Plyushch • The case of Marchenko • The trial of Vins • The trial of Maramzin • The investigation of Case No. 345 • From the *Chronicle of the Lithuanian Catholic Church* • In the prisons and camps • Bukovsky Day • Letters and statements • News in brief • Threats to Sakharov • *Samizdat* news • Final speech of Ilya Gabai • Biographies • Official documents • Corrections to a list of prisoners.

No. 36   May 31, 1975
The arrest of Andrei Tverdokhlebov • The eighteenth of April • The arrests in Tallin • The trial of Nashpits and Tsitlyonok • The treatment of Leonid Plyushch continues • In the camps and prisons • A list of political prisoners in Vladimir Prison • Torture in the investigation prisons of Georgia • Events in Lithuania • The persecution of religious believers • Extra-judicial persecution • News in brief • Letters and statements • *Samizdat* news • A letter to the *Chronicle* • Addenda and corrigenda.

No. 37   September 30, 1975
Mustafa Dzhemilev has not been freed • The trial of Osipov • Trials ... The trial of Roitburd ... Trials for refusal to do military service (Malkin, Slinin, Vinarov) ... The trial of Mukhametshin ... The trial of Gilyutin • Pre-trial investigations ... The case of Kovalev ... The case of Tverdokhlebov ... A case concerning a journal (*Jews in the USSR*) ... The case of Igrunov • In the camps and prisons ... The Mordovian camps ... The Perm camps ... Vladimir

Prison • In the psychiatric hospitals • About the Crimean
Tatars • Events in Lithuania ... The trial of Nijole
Sadunaite ... Other events • Persecution of religious be-
lievers • Extra-judicial persecution • State security and
artificial intelligence • The right to marry • About P. G.
Grigorenko's pension • News in brief • Letters and state-
ments • Official documents • *Samizdat* news • *Tamizdat* news
• Trials of recent years (I. A. Vernik).

No. 38   December 31, 1975
Sakharov's friends and enemies • Before the trials of
Kovalev and Tverdokhlebov • The trial of Sergei Kovalev •
The trial in Tallinn • The trial of Leonid Tymchuk • The
appeal hearing in Osipov's case • The trial of Grigoryants •
The case of Vyacheslav Igrunov • Leonid Plyushch is
released to go abroad • A forcible hospitalization (A. D.
Ponomaryov) • The arrest of Mikhail Naritsa • In the camps
and prisons ... Political Prisoners' Day ... Diary of camp
35 ... Perm camp 36 ... Perm camp 37 ... Mordovia ...
Vladimir Prison...Byelorussia, Georgia, Krasnoyarsk territory ... Letters and appeals from political prisoners • In
defense of Vladimir Bukovsky • Mustafa Dzhemilev continues
his hunger strike • The movement of the Crimean Tatars
... Simferopol ... 'The Crimean Hills are in Danger' ...
Information Bulletin No. 115 • Events in Georgia • The
persecution of believers ... The position of religious prisoners ... Public statements by priests and believers • Exit
visas and call-up papers • News in brief • *Samizdat* news •
Trials of past years (the case of A. Sergienko) • Addenda
and corrigenda.

No. 39   March 12, 1976
Obituary (Grigory Podyapolsky) • In the camps and prisons
... Political Prisoners' Day ... The Mordovian camps ...
The Perm camps ... Diary of camp 35 (September 1975-Jan-
uary 1976) ... Camp 36 ... Camp 37 • Vladimir Prison ...
Ordinary-regime camps • Releases ... Letters and appeals
from political prisoners • In the psychiatric hospitals ...
Dnepropetrovsk Special Psychiatric Hospital ... Sychyovka
Special Psychiatric Hospital (Smolensk region) ... Kazan
Special Psychiatric Hospital ... Leningrad and
Chernyakhovsk Special Psychiatric Hospitals ... Releases
from special psychiatric hospitals ... Psychiatric hospitals
of ordinary type • In defense of Efim Davidovich • In
defense of Mustafa Dzhemilev • Crimean Tatars continue to
return to their homeland • Persecution of religious believers
• Events in Lithuania • A case of refusal to give evidence
(V. Maresin) • Polemics with Sukharev • Letters and

statements · *Samizdat* news · News in brief · Addenda and corrigenda.

No. 40   May 20, 1976
Statement by Tatyana Khodorovich · The trial of Andrei Tverdokhlebov ... In defense of Andrei Tverdokhlebov ... The trial of Mustafa Dzhemilev ... Protests and appeals ... Two more documents ... The trial of Vyacheslav Igrunov · The trial of Valery Maresin · In memory of Efim Davidovich · Psychiatric diagnosis of Valentin Moroz · In the prisons and camps ... Vladimir Prison ... In the Mordovian camps ... In the Perm camps ... In camps for common criminals in the Ukraine ... Releases · Events in Lithuania · Persecution in the Crimea · Negotiations in the Central Committee of the *CPSU* · Problems in the field of linguistics ... At the USSR Academy of Sciences' Institute of Linguistics ... At the M. Thorez Moscow State Pedagogical Institute of Foreign Languages · A new public association · News in brief · Letters and statements · Concerning public statements by Leonid Plyushch · Open letter to Leonid Plyushch from T. S. Khodorovich · From the pages of the Soviet press.

No. 41   August 3, 1976
Suspension of the case against Naritsa · Religion in the USSR ... A lecture by Furov ... A letter by Regelson and Yakunin ... A new way of fighting against religion ... Evangelical Christians and Baptists ... Pentecostals · Events in Lithuania · Tverdokhlebov in exile · Arrests, searches and interrogations · In the prisons and camps ... Vladimir Prison ... The Mordovian camps ... The Perm camps ... Letters and statements by political prisoners ... In defense of political prisoners ... Releases · In the psychiatric hospitals ... Chernyakhovsk Special Psychiatric Hospital ... Sychyovka Special Psychiatric Hospital ... Dnepropetrovsk Special Psychiatric Hospital ... Kazan Special Psychiatric Hospital · The Helsinki Monitoring Group · Persecution of the Crimean Tatars ... Evictions ... No residence permit—no work ... Trials · The emigration movement of the Germans · The struggle of the Meskhetians to return to Georgia · In Pushkin house · Unofficial entertainment · News in brief · Addenda and corrigenda.

No. 42   October 8, 1976
Sent to hospital for his songs · The case of Bashkirov · Arrests, searches and interrogations ... Slogans in Leningrad ... Declaration by Vladimir Borisov ... The persecution of Ilya Levin ... Arrest of Gennady Trifonov

... Arrested for his decency ... The arrest of Mart Niklus
... Verification of identity ... A search at Viktor
Nekipelov's • In the prisons and camps ... A visit to
Dzhemilev ... Vladimir Prison ... The Mordovian camps ...
The Perm camps ... In camps for common criminals ...
Letters and declarations from political prisoners ... In
defense of political prisoners ... Releases • In the psychi-
atric hospitals ... Dnepropetrovsk Special Psychiatric
Hospital • Persecution of Believers • Persecution of the
Crimean Tatars ... Evictions ... Trials • Events in Georgia
• News in brief • The Helsinki Monitoring Group • Letters
and Statements • *Samizdat* news • Two obituaries ... In
memory of Konstantin Bogatyrev ... Mikhail Dyak.

No. 43   December 31, 1976
The Release of Vladimir Bukovsky ... A victory for the
forces of reason and humanity • Traditional days of protest
... October 30 Political Prisoner's Day ... December 5
Soviet Constitution Day ... December 10 Human Rights Day
• In the prisons and camps ... Vladimir Prison ... In the
camps ... Concerning Mustafa Dzhemilev • The trial of
Bashkirov • The trial of Voznesenskaya • The Helsinki
groups • Arrests, searches, interrogations ... The release
of Mart Niklus • The psychiatric arrest of Vladimir Borisov
• In the psychiatric hospitals • The release of Pyotr
Starchik • Persecution of participants in a religious seminar
• Events in Lithuania • Persecution of the Crimean Tatars •
The Jewish movement ... The struggle for emigration ...
The case of ass and Chernobylsky ... Jewish seminars ...
A Jewish cultural symposium • The right to leave one's
country ... In defense of Zosimov • Extra-judicial perse-
cution ... Problems of linguistics • News in brief ... Dirt
by post • *Samizdat* news • Letters and statements • Letters
to the *Chronicle* • Addenda and corrigenda.

No. 44   March 16, 1977
A chronological summary • Reprisals against Helsinki
groups: arrest of Ginzburg, Orlov, Rudenko, Tikhy,
Shcharansky ... Search at home of Alexander Ginzburg ...
Search at home of Ludmilla Alexeyeva ... Search at home of
Lydia Voronina ... Search at home of Yury Orlov ...
Interrogations, shadowing and protests ... Arrest of
Alexander Ginzburg ... Arrest of Rudenko and Tikhy ...
Search at home of O. Ya. Meshko ... Search at home of
Yury Minyukh ... Arrest of Yury Orlov ... Assistance with
departures ... Arrest of Anatoly Shcharansky • Activities
of Helsinki groups • The case of Amner Zavurov • Arrests,
searches, interrogations ... Arrest of Vasily Barladyanu

... Arrest of Iosif Begun ... Persecution of Ilya Levin •
Concerning the explosions in Moscow • In the prisons and
camps ... Vladimir Prison ... The Mordovian camps ... The
Perm camps ... In other camps • Letters and statements of
political prisoners ... In defense of political prisoners ...
Releases • A list of political prisoners in Vladimir Prison •
After release ... Kronid Lyubarsky ... Surveillance of
Strokatova • In exile • The release of Vladimir Borisov •
Persecution of believers ... Adventists ... Pentecostalists •
Events in Lithuania ... The Lithuanian Helsinki Group ...
From *Chronicle of the Lithuanian Catholic Church No. 25* •
Persecution of Crimean Tatars ... A procurator speaks •
The right to leave one's country ... Germans ...
Pentecostalists ... Jews • A fire at the home of Landa •
News in brief ... Registration and exchange ... Trial of
Pyotr Naritsa • Statements by Sakharov ... Correspondence
with Carter ... Six interviews • Letters and statements ...
In defense of Ginzburg, Orlov, Rudenko and Tikhy •
Addenda and corrigenda.

No 45   May 25, 1977
The trial of Anton Pype • The trial of Volkov and Rybakov
• The trial of Pyotr Ruban • The Ginzburg-Orlov case •
The Shcharansky case • The Rudenko-Tikhy case • The
arrest of Marinovich and Matusevich • The Barladyanu case
• The arrest of Gamsakhurdia and Kostava • Arrests,
searches, interrogations ... In Lithuania ... 15 days for
Alexander Podrabinek • In the prisons and camps ...
Vladimir Prison ... The Mordovian camps ... The Perm
camps ... In other camps ... Statute on political prisoners
... Letters and statements by political prisoners ... Re-
leases • After release • In exile • In the psychiatric hos-
pitals • The right to leave one's country ... Persecution of
Soviet Germans ... Pentecostalists and Baptists • The
Jewish movement • Expulsion of writers • News in brief ...
A month of 'preventive conversations' in Moscow ... A talk
with a procurator • Letters and statements • *Samizdat* news
• Obituary • Addenda and corrigenda.

No. 46   August 15, 1977
The trial of Landa • The trial of Begun • The trial of
Barladyanu • The trial of Rudenko and Tikhy • 'Helsinki
groups' under investigation ... The Ginzburg case ... The
Orlov case ... The Shcharansky case ... In Georgia ... In
the Ukraine • Arrests, searches, interrogations • Events in
Lithuania ... Searches and interrogations ... Persecution of
religious believers • Persecution of religious believers ...
Adventists ... Pentecostals and Baptists • The right to

leave one's country ... Pentecostals and Baptists ...
Germans ... Have left • In the prisons and camps ... *MVD*
directives on conditions of detention ... Vladimir Prison ...
The Mordovian camps ... The Perm camps ... Letters and
statements by political prisoners ... Releases • After re-
lease ... In Tarusa • In exile • In the psychiatric hospitals
... Kazan Special Psychiatric Hospital ... Chernyakhovsk
Special Psychiatric Hospital ... In ordinary hospitals •
Extra-judicial persecution • Miscellaneous reports ... A
refusal to give evidence • Relief fund for political prisoners
• Letters and statements • Discussion of the Draft
constitution • An independent news agency • *Samizdat* news
• Trials of former years ... The case of Tikhy (1957) ...
The case of Suslensky and Meshener • Addenda and
corrigenda.

No. 47   November 30, 1977
The trial of Serebrov • The trial of Rozhdestvov • The
Helsinki groups under investigation ... The case of
Ginzburg ... The case of Orlov ... The persecution of the
Working Commission ... The case of Shcharansky ... The
case of Matusevich and Marinovich • Arrests, searches,
interrogations ... The arrest of Snegiryov ... The arrest
of Valentina Pailodze ... Case number 186 • Events in
Lithuania ... The trial of Lapienis, Matulionis and
Pranskunaite ... The arrest of Petkus ... Searches and
interrogations ... Disturbances in Vilnius ... The
Lithuanian Helsinki Group • Persecution of believers ...
Catholics ... Adventists ... Baptists ... Pentecostalists •
Persecution of Crimean Tatars ... Petitions • The right to
leave ... Pentecostalists ... Have left • The Jewish move-
ment • In the prisons and camps ... Vladimir Prison ...
The Mordovian camps ... The Perm camps ... In other
camps and prisons ... Letters and statements of political
prisoners ... In defense of political prisoners ... Releases
• After release • In exile • In the psychiatric hospitals ...
Kazan Special Psychiatric Hospital ... Chernyakhovsk
Special Psychiatric Hospital ... Dnepropetrovsk Special
Psychiatric Hospital ... Leningrad Special Psychiatric
Hospital ... In ordinary hospitals • Extra-judicial perse-
cution • Miscellaneous news • Letters and statements •
Discussion of the draft constitution (Conclusion) • Official
documents • *Samizdat* news • Trials of recent years •
Addenda and corrigenda.

No. 48   March 14, 1978
The expulsion of Pyotr Grigorenko • Repressions against
the Helsinki Group ... The Moscow Group ... Extension of

pre-trial detention ... The Ginzburg case ... The Orlov case ... The Shcharansky case • The Ukrainian Group ... Pressure on Rudenko ... The arrest of Lukyanenko ... The arrest of Pyotr Vins • The Lithuanian Group ... The Petkus case • The Georgian Group ... The case of Gamsakhurdia, Kostava and Rtskhiladze ... The case of Grigory Goldshtein • The Armenian Group ... The arrest of Nazaryan ... The trial of Shagen Arutyunyan • The case of the Podrabineks • Arrests, searches, interrogations • The trial of Anatoly Ivanov • In the prisons and camps ... A meeting before execution ... *MVD* directives on conditions of detention ... Vladimir Prison ... The Mordovian camps ... The Perm camps ... In other Prisons and camps ... Letters and statements by political prisoners ... Releases • In exile • In the psychiatric hospitals ... In special psychiatric hospitals ... Forcible hospitalizations ... The release of Yury Belov • After release ... Mikhail Makarenko • Persecution of the Crimean Tatars ... Mustafa Dzhemilev at liberty ... Threats to Reshat Dzhemilev ... In the Crimea • Events in Lithuania ... The trial of Jaškunas ... Searches and interrogations ... The *Chronicle of the Lithuanian Catholic Church* on the situation of religious believers ... The disturbances in Vilnius • Persecution of believers ... Catholics in Moldavia ... Adventists ... Pentecostals ... Baptists • The right to leave one's country ... The case of Smogitel ... Germans ... Jews ... Pentecostals ... Have left • Extra-judicial persecution • Writer-Parasites • In the Central House of Writers • Miscellaneous Reports ... Demonstrations ... A free trade union • In the pages of the Soviet press • Letters and statements • Documents of the Moscow Helsinki Group • *Samizdat* news • Addenda and corrigenda.

No. 49   May 14, 1978
The trial of Kirill Podrabinek • The trial of Grigory Goldshtein • The trial of Marinovich and Matusevich • The trial of Pyotr Vins • The trial of Gajauskas • The Helsinki groups under investigation ... The case of Ginzburg ... The case of Orlov ... The case of Shcharansky ... The case of Lukyanenko • Arrests, searches, interrogations • In the prisons and camps ... Vladimir Prison ... The Mordovian camps ... The Perm camps ... Letters and statements of political prisoners ... Releases • In exile • In the psychiatric hospitals ... In special psychiatric hospitals ... In ordinary hospitals • After release • Persecution of Crimean Tatars ... In the Crimea ... In Uzbekistan • Events in Lithuania ... Arrests and interrogations ... Persecution of believers • Persecution of believers ...

Orthodox Christians ... Catholics in Georgia ... Advent-
ists: the arrest of Shelkov ... Pentecostals ... Baptists ...
From the pages of the Soviet press • The right to leave ...
Jews ... Pentecostals ... Germans ... Have left • Alter-
native culture ... The trial of Gooss • Discussion of the
draft constitution in Georgia • Miscellaneous reports ...
Interrogations in police stations ... The free trade union
... The end of Snegiryov's case • Letters and statements
... The *Chronicle* is Ten Years Old ... Documents of the
Moscow Helsinki Group • *Samizdat* news.

No. 50   November, 1978
The trial of Orlov • The trial of Gamsakhurdia and Kostava
• The trial of Ginzburg ... The appeal of Ginzburg • The
trial of Shcharansky ... The indictment ... The trial • The
trial of Petkus • The trial of Lukyanenko • The trial of
Alexander Podrabinek ... Arrest and investigation ... Trial
• Trials of Jewish activists ... Demonstrations ... The trial
of Ida Nudel ... The trial of Vladimir Slepak ... The trial
of Maria Slepak ... The trial of Iosif Begun.

No. 51   December 1, 1978
The trial of Nazaryan • The trial of Pailodze • The trial of
Buzinnikov • The trial of Shatalov • The trial of
Konovalikhin • The trial of Bedarev and Raksha • The trial
of Bolonkin • Arrests, searches, interrogations ... The
explosions case • In the prisons and camps ... Order No.
37 ... Vladimir Prison ... Chistopol Prison ... The Mordovian camps ... The Perm camps ... In other camps ...
In transit prisons ... Letters and statements of political
prisoners ... Releases • In exile ... Releases • In the
psychiatric hospitals ... In special psychiatric hospitals ...
In ordinary hospitals ... Releases • After release • Persecution of Crimean Tatars ... In the Crimea ... In Krasnodar territory ... In Uzbekistan • Events in Lithuania ...
Arrests, searches, interrogations ... Persecution of believers • Persecution of believers ... Orthodox Christians
... Pentecostalists ... Baptists ... Jehovah's witnesses ...
Adventists • The right to leave ... Pentecostalists and
Baptists ... Germans ... Jews ... Have left • Defense of
the rights of the disabled • Extra-judicial persecution •
Miscellaneous reports ... Political Prisoner Day ... Items
related to the summer trials ... Dirty tricks ... The Free
Inter-Trade Association of Working People • Letters and
statements ... On the trial of Yu. Orlov ... Documents of
the Moscow Helsinki Group • *Samizdat* news • Biographies

... M. P. Lutsik ... N. I. Budulak-Sharygin • Addenda and corrigenda.

No. 52   March 1, 1979
The case of the explosion on the underground • The death of Gely Snegiryov • The trial of Ovsienko • Arrests, searches, interrogations ... The Zisels case ... The Kuleshov case ... The Morozov case ... The case of the journal *Searches* ... The case of the journal *Jews in the USSR* • In the prisons and camps ... Chistopol Prison ... The Mordovian camps ... The Perm camps ... In other prisons and camps ... Letters and statements of political prisoners ... In defense of political prisoners ... Releases • In exile • In the psychiatric hospitals ... In special psychiatric hospitals ... In ordinary hospitals ... Releases • After release • Persecution of Crimean Tatars ... Resolution No. 700 ... Deportations from the Crimea ... Delegations of Crimean Tatars in Moscow ... The arrest of Seidamet Memetov ... The arrest of Mustafa Dzhemilev • Events in Lithuania ... The arrest of Ragaisis • Persecution of believers ... Orthodox Christians ... Adventists ... Baptists ... Pentecostalists • The right to leave ... Have left • Defense of the rights of the disabled ... On the *Metropol* almanac • Miscellaneous reports ... Human Rights Day ... One more deported national group ... The right to marry • Letters and statements ... Documents of the Moscow Helsinki Group • *Samizdat* news ... Lithuanian *Samizdat* ... Estonian *Samizdat* • Official documents • Addenda and corrigenda.

No. 53   August 1, 1979
Political releases ... Pardons ... An exchange ... On the departure of Ginzburg family • Trials ... The trial of Mustafa Dzhemiev ... Trials of Adventists ... The case of Shelkov, Lepshin, Spalin, Furlet and Maslov ... The end of the Raksha case ... A case about bribery ... The trial of Skornyakov ... The trial of Zisels ... The trials of Tsurkov and Skobov ... The trial of Makeyeva ... The trial of Monblanov ... The trial of Skvirsky ... The trial of Kuleshov ... The trial of Volokhonsky ... The trial of Bebko ... The trial of Kukobaka ... The trial of Morozov • Arrests, searches, interrogations ... Case No. 46012 ... The case of the journal *Searches* ... Events in the Ukraine ... The arrest of Alexander Berdnik ... The suicide of Mikhail Melnik ... The arrest of Taras Melnichuk ... The arrest of Yury Badzyo ... The death of Vladimir Ivasyuk ... The arrest of Pyotr and Vasily Sichko ... The arrest of Monakov ... Exiles on holiday • The arrest of Eduard

Arutunyan • In the prisons and camps ... Chistopol Prison ... The Mordovian camps ... The Perm camps ... The other camps ... In defense of political prisoners ... Releases ... Persecution of Crimean Tatars ... The expulsion of delegates from Moscow ... Arrests, searches, interrogations ... The arrest of Reshat Dzhemilev ... Deportations from the Crimea ... Trials in the Crimea ... The trial of Seidamet Memetov ... The trial of Gulizar Yunysova ... The trial of L. Bekirov, I. Usta, S. Khyrkhara and Ya. Beitullayev ... The trial of Eldar Shabanov • Events in Lithuania • Persecution of believers ... Orthodox Christians ... Adventists ... Pentecostalists ... Baptists ... Catholics in Moldavia • The right to leave ... Jews ... Germans ... Pentecostalists ... A journey to visit friends ... Have left • Defense of the rights of the disabled • Extra-judicial persecution • A labor conflict • Miscellaneous reports ... Beatings in the Ukraine ... The Khavin case ... The arts festival that did not take place • Letters and statements ... Documents of the Moscow Helsinki Group • *Samizdat* news ... Lithuanian *samizdat* • Addenda and corrigenda ... The Ruban case.

No. 54   November 15, 1979
November 1 ... The arrest of Tatyana Velikanova ... The arrest of Gleb Yakunin ... First responses • Arrests, searches, interrogations ... Case No. 46012 ... The case of the journal *Searches* ... The case of the journal *Community* ... The arrest of Poresh ... The Guberman case ... The Zubakhin case ... The interrogation of Tarto ... Persecution of members of the FIAWP Council of Representatives ... Voloshanovich and Kovner are searched ... Events in the Ukraine ... The Goncharov case ... The Monakov case ... The arrest of Litvin ... The Sichko case ... A search at the home of Surovtseva ... The arrest of Rozumny ... The arrest of Gorbal ... Persecution of Kirichenko ... Mafia-like actions ... The arrest of Streltsov • Trials ... The trial of G. Mikhailov ... The trial of Ermolayev and Polyakov ... The trial of Nikitin ... The trial of Rossiisky • In the prisons and camps ... Chistopol Prison ... The Mordovian camps ... The Perm camps ... In other prisons and camps ... In defense of political prisoners ... Releases • In exile ... Releases • In the psychiatric hospitals ... In special psychiatric hospitals ... In ordinary hospitals ... Releases • After release • Persecution of Crimean Tatars ... Deportations from the Crimea ... The case of Reshat Dzhemilev • Events in Lithuania ... The trial of Ragaisis ... The case of Ramanauskaite ... The story of Kelmeliene's illness ... After the priests' statement ... Tamkevicius and

Svarinskas are warned ... Arrests, searches, interrogations ... The arrest of Terteckas • Persecution of believers ... Orthodox Christians ... Adventists ... Pentecostalists ... Jehovah's Witnesses ... Baptists • The right to leave ... Jews ... Germans ... The trials of Noi and Repp • Pentecostalists ... The death of Boris Evdokimov ... Have left • More about the *Metropol* almanac • Miscellaneous reports ... The trial of Tsurkova ... A conversation with Bakhmin ... A conversation with Meiman ... A conversation with Ostrovskaya ... Letters and statements ... Documents of the Catholic Committee for the Defense of Believers' Rights ... Documents of the Moscow Helsinki Group • *Samizdat* news ... Lithuanian *samizdat* ... Estonian *samizdat* • Addenda and corrigenda ... The case of Lubman.

No. 55   December 31, 1979

Trials ... The trial of Streltsov ... The trial of Pëtr and Vasily Sichko ... The trial of Litvin ... The trial of Berdnik ... The trial of Badzë [previously transliterated Badzyo] ... The trial of Reshat Dzhemilev ... The trial of Stasevich, V. Mikhailov and Kochneva • Arrests, searches, interrogations ... The case of T. Velikanova ... The Yakunin case ... The case of the journal *Searches* ... The arrest of Abramkin ... The case of the journal *Community* ... The arrest of Lesiv ... The arrest of Ryzhov-Davydov ... The arrest of Kadiyev ... The arrest of Kalinichenko ... A search at the home of Lisovaya ... The arrest of Nekipelov ... The arrest of Solovov ... A search at the home of Niklus ... The arrest of Regelson • In the prisons and camps ... Chistopol Prison ... The Mordovian camps ... The Perm camps ... In other prisons and camps ... In defense of political prisoners ... Releases • In exile ... Releases • After release • Events in Lithuania ... Searches in Vilnius ... The arrest of Sasnauskas ... Persecution of believers ... Orthodox Christians ... Adventists ... Baptists ... Trials ... Arrests ... Searches ... Breaking-up of prayer-meetings, confiscation of houses ... Dismissals from work ... Schools and religion ... The family and religion • Pentecostalists ... The breaking-up of weddings ... School and religion ... Fines ... Catholics in Moldavia • The right to leave ... Jews ... Germans ... Pentecostalists ... The arrest of N. P. Goretoi ... The trial of I. Korchnoi ... Have left • Miscellaneous reports ... Human Rights Day in Moscow (December 10) ... Beatings in the Ukraine • Letters and statements ... Documents of the Moscow Helsinki Group • *Samizdat* news ... Lithuanian *samizdat* • Addenda and corrigenda.

No. 56   April 30, 1980
The exile of Sakharov • The death of Shelkov • Persecution
of the Moscow Helsinki Group ... The administrative arrest
of Osipova ... The trial of Landa ... A search at the home
of Osipova and I. Kovalëv ... The case of Nekipelov •
Persecution of the Working Commission [on psychiatric
abuse] ... A search at the home of Grivnina ... A search
at the home of A. Podrabinek ... The arrest of Bakhmin
... The administrative arrest of Serebov ... The arrest of
Ternovsky • The case of the journal *Searches* ... The
arrest of Grimm and Sokirko • The arrest of Lavut • The
case of T. Velikanova • A week of preventive talks in
Moscow • The arrest of Dudko • Persecution of the Chris-
tian Committee ... The arrest of Kapitanchuk ... Interro-
gations of Shcheglov • Persecution of the Christian Seminar
... The trial of Shchipkova ... The trial of Popkov and
Burtsev ... Pre-trial investigation • Trials ... The trial of
Kadiyev ... The trial of Zubakhin ... The trial of
Guberman ... The trial of Solovov • Arrests ... The arrest
of G. Fedotov ... The arrest of Meilanov ... The arrest of
Kuzkin ... The arrest of Dyadkin • Searches ... A search
of Zotov ... Searches in Leningrad ... A search of
Danilyuk ... The case of Brailovsky ... A search at the
home of Kormer • Events in the Ukraine ... Trials ... The
trial of Rozumny ... The trial of Gorbal ... The trial of
Goncharov ... The trial of Lesiv ... Arrests ... The arrest
of Krainik ... The arrest of Mikhailenko ... The arrest of
O. Matusevich ... The arrest of Sokulsky ... The arrest of
V. Shevchenko ... The arrest of A. Shevchenko • After
release • Miscellaneous ... Tokayuk is beaten up ... Perse-
cution of the Sichko family • Events in Armenia ... Trials
... The trial of Eduard Arutyunyan ... The trial of
Avakyan ... Biographies • Events in Estonia ... Arrests
... The arrest of Kukk ... The arrest of Niklus ...
Estonian *samizdat* • Events in Lithuania ... Persecution of
the Lithuanian Helsinki Group ... The arrests of Skuodis
... The case of Jurevicius ... A search at the home of
Laurinavičius ... The arrest of Statkevičius ... Arrests ...
The arrest of Pečeliunas ... The arrest of Janulis ... The
arrest of Buzas ... Searches ... A search at the home of
Žarskus ... A search at the home of Mandrit ... A search
at the home of Sereikaite ... A search at the home of
Sabaliauskas ... Interrogations and chats ... A chat with
Patackas ... An interrogation of Zvikaite ... The case of
Terleckas ... The death of V. Jaugelis ... Miscellaneous
... The dismissal of Keršiute ... Wreaths are laid • Perse-
cution of believers ... Catholics in Lithuania ... A search
at the home of Gražulis ... Arrests and searches on April

17-18 ... Documents of the Catholic Committee for the
Defence of Believers' Rights ... Miscellaneous ... Baptists
... The trial of Valentin Naprienko ... The trial of Runov
... The trial of Kinash ... Arrests in Elektrostal ...
Arrests in Krasnodar ... Arrests in Chernovtsy region ...
Arrest of printers of the 'Christian' publishing house ...
The arrest of Khorev ... Searches ... Miscellaneous ...
Pentecostalists ... Trials ... The breaking-up of prayer
meetings ... Miscellaneous • The right to leave ... Jews
... Germans ... Baptists ... Pentecostalists ... Have left •
Between emigration and prison ... In the prisons and camps
... Chistopol Prison ... The Mordovian camps ... The Perm
camps ... In other prisons and camps ... In defense of
political prisoners ... Releases • In exile ... Releases ...
In the psychiatric hospitals ... In special psychiatric
hospitals ... In ordinary hospitals ... Releases • After
release ... Miscellaneous reports ... From the Writer's
Union • Letters and statements ... Documents of the
Moscow Helsinki Group • *Samizdat* news • Official documents
• Addenda and corrigenda.

No. 57   August 3, 1980
The trial of Poresh • Persecution of the Moscow Helsinki
Group ... The arrest of Osipova ... A warning to the
group ... The trial of V. Nekipelov • Persecution of the
Working Commission [on Psychiatric Abuse] ... The case of
Vyacheslav Bakhmin ... The case of Ternovsky ... The
arrest of A. Podrabinek • The deportation of Vladimir
Borisov ... Persecution of the Initiative Group to Defend
the Rights of the Disabled • The case of the journal
Searches • The case of Lavut • The repentance of Dudko •
Pre-trial investigations ... The Yakunin-Kapitanchuk-
Regelson-Dudko case ... The case of Dyadkin ... The
arrest of Gorbachëv ... The case of Morozov ... The case
of Kuzkin ... An interrogation of A. Daniel ... The case of
Terleckas and Sasnauskas • Arrests ... The arrest of
Milyutin ... The arrest of Sarbayev • Sakharov in adminis-
trative exile • Persecution of Crimean Tatars • Events in
the Ukraine ... The trial of Kalinichenko ... Arrests ...
The arrest of Kurilo ... The arrest of Stus ... Psychiatric
arrest of Meshko ... The arrest of Mazur ... The arrest of
Prikhodko ... Searches in Kharkov ... Persecution of the
Sichko family • Events in Armenia ... The arrest of
Manucharyan ... The case of M. Arutyunyan • Events in
Estonia • Events in Lithuania • Persecution of believers ...
Orthodox Christians ... Pentecostalists ... Adventists •
The right to leave ... Jews ... Germans ... Pentecostalists
... Have left • In the prisons and camps ... Chistopol

Prison ... The Mordovian camps ... The Perm camps ... In
other prisons and camps • In exile ... The trial of
Chornovil ... The trial of Lisovoi ... Releases • In the
psychiatric hospitals ... Biographies ... A. I. Lupinos ...
N. G. Plakhotnvuk ... Forcible hospitalizations ... Releases
• After release ... The trial of Chuiko ... The trial of
Khramtsov • Miscellaneous reports • Letters and statements
... Documents of the Moscow Helsinki Group • *Samizdat*
news • Official documents • Addenda and corrigenda • The
death of Shelkov.

No. 58   November, 1980
Dates of trials • The trial of Tatyana Velikanova • The trial
of Vyacheslav Bakhmin • The trial of Yakunin • The trial of
Regelson • The trial of Kapitanchuk • The trial of
Ogorodnikov • The case of the journal *Searches* • The trial
of Sokirko • The trial of Abramkin • The trial of Grimm •
The trial of Statkevicius • The trial of Terleckas and
Sasnauskas • The trial of Barladyanu • The trial of Olga
Matusevich • The trial of Stus • The trial of Goncharov •
The trial of Treskunov • The trial of Goretoi • The trial of
Markosyan • The trial of Kuzkin • The trial of Dyadkin and
Gorbachёv • The trial of Davydov.

No. 59   November 15, 1980
(Manuscript confiscated by KGB agents February 20, 1981
during search of Moscow apartment of Leonid Vul. Issue
never published.)

No. 60   December 31, 1980
The trial of Lavut • The trial of Meilanov • Persecution of
the Working Group ... The arrest of Grivnina ... The trial
of Ternovsky • The Case No. 50611 - 14/79 • The case of
the journal *Searches* • The trial of Sorokin • Miscellaneous
• Around the literary club *Belletrist* • Search for the novel
Enych ... The search of the home of Kirill Popov • Persecution of the Initiative Group in Defense of Rights of the
Handicapped • Arrests ... Arrest of Myasnikov ... Arrests
of Lazareva and Maltsev ... Arrest of Brailovsky ... Arrests of Bogolyubov and Yeremenko ... Arrest of
Azadovsky • Searches • The case of Osipova • The perse-
cution of the Crimean Tatars • Events in Ukraine ... The
trial of Sas-Zhurakovsky ... The trial of Krainik ... The
trial of Mazur ... The trial of Khmara, V. Shevchenko and
A. Shevchenko • The arrest of Meshko ... The arrest of
Vladimir Sychko ... The arrests of Zinchenko and Altunyan
... Miscellaneous • Events in Estonia • Events in Lithuania
... The trial of Yanulis and Buzas ... The trial of

Navitskaite and Vitkauskaite ... The trial of Abrutis ...
The trial of Skuodis, Yeshmantas and Pechelyunas ... The
trial of Stanelite ... Miscellaneous • Persecution of the
believers ... Catholics in Lithuania ... The documents of
the Catholic committee in defense of the rights of believers
... Adventists ... The trial of Zvyagin ... Baptists ...
The trial of V. Rytikov and Vilchinsky ... The arrest of
Rumachik ... Orthodox • The right to leave ... The tenth
anniversary of the sentencing in the case of the "airplane"
... Moscow ... Kiev ... Lvov ... Armenia ... Have left •
In prisons and in camps ... Chistopol Prison ... Camps in
Mordovia ... Camps in Perm ... In other prisons and camps
... The letters and statements of the political prisoners ...
In defense of the political prisoners ... Releases • In exile
... Releases • In psychiatric hospitals ... Releases • After
release • Extra-judiciary persecutions • Miscellaneous ...
Human Rights Day in Moscow ... Dispersal of unofficial
seminars ... The right to emigrate • Letters and statements
... Letters of Andrei Sakharov ... After the trial of
Sokirko ... Documents of the Moscow Helsinki Group •
Samizdat news • Addenda and corrigenda • The case of
Gorbal • The case of Chernovol.

No. 61   March 16, 1981
The trial of Morozov • The repressions of the Working
Commission ... The trial of Alexander Podrabinek ... The
arrest of Serebrov ... The arrest of Koryagin ... The case
of Grivnina and Serebrov • the trials ... The trial of
Lazarev ... The trial of Magidovich ... The trial of
Myasnikov • The arrests ... The arrest of Batarevsky ...
The arrest of Zotov ... The arrest of Georgy Shepelev •
House searches ... The search in the home of Alexei
Smirnov ... The search in the home of Vul ... Miscel-
laneous • The case of Brailovsky ... The interrogations •
Events in the Ukraine ... The trial of Meshko ... The trial
of Vladimir Sychko ... The trial of Zinchenko ... Arrests
... The arrest of the five residents of Kiev ... The arrest
of Gandzuk ... The arrest of Genchu. The case of
Altunyan ... Miscellaneous • The events in Armenia ... The
arrest of Navasardyan and Arshakyan • The events in
Georgia ... The trial of Zhgenti, Gogiya and Chitanava ...
The arrest of Samkharadze ... The letters of Gamzakhurdia
• The events in Estonia ... The trial of Niklus and Kukk •
The events in Lithuania • The persecution of believers ...
Catholics in Lithuania ... Baptists ... The arrest of
Minyakov ... The arrest of Khomenko • Adventists ... The
arrest of Atsuta ... The arrest of Neverova ... The right
to leave ... Pentecostalists ... Jews ... Moscow ... Kiev

... Tbilisi ... Have left • In prisons and labor camps ...
The trial of Kirill Podrabinek ... The trial of Kazachkov
... The case of Airykyan ... The Chistopol Prison ... The
camps in Mordovia ... The camps in Perm ... In transitory
prisons ... In other camps ... The letters and statements
of the political prisoners ... Releases • In exile • In psychiatric hospitals ... In special hospitals ... In ordinary
hospitals ... Releases • After release • The right to emigrate ... Miscellaneous ... Letters and statements of the
Moscow Helsinki Group • *Samizdat* news • Official documents
• Addenda.

No. 62   July 14, 1981
The death of Kukk • The arrest of Anatoly Marchenko •
The trial of Osipova • Persecutions of the Working Commission ... The trial of Koryagin ... The case of Grivnina and
Serebrov • The trials ... The trial of Azadovsky ... The
trial of Georgy Shepelev ... The trial of Yeremenko ...
The trial of Sarbayev ... The trial of Zotov • The case of
the journal *Searches* ... The arrest of Yakovlev ... Interrogation of Gefter • Arrests ... The arrest of Pavlov ...
The arrest of Kuvakin • Searches, interrogations ... The
searches of the homes of the members of the editorial board
of the journal *Poyedinok* • The search of the home of
Gotovtsev ... The interrogation of Vul ... The Case No.
50611 - 14/79 ... The search of the home of Legler ... The
search of the home of Romanov ... The search of the home
of Khodorovich ... The case of the greenhouse in Tomsk
... The interrogations concerning Alexei Smirnov ... The
searches and interrogation of Sannikova and Probatova •
The persecution of the Initiative Group in Defense of the
Rights of the Handicapped • Events in Ukraine ... The
trial of Altunyan ... The trial of Naboka, Milyavsky,
Lokhvitsky and Chernyavskaya • Arrests ... The arrest of
Lidenko ... The arrest of Kandyba ... The arrest of Raisa
Rudenko ... The arrest of Attsupov ... Miscellaneous •
Events in Armenia ... The trial of Manucharyan ...
Apikayan and Melkonyan ... The trial of Mrzapet Arutunyan
and Vartan Arutunyan ... Mkptchyano, Yegiazaryan and
Agababyan • Events in Estonia ... The trial of Kalep,
Niytsoo and Madisson • Events in Lithuania ... The trial of
Vaichunas ... The trial of Yuryavichus ... The persecution
of believers ... Lutherans in Estonia ... Catholics in
Lithuania ... Adventists ... The trial of Ivan Fokanov ...
The trial of Ardzhevanitse and Sayapin ... The trial of
Vladimir Fokanov, Kovalchuk and Kaduk ... The trial of
Galetsky and Chulkova ... The trial of Didenko ... The
trial of Genchu ... Miscellaneous ... Baptists ... The trials

of Vladimir Hailo ... The trial of Boiko ... The trial of
Lakatosh, Deshko and Fenchak ... The trial of Levtsenyuk
... The trial of Kozorezov ... The trial of Kozorezova ...
The arrests ... Dispersal of prayer meetings ... Miscella-
neous • Orthodox • The right to leave ... Moscow ... The
trial of Kurnosov ... The trial of Brailovsky ... The case
of Chernobylsky ... Miscellaneous • Leningrad ... The
arrest of Leyna ... Miscellaneous • Kiev ... The trial of
Fridman ... The trial of Kislik ... The arrest of Zubko ...
Miscellaneous ... Kharkov ... Kishinev ... The arrest of
Lokshin and Zukerman ... Tbilisi ...Dushambe ... The
arrest of Marsala ... Estonia ... Bilnius ... Armenia ...
Have left • In prisons and camps ... The case of Airykyan
... The case of Ovsiyenko ... The case of Bolonkin ...
The Chistopol Prison ... The camps in Mordovia ... The
camps in Perm ... In other prisons and camps ... The
letters and statements of the political prisoners ... In
defense of the political prisoners ... Releases • Sakharov in
administrative exile • In exile ... Releases ... In psychiatric hospitals ... In special hospitals ... In ordinary hospitals ... After release • Miscellaneous • Letters and statements • The documents of the Moscow Helsinki Group •
Samizdat news • Addenda and corrigenda • The case of
Lupinos.

References and Bibliography

INTERVIEWS

The following persons have been associated with the *Chronicle* in one way or another. They were interviewed for periods of one to four hours at the times and places indicated. Most of the interviews were tape-recorded.

Alexeyeva, Ludmilla. July 25, 1981, Tarrytown, N.Y.; February 14, 1982, Tarrytown, N.Y.; May 10, 1982, Washington, D.C.; October 17 and 18, 1982, Washington, D.C.

Bukovsky, Vladimir. June 4, 1982, Paris.
Chalidze, Valery. May 11, 1982, Washington, D.C.
Corti, Mario. June 7, 1982, Munich.
Gabai, Galina. February 13, 1982, Waltham, Mass.
Gastev, Yuri. June 5, 1982, Paris.
Ginzburg, Alexander. June 5, 1982, Paris.
Ginzburg, Arina. June 5, 1982, Paris.
Gorbanevskaya, Natalia. June 3 and 4, 1982, Paris.
Khodorovich, Tatyana. June 5, 1982, Paris.
Krasin, Victor. May 12, 1982, New York.
Litvinov, Pavel. July 26, 1981, Tarrytown, N.Y.
Lyubarsky, Kronid. June 8, 1982, Munich.
Reddaway, Peter. June 2, 1982, London.
Salova, Galina. June 9, 1982, Munich.
Shragin, Boris. May 8, 1982, Boston.
Voinovich, Vladimir. May 8, 1982, Boston.
Yankelevich, Yefrem. February 12 and 13, 1982, Newton, Mass.

TRANSLATIONS AND PERIODICALS

A *Chronicle of Current Events*. Nos. 13, 14, 15, translated by Peter Reddaway. London. Mimeographed.
A *Chronicle of Current Events*. Nos. 17-58. London, Amnesty International.
A *Chronicle of Human Rights in the USSR*, edited by Valery Chalidze, Edward Kline, and Peter Reddaway. New

York: Khronika Press, 1973-82.

Khronika Tekushchikh Sobytii. Nos. 1-15. Amsterdam: Alexander Herzen Foundation, 1979.

Khronika Tekushchikh Sobytii. Nos. 60, 61, 62. New York: Khronika Press, 1981 and 1982.

USSR News Brief, edited by Kronid Lyubarsky. Brussels: Cahiers du Samizdat, 1978-82.

BOOKS

Amalrik, Andrei. *Notes of a Revolutionary.* New York: Knopf, 1982.

Barron, John. *KGB: The Secret Work of Soviet Secret Agents.* New York: Readers Digest Press, 1974.

Bloch, Sidney, and Peter Reddaway. *Psychiatric Terror: How Soviet Psychiatry Is Used to Suppress Dissent.* New York: Basic Books, 1977.

Bukovsky, Vladimir. *To Build a Castle—My Life as a Dissenter.* New York: Viking Press, 1979.

Chalidze, Valery. *To Defend These Rights: Human Rights and the Soviet Union.* New York: Random House, 1974.

Dornberg, John. *The New Tsars: Russia Under Stalin's Heirs.* New York: Doubleday, 1972.

Gorbanevskaya, Natalia. *Poberezhye: Stikhi.* Ann Arbor, Mich.: Ardis, 1973.

————. *Red Square at Noon,* translated by Alexander Lieven. London: Andre Deutsch, 1972.

Litvinov, Pavel. *Dear Comrade,* edited and annotated by Karel Van Het Reve. New York: Putman, 1969.

————. *The Demonstration in Pushkin Square.* Boston: Gambit, 1969.

Reddaway, Peter. *Uncensored Russia: Protest and Dissent in the Soviet Union.* New York: American Heritage Press, 1972.

Rositzke, Harry. *The KGB: The Eyes of Russia.* New York: Doubleday, 1981.

Rubenstein, Joshua. *Soviet Dissidents: Their Struggle for Human Rights.* Boston: Beacon Press, 1980.

Smith, Hedrick. *The Russians.* New York: Quadrangle, 1976.

Index

About the Author

MARK W. HOPKINS has traveled in and written about the Soviet Union for more than 20 years. As a correspondent for the *Milwaukee Journal* and then the Voice of America, he has reported from Moscow, Leningrad, Kiev, and a dozen other Soviet cities in more than 30 trips to the Soviet Union. For most of the years covered in the history of the *Chronicle*, he was reporting Soviet international and domestic developments from Moscow, as well as from VOA bureaus in Belgrade and Munich.

Hopkins is the author of *Mass Media in the Soviet Union* (New York: Pegasus, 1970). Numerous of his articles on Soviet and East European affairs have appeared in *The New Leader*.

Hopkins graduated with a B.A. from Middlebury College and an M.A. from the University of Wisconsin. He also holds the Certificate of the Russian Studies Program of the University of Wisconsin. He has done advanced research in the Soviet Union as a Ford Foundation fellow and in Eastern Europe as an Alicia Patterson Foundation fellow.